D1795893

CENTRE OF REMEMBRANCE

Memory and Caribbean
Women's Literature

Centre of Remembrance

Memory and Caribbean Women's Literature

EDITED BY

JOAN ANIM-ADDO

MANGO PUBLISHING
2002

©The authors and Mango Publishing 2002

All rights reserved. No reproduction, copy or transmission of this
publication may be made without written permission. Mango Publishing is
registered with the Publishers Licensing Society, London, England and the
Copyright Clearance Centre, Salem, Mass, USA.

First published 2002

Published by Mango Publishing, London UK
P.O. Box 13378, London SE27 OZN

ISBN 1 902294 02 5

British Library Cataloguing in Publication Data
A CIP catalogue record for this book is available from the British Library

Printed in the UK by Print Solutions Partnership
Cover design by Reggie Freeman

CONTENTS

In memory
of
Beryl Gilroy
(1926-2001)

Acknowledgements

This book would not have been possible without the collaboration of many people who made possible the 1996 London conference, 'Centre of Remembrance'. Thanks are due to the conference organisers, all members of the Caribbean Women Writers' Alliance (CWWA) who worked unstintingly against remarkable odds to bring together writers, academics and a range of enthusiastic readers for this event. A deep gratitude is owed to Mary Boley and Diana Birch. I would like to thank, also, the London Arts Board and the British Academy whose funds allowed the visit of guest writers M. Nourbese Philip (Tobago), Aida Bahr (Cuba) Merle Hodge (Trinidad) and Olive Senior (Jamaica) thus ensuring a very special literary dialogue.

My deepest appreciation is extended to the authors of the essays included in this collection. I thank you all for your commitment and patience.

Special thanks to Kofi Anim-Addo for his work on the Index.

INTRODUCTION

Remembrance: A Bridge from Past to Future

JOAN ANIM-ADDO

The twentieth century witnessed a significant breaking of publication silence by Caribbean women writers for whom collective memory has been crucial. This collection of critical essays, which draws its title from M. Nourbese Philip's seminal text, *She Tries Her Tongue Her Silence Softly Breaks* (1993), treats both silence and memory.[1] Philip writes:

> Hold we to the *centre of remembrance*
> that forgets the never that severs
> word from source
> and never forgets the witness
> of broken utterances that passed
> before and now
> breaks the culture of silence
> in the ordeal of testimony[2]

'Centre of remembrance', borrowed from the text, above, entitled the 1996 London-based conference on Caribbean women's literature[3] and serves here as the thematic 'centre' holding together this book. If Caribbean women's literature 'holds' to Philip's notion of the 'centre of remembrance' as texts from across the region suggest, what are some of the meanings?[4] Does literary production situate 'an effort or passion of memory' as Édouard Glissant has indicated?[5] In the work of poets such as Georgina Herrera, Grace Nichols, and Olive Senior there is evidence of such 'passion' and this holds true, also, for fiction by Maryse Condé, Jamaica Kincaid, Simone Schwarz-Bart, Beryl Gilroy and Erna Brodber, among many women authors from the archipelago. Noticeably, through the texts, the centrality of 'remembrance' may be understood first in relation to the region's traumatic past. That 'remembrance' of *that history* informs the writing in diverse ways is a concern central to the debate which this volume explores.

While Caribbean history speaks directly to the function of memory within the literature, it has left, also, a legacy of 'Relation' for which we are finally beginning to account in terms of a plurality of voices reflecting the region's diversity.[6] *Centre of Remembrance: Memory and Caribbean Women's Literature* reflects a pan-Caribbean concern which is alert to this plurality. This volume is the second of its kind to be published as a result of literary and academic interest in Caribbean women's literature within the UK.[7] It is perhaps surprising that despite Britain's role in the shaping of present-day anglophone Caribbean culture, including its literary culture, current UK debate about Literature in English continues to take little cognisance of the growing body of writing by Caribbean heritage women who share a common history[8] or of their contemporaries in the French, Spanish and Dutch-speaking Caribbean.[9]

Significantly, the literature is marked by the impact of a specific colonial heritage central to which is endemic slavery and its racialised meanings. How this informs the reading of recent as well as earlier texts is important. That much of the writing is also part of a late twentieth century explosion of women's writing cannot be ignored. The book is divided into two sections. Part One focuses on 'Memory and Diaspora Discourses' foregrounding a diversity of approaches to the literature. This is because, while the common denominator is writing by Caribbean women, the reading of these texts constitutes a new, exciting and heterogeneous field. Overall, therefore, this collection seeks to represent a range of current approaches to the texts, rather than a unified theoretical stance.

It is appropriate that the Prologue goes to M. Nourbese Philip whose 'In the Matter of Memory' highlights some of the tensions between the 'nightmare' of Caribbean history and the memory of it which fuels much of her writing. Philip locates the African-heritage woman's body as a central textual site of both history and memory and indicates some of the meanings of this, particularly given the absence of material 'markers' of African history in the Caribbean. Following this, Beverley Ormerod, in 'Attitudes to Memory: Reappraisal and Self-Discovery in the Works of French Caribbean Women Writers', distinguishes between two types of interlinked memory: the 'collectively shared' historical memory and the private, individual memory. Ormerod examines fiction and drama by authors from Guadeloupe and Martinique, principally Maryse Condé, Simone Schwarz-Bart, Michèle Lacrosil and Gisèle Pineau whose writing collectively indicates the complexities of remembrance in Caribbean society as written by Francophone Caribbean women. While this writing bears features similar to that of the Créolité movement inspired by Glissant, Ormerod argues that there is also a more individualist and perhaps well established tradition fashioned by these women writers.

One of the most widely read Caribbean authors currently is Jamaica Kincaid and two papers are devoted here to her work. Denise deCaires Narain's 'Living in the Spell of History: The Novels of Jamaica Kincaid' offers a post-colonial exploration of Kincaid's 'engagement with history' in *Annie John*, *Lucy* and *The Autobiography of My Mother*. DeCaires Narain argues for recognition of the significance of Kincaid's 'muting of voice'. In comparison, Giovanna Covi's emphases are different. She argues in 'Re-memorying, Decolonising and Translating in Jamaica Kincaid's *The Autobiography of My Mother*' that Kincaid contributes to a 'new' resistant 'culture' informed by the 'process of re-memory' in which history is perceived as discourse. Covi's feminist reading insists upon a focus on subjectivity albeit within a specificity that is Caribbean.

Theoretical concerns are central to Alison Donnell's 'Here and There in the Work of Olive Senior: Relocating Diaspora Discourses in Relation to Caribbean Women's Writing'. Donnell takes issue with a 'dismantling of geographical belonging' which relocates Caribbean women's writing more within the diaspora, and therefore in relation to migration and exile, rather than in the region. If Donnell rearticulates a regional position, Maria Cristina Fumagalli adopts a bold stance in her comparison of the writing of twentieth century Erna Brodber and that of Lady Mary Roth, the Renaissance aristocrat, in order to re-member a 'dis-membered' past, the legacy of each writer, albeit in differentiated circumstances. Paulette Brown-Hinds's 'In the Blood: Performing Memory in Paule Marshall's *Praisesong for the Widow*' examines a specific coming to terms in which the Caribbean functions as a 'site of liberation and diasporic memory'. Brown-Hinds focuses on how the body of the protagonist, Avey Johnson, through dance, re-memories, reconnects and heals following the adjustment of a more recent dislocation and migration. Beryl Gilroy's 'Creativity, Autarchy and Memory' highlights, in contradistinction, both the autobiographical and psychological underpinnings of a range of writing. Most informatively, Gilroy makes connections with the writing of her own novels in which memory, migration and history play important parts. Like Brown-Hinds, Mary Condé extends the boundaries of Caribbean women's writing, this time to black Caribbean Canadian authors. Raising questions of Caribbeanness and 'home', Condé's 'Complex Identities: Caribbean Canadian Women Fiction Writers' foregrounds issues of identity and the construction of both Caribbean and Canadian locations in the new literature. Similarly, Sarah Lawson Welsh, in 'Out from under the Shadow of Jean', seeks to extend perceived boundaries. She draws attention specifically to Elma Napier's 'neglected' novels of the 1930s and 1940s, some of which were published under the pseudonym E. Garner.

In Part Two, 'Textual Space and Remembrance', the focus shifts to emphasise the writer and the type of textual spaces she creates. Sheila Rampersad, for example, explores the 'Revolutionary Dougla Poetics' characteristic of Merle Hodge's fiction. Rampersad contends that this dynamic in Hodge's writing makes for an 'organic integration' of Trinidadian Indian and African communities in *Crick Crack Monkey* (1970) and that this is further and distinctly developed in Hodge's later text, *For the Life of Laetitia* (1993). If Rampersad's focus is a textual Trinidad, Velma Pollard's is Jamaica. 'Pollard's 'To Us All Flowers Are Roses' offers a linguistic perspective as she explores the creole voice in Jamaican women's writing. While Pollard refers to both the poets, Olive Senior and Lorna Goodison, the central focus of Aida Bahr's essay is Olive Senior's fiction. In 'Olive Senior's Female Characters and the Expression of Cultural Duality in *Discerner of Hearts*', Bahr's exploration is attentive to details of characterisation and the socialisation which fuel the duality expressed in Senior's narratives. Moving from Jamaica to Britain, Roshi Naidoo contextualises Joan Riley's work within Black British writing. Central to Naidoo's essay is a reading of Riley's ironically titled *Romance* (1988) which is set in London. Naidoo argues for an appreciation of Riley's contribution to 'black women's experience', without the burden of 'representation' as an African-Caribbean woman writer in Britain. Further, she argues that *Romance* offers a distinctive writing of collective memory complicated by relationship with the 'self' as well as with black and white communities.

Sam Haigh engages with an 'older' generation of 'Guadeloupean Women Writers and the Representation of Black Female Desire'. Haigh focuses principally upon Jacqueline Manicom and Michèle Lacrosil who succeed, she argues, in not only 'complicating Fanon's analysis of the lactification complex'. Rather, these authors, she suggests, also write a form of desire which resists reductive analysis including that of the gaze. Conrad James's essay engages with a reading of the equally complex 'maternal desire' in texts by black Cuban poet, Georgina Herrera. James foregrounds the contradiction which Herrera's poetry illustrates in the writing of the mother / daughter bond and particularly filial resentment. While much of Herrera's poetry 'goes against the grain' of ideals of motherhood, James argues, Herrera also represents motherhood as liberating. Following James's close attention to

Herrera's writing, Evelyn O'Callaghan's focus is more wide-ranging. In 'Politically Correct' Marginalisation and Early Narratives of the West Indies by White Women', she takes up the debate concerning the place of 'early' white women writers within the tradition of West Indian women's writing. Specifically, O'Callaghan questions the significance of race and notions of 'political correctness' in determining the marginalisation of some texts, particularly the 'early narratives'.

Like O'Callaghan, Paula E. Morgan, begins her paper with a focus on Jean Rhys. In 'Dark and Fathomable Beyond Control: Women Writing the Deviant Male' Morgan's central concern is with the 'portrayal of the deviant male as criminal'. While Jamaica is the primary locational setting of interest to Morgan, she explores writing by a range of authors including Olive Senior, Michelle Cliff and Barbara Lalla. Morgan argues that crucial to an understanding of male violence is an appreciation of 'interlocking concepts of gender and power', including those related to ethnicity.

In the final chapter, Joan Anim-Addo's 'Long Memoried Meanings' focuses on texts by African-Caribbean authors Beryl Gilroy, Grace Nichols and Merle Collins in order to explore some of the underpinnings of the writing of memory, principally the gaze, voice and testimony within specific texts. Closing the collection, Alba Ambert's 'In Reflection' privileges the direct voice between writer and Caribbean home place, in a differentiated and nuanced rendering of memory, which serves as an Epilogue to this volume.

Notes

1. M. Nourbese Philip, *She Tries Her Tongue Her Silence Softly Breaks*, London: Women's Press, 1993.
2. Ibid., p.70 (my italics).
3. I refer to the International conference hosted by the Caribbean Centre at Goldsmiths, University of London on 28-29 June, 1996.
4. Philip, ibid.
5. Édouard Glissant, *Poetics of Relation*, (*Poétique de la relation*, Gallimard, 1990), trans. Betsy Wing, Michigan: University of Michigan Press, 1997.

6. Ibid.
7. See Joan Anim-Addo (ed.) *Framing the Word : Gender and Genre in Caribbean Women's Writing*, London: Whiting and Birch, 1996.
8. See also Mary Condé and Thorunn Lonsdale, (eds.), *Caribbean Women Writers: Fiction in English*, Hampshire and London: Macmillan, 1999.
9. While it is true that there are publications about the literature, my focus here is on inclusion of Caribbean women's literature within 'mainstream' debate.

PROLOGUE

In the Matter of Memory

(A work in progress)[1]

M. NOURBESE PHILIP

A person who has no past, only a future is a person with little reality.

Octavio Paz

The yearning to transcend the insubstantialities of memory and return to a full knowledge of the past (and an unspoiled sense of the future) is an impossible one, but can be a rich source of imaginative insights.

Liz Heron

History is a dream from which I'm trying to awaken.

James Joyce

The Nightmare of History

For me history is not so much a dream from which I am trying to awaken as a nightmare. As a writer in the process of writing and re—writing the essentials of my reality, I use memory to awaken from this nightmare. Carlos Fuentes writes that 'we remember the future (and) imagine the past'; much of my work as poet and writer takes place within the boundaries delimited by a remembrance of the future and imagination of the past. There can, however, be no imagining of the past or remembrance of the future without a confrontation with history, a history or histories stolen, lost, mislaid, erased, embellished, hidden or found.

3

Memory, I suggest, is the activity that fuels the imagining of the past and the remembrance of the future, but is there any validity to memory in and of itself, or do we indulge in it for the sake of nostalgia? The English critic Terry Eagleton writes:

It is sentimentalism to believe that memories are valuable in themselves. To write of regional or rural memories...is often a way of evading the struggle with meaning, for such lovingly preserved experiences seem deceptively meaningful in themselves, and the act of narrating them assumes an auratic significance for which it has not sufficiently paid.[2]

Memory, however, can be a way of coming to terms with meaning, or even discovering meaning, as well as serving many other purposes:

- compensation for the earlier erasure of memories
- prevention of future mistakes
- to understand the why of something
- to grieve at a later time when earlier grief was not possible
- to correct mistakes and write the 'truth' of history
- to dispute lies
- for those whose lives appear meaningless, memory may be the only place to begin.

When the African came to the New World, she brought with her nothing but her body and all the memory and history which that body could contain. I use body here to include mind which is, in my opinion, very much a part of *and* an extension of body; I also believe that within the 'body', as the word is commonly used, resides an intelligence — including memory and knowledge — which is as important to the whole existence of the person as the intelligence we have come to associate with the mind.

What I learned from the slave is that I *can* control my body. Music, movement — this was outside the reach of the oppressor. The creative mind. The body intelligence. The imagination. This we could control. When I'm dancing, I'm dancing for my self and my people.[3]

The text of the African's history and memory was inscribed upon and within that body which would become the repository of all the tools necessary for spiritual and cultural survival. At her most unmanageable, the slave removed her body from control of the white master, either by suicide, or by maroonage, running away, where the terrain allowed, to highlands and mountains to survive with others as whole people and not as chattel.

And the body with its remembered and forgotten texts is of supreme importance in negotiating and balancing the relationships between history and memory.

How does one make memory 'matter' and what is the nature of the impulse that attempts to make memory material? One of the most obvious manifestations of this materiality is the erection of memorials. The many statues along University Avenue commemorating Canada's involvement in World War I and II for instance; the Vietnam war memorial in the United States and the AIDS quilt are examples that come to mind. And in making memory material, culture plays a profound role. Further, *in the absence of material evidence of the events being remembered,* such as slavery, for instance, how is memory made material?

Some of the most enduring and powerful images in modern times have been those associated with the Jewish Holocaust. For those of us who are not Jews these images have enabled us to enter this experience and to come to some point of sharing in the pain, the outrage and horror of these events. And among these images some of the most poignantly powerful have been those of piles of ordinary things like shoes, toothbrushes, household utensils and so on. The power of these images lies in their ability to underscore the absence and loss of the humans to whom these things once belonged. And so they become tangible evidence of the event that one wants remembered or to remember. Thinking of the cataclysmic events around the enslavement of Africans in the

New World, it appears to me that there exist no similar markers — and certainly not on the same scale — of these historical events, or of the memories generated by them. How then does memory function in the virtual absence of these markers? This work will explore the reasons for these absences as well as how memory functions in such circumstances and more particularly how the body becomes implicated in the materializing of memory. Although the events to which I refer have been recorded by history, for many reasons, not the least of which is the tension between history and memory (explored later), this fails to satisfy that impulse to materialize memory. Memory, I suggest, is to be found in the interstices, the silences, the half said, the stories that are passed on, the markers of absence.

Pierre Nora writes in his work: 'Between Memory and History':

Memory and history, far from being synonymous, appear now to be in fundamental opposition... At the heart of history is a critical discourse that is antithetical to spontaneous memory. History is perpetually suspicious of memory, and its true mission is to suppress and destroy it.[4]

The tensions between memory and history, I suggest, become particularly visible in certain cultural conflicts. For instance, among the arguments put forward by the supporters of the production of *Show Boat* was the historical one: 'This is the way things were'. Those opposed to the event not only questioned the historical accuracy of events, but also drew on the language of memory — the memory of slavery and what it meant to those who have suffered through it. This becomes particularly significant, given that those opposed to the show were not themselves African Americans but were from the Caribbean. The collision of these two languages: the language of history and that of memory was also evident in the issue of appropriation, where the history of the novel — freedom of the imagination for instance — came into conflict with the language of story—telling at the heart of which is memory.

MEMORY AND DIASPORA

DISCOURSES

Attitudes to Memory: Reappraisal and Self-Discovery in the Works of French Caribbean Women Writers

BEVERLEY ORMEROD

In French Caribbean writing by women, two kinds of memory are evoked and sometimes interwoven. There is the historical memory — collectively shared — of the Caribbean past, the loss of Africa, the centuries of slavery and French colonial rule, and the psychological and economic consequences of all this for West Indian society. And there are the private memories of a particular individual whose life is conditioned, or even dominated, by what has happened in some personal past. Sometimes such an individual is able to use memory creatively, in order to confront the past and reappraise it in a way that brings about spiritual healing or helps a character towards self-discovery and positive action. When this does not occur, memory may become the instrument of self-destruction, because of the individual's inability to break free, to separate a former state of helplessness and passivity from a potential movement towards independence.

In the works of fiction and drama to be discussed here, French Caribbean women writers deal with both kinds of memory, while sharing with the reader their perception that the victims of a crippling personal past are also the products of a historical situation. Individual obsessions and failures cannot readily be separated from social factors set in motion by Caribbean history. In exploring this dimension of remembrance, women authors from Guadeloupe and Martinique often focus on female experience,[1] sometimes in texts that highlight a contemporary individual's predicament when faced with a situation that reflects the female slave's historical lack of power to dispose of her body, her skills, or her children. The weight of memory may be felt as a burden, or it may be an agent of transcendence, a decisive element in determining a psychological outcome.

When choosing to illustrate historical memory, women writers have generally avoided the traditional approach of *Négritude* with its deliberate evocations of exceptional Caribbean male figures such as Toussaint L'Ouverture or Henri Christophe. Female Francophone authors in the second half of the twentieth century have opted rather to feature those ordinary individuals who would have been ignored by early archivists or keepers of upper-middle-class travel journals. In this respect, their stance resembles that of the contemporary, male-dominated *Créolité* movement inspired by Edouard Glissant and associated chiefly with the Martinican writers Patrick Chamoiseau and Raphaël Confiant.[2] But women writers in this region are on the whole individualists rather than members of official literary groups. They have long independently pursued the goal of recovering unrecorded aspects of West Indian social history through the fictional recreation of the individual feminine experience in earlier decades, while also seeking to capture the nuances of contemporary life in the French Caribbean.

Maryse Condé, the prolific Guadeloupean novelist and playwright, has drawn on her long personal experience of Africa in her imaginary reconstructions of the lives of the African ancestors and of an African female slave in the seventeenth century Caribbean and North America.[3] Her two-volume saga, *Ségou*, dedicated 'To my Bambara ancestress', reveals Condé's fascination with the historical conflicts within West Africa just before and during the establishment of the Atlantic slave trade: an Africa caught up in the struggle between indigenous tradition, Muslim penetration from the north and the first impact of European trade and expansion. The commitment and detail evident in her evocation of a distant African way of life do not, however, prevent her sounding a warning note elsewhere about the danger of West Indians' romanticising a false concept of the ancestral continent. In *Heremakhonon* she sardonically charts the disillusionment of a young Caribbean teacher who falls in love with an African politician. His power and glamour derive, for her, from the fact that he is a 'black man with ancestors', a genuine, authentic African, unlike those descended from slaves in her native West Indies. The politician, on the other hand, has no sense of racial or historical bonding with his admirer, and no comprehension of the psychological drives that motivate her interest in him. She seems to be simply another foreign groupie aspiring to his bed. A similarly ironic treatment of the notion that a shared culture and spiritual kinship exist between Africans and the black diaspora is evident in Condé's depiction of other failed relationships: the unhappy African/Caribbean marriage of *Une Saison à Rihata* (*A Season in Rihata*) and, in *Les Derniers Rois mages* (*The Last of the Magi*), the self-destructive union between a working-class West Indian man and the African-American college graduate who finds him desirable because his family is said to trace its ancestry directly to an African patriarch.[4] The same kind of frustrated yearning to be reintegrated with an African identity is a poignant theme in *L'Autre qui danse* (*The Other One, Who Dances*), a novel by the Martinican Suzanne Dracius-Pinalie. A student in Paris is drawn into a group of African squatters and conceives a child by one of them. But her lack of success in adopting, other than superficially, the signs of an African origin is contrasted with her sister's contented choice to embrace her own Caribbean identity.[5]

Simone Schwarz-Bart, another well-known Guadeloupean writer, is also concerned with the difficulties that Caribbean people face in relating to an imperfectly understood Africa. In *Ti Jean l'Horizon*, a novel of fantasy loosely based on the Eastern Caribbean folktale figure, she suggests some basic contradictions between West Indian and African perceptions of each other.[6] Ti Jean's fiercely proud Maroon grandfather assures him that a warm welcome awaits them some day in their ancestral village on the banks of the River Niger. But when they are magically returned to eighteenth century Africa, their native tribe treats them with violent hostility; they are regarded as being tainted by the disgrace of captivity and exile. The thrust of this novel is not to imply a real rejection by Africa of the blameless victims of slavery, but rather to suggest that returning to Africa should not be an end in itself, but only an initiatory step in the process of fully assuming one's Caribbean identity. While the traumatic uprooting from Africa is a key motif in both of Schwarz-Bart's novels, her dominant theme is the importance of a firmly-rooted national identity. Her best-known work, *Pluie et vent sur Télumée Miracle (The Bridge of Beyond)*, has as its iconic introductory figure an old woman who stands up in her little garden in order to assert her pride in belonging to her native Guadeloupe.[7]

The importance of the search for ancestry in the Caribbean is recognised by Schwarz-Bart through the way in which Télumée's maternal ancestry is carefully retraced over four generations. But slavery and the loss of Africa are present above all as background material that serves to alert the reader to the social and historical forces underlying the poverty of Télumée's village and the peasants' tendency to resignation and pessimism. The implication is always present that every hard-won moment of happiness is something rescued from the immense disaster of the past. Although Télumée's grandmother sings her a song of the girl child sold away from the plantation where her slave mother and siblings mourn her, Télumée's very presence at her grandmother's knee is an affirmation that family links can sometimes be restored. *Télumée Miracle* retraces the decades since 1848, the year when slavery ended in the French Caribbean, using the story of a female dynasty to show the choices and constraints that have determined the lives of the rural poor during an era of theoretical freedom. While indicating the strength of the Lougandor women, Schwarz-Bart acknowledges the general fragility of a sense of identity among the scattered descendants of uprooted slaves. Télumée's firm allegiance to her particular, known, female line contrasts with the other peasants' difficulty in assuming family responsibilities, their tenuous links with older generations, and their view of themselves as a handful of orphans.

Condé's *La Vie scélérate (The Tree of Life)* is another text preoccupied with the idea of ancestry and the recovery of a sense of identity rendered problematic by the enforced separation of families during slavery.[8] In this novel, the joyful transition from exile to repatriation — like an echo of the dream of those displaced by slavery, who traditionally awaited a spiritual return to ancestral Guinea at the end of their lives — is mirrored in the situation of an illegitimate Caribbean girl, left forgotten for years with a foster-mother in France while her real mother tries to escape her own racial and national identity. The child's long-delayed discovery of Guadeloupe and of her grandfather allows her to gain a healing knowledge of her cultural origins. Her emotional flag is firmly planted in the island that her mother had renounced in favour of France. Her feeling of belonging is patiently cultivated by the old man, whose sharing of family photographs and anecdotes — a domestic equivalent of traditional oral history — is designed to expunge the memory of her mother's rejection, establishing her in the heart of his family and implicating her in all its lines of descent.

The work of Condé and Schwarz-Bart is infused with a sharp awareness of the consequences for West Indian society not only of the historic loss of Africa, but also of the imposition of European colonial attitudes with regard to race and class hierarchies. In *Mémoires d'Isles (Memories of Isles)*, the Martinican playwright Ina Césaire interweaves personal and historical memory, dramatising colour and class conflicts which are the undeniable heritage of the slave past.[9] These conflicts are evoked through an encounter between two elderly Martinican half-sisters. Remembrance is the substance of their conversation; and the richness of their memories is compared to the soft, juicy flesh of a guinep, concealed beneath the dry outer shell of old age. But their recollections are of two very different pasts. The darker-skinned sister was illegitimate, and was never recognised as her father's daughter. This motif, briefly touched on in the published version of the play, is developed more fully in the extensively improvised stage version, where the protagonists' stories are specifically related to their place and position in Caribbean history. The prologue, recalling the suffering of those in the canefields, goes on to remind the audience of the unenviable lot of the female slave who worked in the Great House and was obliged to have children by her master. The theme of enforced race mixing leads on to more personal passages where the old women compare notes on their experience of class, skin colour and social acceptability. This reappraisal of their past has wider implications concerning the ways in which prejudices tied to race and illegitimacy have historically conditioned West Indian society and influenced events in twentieth century Martinique.

Other texts by Francophone Caribbean women writers have used the motif of the past in a less overt way, yet one guaranteed to arouse echoes in the mind of a public familiar with the region's history. Simone Schwarz-Bart's play, *Ton Beau Capitaine (Your Fine Captain)* is about a tangible form of memory, the one recorded in the cassettes which a Haitian couple exchange as the woman waits at home while the man works as an unskilled labourer in Guadeloupe.[10] Their past relationship is seldom directly evoked: it is their present situation, one of separation, distancing and loss, that conveys to the spectator all the pain of their charged memories. As Wilnor plays his wife's last cassette, there emerges the slow revelation of a betrayal of trust. Parallel to this personal blow, there is an implicit reminder of the fall from grace of Haiti itself, once the proud leader of a Caribbean revolution that showed the way to liberty and equality for all former slaves. Now Haiti is destitute, betrayed by generations of corrupt or ill-advised leaders. Ironically, the first island to be independent must now seek the patronage of islands that are themselves still dependent on France. The Haitian abroad has become a source of cheap labour and an object of contempt: Wilnor, in Guadeloupe, sees himself as '*their* black man, the black man's black, if you want to know'. The link between national and individual fate is suggested by the dimming memory of former pride and by the contrast, at both levels, between past confidence and present despair.

When presenting contemporary Caribbean society, women writers have been drawn to the exploration of characters whose minds are governed by their own past, trapped in the involuntary recollection of events, or situations that they cannot accept. Hindering their personal growth, memory serves the negative function of impelling them towards wrong choices. Writing over thirty years ago, the Guadeloupean novelist Michèle Lacrosil dramatised the fate of unhappy protagonists neurotically obsessed by a conviction of their own unworthiness, an assumption based entirely on childhood experiences that have reinforced their perception of their non-white skin as being inferior.[11] In their early contacts with teachers and schoolmates during the colonial era, all have undergone destructive indoctrination with regard to white 'superiority', sometimes unintentional, sometimes deliberately cruel. The fanciful fruit-names of some of Lacrosil's characters — *Sapotille*, the brown sapodilla or naseberry; *Cajou*, the reddish-brown cashew, with its underlying echo of Creole *kajou*, mahogany — are, to the bearers, the shameful designations of an unwanted skin colour. Unable to relate successfully to those of any race, their ways of coping with the unacceptable label of inferior 'Other' range from flight, to suicide, to murder.

But recent fiction by women is more optimistic about the possibility of coping with the memory of past trauma. Although writing from Haiti lies outside the scope of this paper, it is interesting to note the strength of the notion of healing in *Breath, Eyes, Memory*, a novel by the young writer Edwidge Danticat (now resident in the United States).[12] Danticat shows three generations of Haitian women struggling to survive against a backdrop of material poverty and retrograde tradition. The youngest is sent to join her immigrant mother in the United States. Haunted by the secret humiliations of her adolescent years, when her mother repeatedly made her undergo tests of her virginity, she escapes from home into an early, unsuitable marriage that is without sexual satisfaction. But, taking her baby back to her native village to stay with her grandmother and aunt, she learns that the virginity tests are part of a repeated pattern, a folk tradition which every female member of her family has had to endure — as inevitably as each female's name has been chosen from the same circle of family gravestones. In Haiti she comes to understand her likeness to the mother she had rejected, the mother who once was forced to submit to the same traditional tests; the mother whose death finally brings her daughter emotional liberation. Thus memory at last becomes, not an inhibiting force, but the point of departure for illumination and personal change.

This theme is also developed in Maryse Condé's *Traversée de la Mangrove (Crossing the Mangrove)*, where a largely female group of mourners is gathered around a coffin.[13] These women have long accepted their own social conditioning and the passive role which they are expected to play in their village. They habitually keep their private suffering and frustrations hidden, even from their own daughters. Their whole existence, including their choices of education or sexual partner, has always been determined by the overall patriarchal bias of their society. But the funeral wake, with its long periods of silent reflection, leads them to re-examine their own past in the context of the dead man's known actions. He becomes for them all an emblem of independence. Although his life certainly provides no model for the successful pursuit of happiness, the recollection of his freedom from conventional considerations is now a trigger for life choices that will bring the women, all victims in various ways of the expectations that tradition has imposed upon them, a much greater measure of hope for personal fulfilment.

Gisèle Pineau's first major novel, *La Grande Drive des esprits (The Great Drifting of the Spirits)*, was compared with the work of the *Créolité* writers Chamoiseau and Confiant, as, like them, she chose to highlight various picturesque elements of folk tradition: Creole cuisine, uninhibited sexuality, and the persistence of magic practices across three generations in early twentieth century Guadeloupe.[14] Her most recent novel, *L'Espérance macadam (The Tarmac of Hope)*, but also, loosely, in another possible reading, *Hope and Poor Man's Rice)*, explores different territory, offering a subtle illustration of the ways in which several layers of memory can control and prompt narrative action.[15] In the background of the novel is the unspoken historical heritage of slavery and dispossession, underlying the present evidence of physical brutality and psychological disturbance in a semi-rural slum district. The community can barely cope with the memory of local events that all have perceived to be both shameful and unavoidable: the mistreatment and abandonment of children, the violence of frustrated men towards their weaker, scapegoat partners, the helplessness of young girls in the face of a father's incestuous demands.

In this narrative the earliest victim, like those around her, has softened or repressed her memories of past trauma, and for much of the novel, her recognition of violence is diverted from the human sphere and projected through nature. Thus the notion of incest is transposed into the image of the violently destructive hurricane. The novel begins and ends with Hurricane Hugo, which devastated Guadeloupe in 1988; but the central character, the ageing Eliette, lives with the shadowy memory of a hurricane sixty years before, in which she was so badly injured that she was unable to speak for three years afterwards. The main action of the novel hinges upon this distant, imperfect memory of physical injury supposedly sustained by a falling beam. It is shot through at times with an inexplicable, alarming flash of recollection: Eliette's mother frantically bundling bloody sheets into a cupboard before carrying her child into the storm in a desperate search for help. But Eliette does not seek to recover full memory. Twice widowed and childless, she chooses to live alone, ignoring all dangerous thoughts, shying away from all hints of latent brutality, as she avoids all emotional contact with others in the district. The novel traces her gradual recovery of knowledge concerning her childhood, which is induced through her unwilling involvement with Angela, the adolescent daughter of her neighbours. Repeatedly raped by her father, Angela eventually denounces him to the police as he is about to turn his attentions to her younger sister. He is arrested and his wife, unable to accept what has happened, attacks her daughter and casts her out. This event is the

25

catalyst that drives Eliette, for the first time in her life, to show compassion and allow herself to be involved in another person's need.

The slow realisation of the parallels between Angela's experience and Eliette's is the counterpoint to other flashbacks through which Pineau demonstrates how subjective and unreliable is the very phenomenon of memory. There are, for instance, several 'true' yet different versions of the rape of Angela, coloured by the emotions of those most closely involved: Angela's own retrospective incomprehension, horror and dread; her imprisoned father's anger and pain as he remembers his own harsh childhood and his hope for a kind of fusion with his daughter's innocence; her mother's shock, visualising a repeated act of abuse which has taken place, incredibly, under her own roof, between her partner and her child; and the different kind of shock felt by Eliette as she relives in imagination a scene which is suddenly, terrifyingly, familiar to her. In this narrative, the act of remembering sears the mind with pain; yet the protagonist ultimately manages to survive the recovery of an intolerable memory. The ability to envisage such a survival might perhaps be interpreted as a metaphor for Caribbean healing, in that it posits the belief that a heritage of violence and dispossession can ultimately be transcended.

These works by French Caribbean women writers show remembrance as a complex phenomenon in Caribbean society. They stress the weight of historical memory, the underlying awareness within communities and individuals of past oppression which is at the root of much present-day suffering and violence. They demonstrate women's place in the past and in contemporary Caribbean society: frequently a disadvantaged place, as victims of male-dominated culture, lacking the physical strength necessary to impose their own choices of partner or way of life. But women are also revealed to be survivors, blessed with the moral energy necessary to confront the past, and generally able to avoid dwelling upon it in a self-destructive way. For Francophone Caribbean women writers, an understanding of the past is essential to a clear and sympathetic vision of contemporary society. At the same time, they suggest that a history of bitter struggle can co-exist with an optimistic vision of the future: the past can be seen not as an obstacle, but as a spur to personal and social transformation.

Notes

1. On the tendency of West Indian women's writing to foreground woman as subject, see Evelyn O'Callaghan's discussion of Anglophone writers in *Woman Version: Theoretical Approaches to West Indian Fiction by Women*, London: Macmillan, 1993, Introduction.

2. See the discussion of 'updating true memory' in Jean Bernabé, Patrick Chamoiseau and Raphaël Confiant, *Eloge de la Créolité*, Paris: Gallimard, 1989, trans. Mohamed B. Taleb Khyar, as 'In Praise of Creoleness', *Callaloo*, 13, (1990) 886-909.

3. Maryse Condé, *Ségou: Les Murailles de terre* and *Ségou: La Terre en miettes*, Paris: Laffont, 1984, 1985; *Moi, Tituba, sorcière noire de Salem*, Paris: Mercure de France, 1986, trans. Richard Philcox, as *I. Tituba, Black Witch of Salem*, Charlottesville: University Press of Virginia, 1992.

4. Maryse Condé, *Heremakhonon*, Paris: Union Générale d'Editions, 1976, trans. Richard Philcox, *Heremakhonon*, Washington: Three Continents Press, 1982; (1981) *Une Saison à Rihata*, Paris: Laffont, 1981, trans. Richard Philcox, *A Season in Rihata*, London: Heinemann, 1988; *Les Derniers Rois mages*, Paris: Mercure de France, 1992.

5. Suzanne Dracius-Pinalie, *L'Autre qui danse*, Paris: Seghers, 1989.

6. Simone Schwarz-Bart, *Ti Jean L'horizon*, Paris: Seuil, 1979, trans. Barbara Bray, *Between Two Worlds*, New York: Harper & Row, 1981.

7. Simone Schwarz-Bart, *Pluie et vent sur Télumée Miracle*, Paris: Seuil, 1972, trans. Barbara Bray,*The Bridge of Beyond*, New York: Atheneum, 1974.

8. Maryse Condé, *La Vie scélérate*, Paris: Seghers, 1987, trans. Victoria Reiter, *The Tree of Life*, New York: Ballantine Books, 1992.

9. Ina Césaire, *Mémoires d'Isles*, Paris: Editions Caribéennes, 1985. First performed in 1983. I am indebted to Bridget Jones for enabling me to consult the unpublished stage version of this play.

10. Simone Schwarz-Bart,*Ton Beau Capitaine*, Paris: Seuil, 1987.

11. Michèle Lacrosil, *Sapotille et le serin d'argile*, *Cajou*, and *Demain Jab-Herma*, Paris: Gallimard, 1960, 1961, 1967.

12. Edwidge Danticat, *Breath, Eyes, Memory*, USA: Soho Press, 1994; London: Abacus, 1995.

13. Maryse Condé, *Traversée de la mangrove*, Paris: Mercure de France, 1989, trans. Richard Philcox, *Crossing the Mangrove*, New York: Anchor Books, 1995.

14. Gisèle Pineau, *La Grande Drive des esprits*, Paris: Le Serpent à plumes, 1993.

15. Gisèle Pineau, *L'Espérance macadam*, Paris: Stock, 1995.

Living in the Spell of History:

The Novels of Jamaica Kincaid

DENISE deCAIRES NARAIN

We make too much of that long groan which underlines the past.

Derek Walcott[1]

But nothing can erase my rage — not an apology, not a large sum of money, not the death of the criminal — for this wrong can never be made right, and only the impossible can make me still: can a way be found to make what happened not have happened?

Jamaica Kincaid[2]

I shall discuss here the increasingly focused engagement with history in Jamaica Kincaid's three novels. Caribbean writers have often, as the quote above from Walcott suggests, looked to 'the terrible muse of history' for inspiration. Many of the texts written recently by Caribbean women writers suggest the continuing centrality of history. In addition, many Caribbean women writers, building on Kamau Brathwaite's experiments with voice in *The Arrivants* and his discussion of Creole language and orality in *A History of the Voice*, have asserted the importance of incorporating Creole in their texts as, amongst other things, a way of challenging dominant voicings and versions of his-story.[3] To some extent, the current emphasis on the literary use of Creole and its status as paramount symbol of survivalism in 'the New World', almost implies that history **is** *the voice*. Kincaid's texts, however, seem at odds with the noisy clamour of contemporary Caribbean women's texts.[4] I will argue, broadly, that Kincaid's texts move towards consolidating a sense of history as a huge immovable weight which severely constrains any articulation of self by the post-colonial woman and results in a muting of *voice* in her texts and a series of silent, self-contained protagonists.

History is important in each of Kincaid's three novels but a sequential reading of *Annie John, Lucy,* and *The Autobiography of My Mother* reveals a gradual but firm insistence on the disabling effects of colonial history.[5] I appreciate that there are risks in reading any writer's œuvre as a straightforwardly teleological progression and of insisting on an incestuous intimacy between their texts. But Kincaid's writing invites such a reading because of the way in which she repeatedly blurs distinctions between her own personal experiences (as described in interviews and various autobiographical pieces) and those represented in her fiction and because there are so many examples in her fiction of similar incidents making their appearance repeatedly, in different guises, in different texts. In addition to this seepage of the personal into the public, political arena, Kincaid's handling of the personal *within* her novels often insists on its location within the broader historical/political context of colonial and post-colonial history. The handling of the connections between the personal and the political is taken to its logical conclusion in Kincaid's novel, *The Autobiography of My Mother*, where History is presented as a bleakly deterministic force which immobilises and silences her protagonist and makes the reader yearn for a return to the worlds of Annie and Lucy where such an ideology has not yet taken hold.

In Kincaid's first novel, *Annie John*, it is the relationship between mother and daughter which is central and the drama which propels the narrative forward is Annie's response to being cast out from the Edenic garden of her mother's love. The mother, in this text, *is* her history and Annie must learn to leave this history behind and negotiate her place in a wider history in order to survive. That it is the onset of puberty which initiates her mother's rejection of her and propels her into 'the wide world', suggests the centrality of the body in Annie's quest for independence. Where, before her 'fall' from the grace of the dyadic relationship with the mother, little Annie had taken sensuous baths with her mother, had eaten with her and dressed like her, the pubescent Annie is constantly warned by her mother to police her body into ladyhood. This 'ladyhood business' is deemed necessary for Annie to avoid becoming a slut and it is here that Kincaid subtly makes a link between the values of the mother and the values of the mother country, so that Annie's rage at being betrayed by her mother is welded to her rage at her mother's insistence on socialising her via colonially-inherited gender roles to take her historically-determined place as a subservient post-colonial girl child.[6] Recognising that she doesn't fit easily into the ladyhood paradigm, Annie stages a series of small rebellions: she plays marbles, farts during piano lessons, plays with the outlawed 'red girl', displays her naked breasts in the graveyard and generally insists on asserting rather than effacing her embodied self throughout the text. Control of her body, then, becomes a way of resisting her 'historical' place in society.

The other crucial aspect of self-determination which appears in *Annie John* is a recognition of the importance of taking control over how one remembers and narrates one's life. In the ritual emptying of the trunk, for example, each of the stories the mother tells connects Annie to a particular item taken out of the trunk and, whether she was actually old enough to remember or not, Annie 'knew exactly what she would say, for I had heard it so many times before'.[7] In this way, she lays claim to these memories as 'events' of her own. Similarly, Annie identifies so powerfully with particular memories of her parents — and remembers and refers to them repeatedly — that she seems to inhabit them herself. After hearing of her father's abandonment by his parents and of his grandmother dying beside him in bed, 'I threw myself at him at the end of it, and we both started to cry — he just a little, I quite a lot'.[8] Her ability to control her response to the telling of these memories marks an important moment in her struggle for autonomy. So, when her mother, in an attempt to get Annie to confess to playing marbles, tells her the story of how she had, as a young girl, unknowinglyly carried a snake on her head amidst a bunch of fig bananas, she is just about to capitulate and reveal the marbles when she decides to resist the sentimental appeal of the story with a cunningly controlling voice of her own:

Summoning my own warm, soft, and newly acquired treacherous voice, I said, 'I don't have any marbles. I have never played marbles, you know'.[9]

The selective erasure of various parts of the photographs, in 'The Long Rain', can also be read as symbolic of this attempt to control the past by controlling memory.

Early on in the novel, the narrator had already neatly demonstrated some of the ways in which a narrative might be 'adjusted' for effect: asked to write an 'autobiographical essay' at school, Annie tells of a dream in which she is distressed at being separated from her mother but, in the version she offers her school mates, her mother does not turn her back on her (telling her not to eat unripe food late at night!) but consoles and reassures her. Here, Kincaid again emphasises the way in which the process of ordering the text compensates for the lack of order and control in the lived world. Stepping back from the detail of the text for a moment, the final chapter in *Annie John*, 'A Walk to the Jetty', in which important bits of information about Annie's life are suddenly given (her father is thirty-five years older than her mother, for example) acts as a prompt to the reader to ask questions about the ordering and re/presentation of self of *Annie John* itself. In other words, Kincaid's strategy here is to alert the reader to the selective and partial way in which memory can be used to construct a particular version of the self.

Towards the end of *Annie John*, the narrator, recovering from a breakdown of sorts, says, 'how much I longed to be in a place where nobody knew a thing about me'.[10] In *Lucy* we are given a narrator who is in a place where she is unknown (she works as a nanny for a middle-class American family), where her own personal history is not mapped onto her surroundings as it is in *Annie John* (where her mother can point to the very tree she sat beneath to embroider Annie's first chemise). But geographical relocation, while it may afford some distance from the immediate hooks of family,[11] serves to heighten the role of memory and to foreground the immutability of History:

I used to think that just a change of venue would banish forever from my life the things I most despised. But that was not to be so. As each day unfolded before me, I could see the sameness in everything; I could see the present take a shape — the shape of my past.
My past was my mother.[12]

Thus, the will to control memory — particularly those associated with mother/home — is even more emphatically articulated in this text. Lucy refuses to open the letters from her mother but keeps them in her bra where they scorch her breasts;[13] an image which captures powerfully the ambivalent forces at work here of simultaneous denial and yearning:

The object of my life now was to put as much distance between myself and the events mentioned in her letter as I could manage. [...] and if I could put enough events between me and the events mentioned in her letter, would I not be free to take everything as it came *and not see hundreds of years in every gesture, every word spoken, every face?* [14]

It is not the case that the narrator does not feel, does not cry, does not miss home; we are told that this happens but it is never dwelt upon and is invariably overridden by a statement of *willed control* over such 'lapses' into expressions of sentiment. So, for example, when Mariah's family and Lucy are all leaving the lake, she announces', — I would not miss anything, for I long ago had decided not to miss anything'.[15]

Instead, the narrator assembles a sense of self which — in shaping itself against the mother's wishes (as 'slut', not 'lady') — reinscribes the mother as absence instead of all-consuming presence. That this absence becomes as powerful as presence is taken further in *The Autobiography of My Mother* which I will discuss below. For the moment, what I want to emphasise is the way in which the focus on the invention of self is fuelled by a desire to exorcise the past in an attempt to exercise control over one's personal history; a kind of control which Kincaid herself demonstrates through the self-conscious manipulation of textual surfaces. One's life, then, becomes a script which can be re-written *at will*. In *Annie John*, in the face of her mother's disappointment with her, Annie carefully rearranges her life, regrouping her friends and reminding herself of her own strengths away from her mother.[16] This sense of manipulating the raw material of experience into the script of one's life story is even more disturbingly exemplified in *Lucy*, when the narrator remembers an incident involving a childhood friend. What Lucy feels now, when she remembers Myrna's story — in which her young friend is sexually abused for a pittance by a fisherman — is that the event is wasted on Myrna; here, Lucy wants to *possess* Myrna's past:

I was almost overcome with jealousy. Why had such an extraordinary thing happened to her and not to me? Why had Mr. Thomas chosen Myrna as the girl he would meet in secret and place his middle finger up inside her and not me?[...] This would have become the experience of my life, the one all others would have to live up to. What a waste! It meant nothing to Myrna; she spoke only of the money.[17]

In another scene, having witnessed her first snow fall, Lucy claims it as her first 'real past':

I could now look back at the winter. It was my past, so to speak, my first real past — a past that was my own and over which I had the final word.[18]

This self-conscious construction of self recalls Derek Walcott's Adamic artist-figure; but where his New World Adam suggests a fresh, appraising gaze, Kincaid's artist-figure has the knowingly scorching gaze of an already-wise Lucifer. In a recent interview in *Wasafiri*, Kincaid describes her writing style: 'So I just now use this slash-and-burn policy of writing, I just say what I have to say and get out'.[19] Where Walcott's texts patiently work towards a dense and complex repertoire of images which might cumulatively suggest a 'New World *tradition*', Kincaid's hit-and-run approach refuses such a teleological destination. Instead, her narrators (all artists of sorts) can only yearn to be 'New World Eves' while their pasts continue to insist on their location as post-colonial subjects.

In a piece published recently in *Transition*[20] Kincaid talks about a brother of hers, recently diagnosed as HIV positive, and she reminds her mother of the time when red ants attacked this brother in his bed:

> I reminded my mother of the ants almost devouring him and she looked at me, her eyes narrowing in suspicion, and she said, *'What a memory you have!'* — for that is perhaps the thing she dislikes most about me.[21]

Throughout Kincaid's texts, the frequent repetition and recycling of particular events gives the reader a sense that these *really are* Kincaid's memories and — by dint of our familiarity with them in their various guises — ours too. She is, in *Annie John* and *Lucy*, 'long-memoried' but in a way which refuses the all-embracing representativeness of Grace Nichols's long-memoried woman[22] and, instead, welds personal history into a tailor-made set of armour. The insistence in *Annie John* and *Lucy* on controlling one's 'life-history' is coupled with a stark recognition of, and confrontation with, colonial His/story. The *knowingness* of the narrators which results from such a vision is bleak:

> I understood that I was inventing myself [...] I did not have position, I did not have money at my disposal. I had memory, I had anger, I had despair.[23]

Kincaid's mother's words,[24] 'What a memory you have!' are echoed in *Lucy* by the words Mariah (a figure sometimes likened to the mother and sometimes precisely not like the mother) uses when Lucy describes her dream of being chased and buried under a pile of (Wordsworthian) daffodils: *What a history you have*'.[25] And it is the sheer weight of this History which Annie and Lucy rail against and which, finally, silences and imprisons Xuela. The fine-tuning of autobiographical detail which characterises the handling of personal history and the frequent rehearsing of versions of self, is always played out within the parameters for the *worlding* of the self which Colonial History has ordained, as in this example from *Lucy*:

I was not a man; I was a young woman from the fringes of the world, and when I left home I had wrapped around my shoulders the mantle of a servant.[26]

But, while Kincaid presents colonial history in bluntly precise essentials in *Annie John* and *Lucy*, she also provides images which overtly resist and challenge that history. So, Annie inscribes her mother's words 'The Great Man Can No Longer Just Get Up and Go' under the picture of Columbus in her *A History of the West Indies*, undermining and mocking his greatness.[27] We are presented with the image of blond-headed Ruth, resplendent in the dunce's cap, as well as the putty-faced princess also from England. In *Lucy*, Kincaid gives us the image of Lucy scything away the daffodils and ruining Mariah's complacent pleasure by transforming the spring scene into 'a scene of conquered and conquests'.[28] Columbus makes a reappearance in *Lucy* as someone who should have been taxed by the effort of having to name so many discoveries, 'A task like that would have killed a thoughtful person, but he went on to live a very long life'.[29]

In response to Mariah's frequent references to 'women in history' and to books, Lucy invokes the intuitive knowing associated with her mother, grandmother and home. In *Annie John*, Annie wishes her father could fashion her a set of clamps to retard her growth into full-blown womanhood.

Escape from the island becomes essential for her survival. In *Lucy* her relocation from Antigua to America allows her to 'talk with her body', to indulge her interest in sex and to reinvent herself as the very slut she was warned against becoming. Sexuality becomes an arena in which she can exercise some agency and her sexual exploits with men are narrated from a position in which Lucy has every aspect of the deal covered; the fact that this is cold comfort is hinted at in the text and more fully released on the final page when she dissolves into tears. Control of her body, like the control of her life via the repeated re-telling and re-shuffling of memories, gives Lucy a self-contained aloofness which is, however, tempered by the glimpses we get in the text of her vulnerability and of the sheer effort of *will* required to sustain the anger necessary for such control to be maintained.

In Kincaid's *The Autobigraphy of My Mother*, there is no such respite for the reader as Kincaid's argument about History works to its logical conclusion. *Lucy* ends with the narrator's tears blurring the line she writes in her pristine notebook: 'I wish I could love someone so much that I could die from it'[30] while *The Autobiography of My Mother* opens with these words:

My mother died at the moment I was born, and so for my whole life there was nothing standing between myself and eternity; at my back was always a bleak, black wind.

and ends, 'Death is the only reality, for it is the only certainty, inevitable to all things'.[31] This image of death punctuates the text as a repeated refrain, reminding the reader again and again of the orphanhood of the narrator, Xuela Claudette Richardson, and — by association — of the orphanhood of *all* Dominicans. That Kincaid returns to the West Indies in this novel, however, has nothing of the tentative optimism of, say, Brathwaite's *The Arrivants*:

now waking/ making/ making/ with their/ rhythms some-/thing torn/and new[32]

The return to an island location (this time, Dominica) two novels later affords Kincaid the opportunity to reiterate even more powerfully the *lack* — of possibilities, of love — inherent to such small places.[33] It is interesting that this novel is dedicated to Derek Walcott for it represents an insistent challenge to Walcott's notion, quoted above, that '...we make too much of that long groan which underlines the past..', for *The Autobiography* presents the past as *eternally* determining one's future. So, just as Xuela constantly circles back to the death of her mother at her birth, so, too, History is presented as an immutable fact which determines forever Xuela's position in the world as one of the 'defeated'.

The novel charts Xuela's birth through to her seventies but each episode narrated confirms the sense of herself as unloved — in her home and in the wider culture. As with the earlier novels, there is an emphasis on asserting and claiming one's embodied and sexual self but where those novels pointed to brief moments of connection between Annie and Gwen or the red girl or between Lucy and Peggy or Mariah, in this novel, Xuela is bleakly and inviolably *alone*. The novel begins with her father bundling the young Xuela out, along with his washing, to Ma Eunice, leaving the child to wonder if he makes any distinction between the two 'bundles'. When she accidentally breaks Ma Eunice's china plate (decorated with an idealised image of England and the word, 'heaven') she is forced to kneel on a pile of stones, holding her hands high with a stone clasped in each hand. Into this punishment Xuela reads history writ large:

Why should this punishment have made a lasting impression on me, redolent as it was in every way of the relationship between captor and captive, master and slave, with its motif of the big and the small, the powerless, the strong and the weak.[34]

When she returns to live with her father, she recognises immediately that her step-mother does not like her:

My spirit rose to meet this challenge. No love: I could live
in a place like this. I knew this atmosphere all too well.
Love would have defeated me. Love would always defeat
me.[35]

and, when she is sent to stay with a friend of her father's so
that she can attend school in Roseau, he exploits her curiosity
about sex and eventually impregnates her. The abortion she
has catapults her into adulthood and the realisation that:

I knew things that you can know only if you have been
through what I had just been through. I had carried my
own life in my hands.[36]

The self-aware *knowingness* of the narrator, familiar to us
from reading *Annie John* and *Lucy*, is given much greater
significance in this text and allows Xuela a bleakly panoramic
vision backwards. In the earlier novels, the known 'biological'
mother is always the focal point of the narrator's existence
and the detailed memories associated with the mother,
however bitter, seem to eclipse the harsh realities of postcoloniality. In *Autobiography*, all that is available of the
mother is the white hem of her skirt as she ascends a ladder
in Xuela's recurring dream and this, coupled with the
ambiguities surrounding the title of the novel — *whose* story
is being told in this *autobiography?* — confirms the sense of
Xuela as an archetypal figure. Without the Janus-faced
mother figure to mediate between herself and her past, the
protagonist in this novel engages head-on with History. It is
the violence of this history which makes love an impossibility:

The people we should naturally have mistrusted were
beyond our influence completely; [...] To mistrust each
other was just one of the many feelings we had for each
other, all of them the opposite of love, all of them
standing in the place of love.[37]

This bereftness of love in both the private and public
arenas of her life, spawns a narcissism of terrifying proportions

which is most compellingly dramatised in the text with reference to the body and to sexuality. Aware that she is not recognised in the eyes of any other as *beloved*, and so 'I came to love myself in defiance, out of despair, because there was nothing else',[38] Xuela learns to treasure the *thereness* of her body, the smells, the dirt, the 'funk':

> Whatever about me caused offense, whatever was native to me, whatever I could not help and was not a moral failing — those things about me I loved with the fervor of the devoted.[39]

Throughout the text, there are scenes in which aspects of her embodied self are described and affirmed:

> I began to worship myself. My black eyes, the shape of half-moons were alluring to me; my nose, half flat, half not, as if painstakingly made that way, I found so beautiful that I saw in it a standard which the noses of the people I did not like failed to meet. I loved my mouth; my lips were thick and wide [...] My own face was a comfort to me, my own body was a comfort to me.[40]

This sense of taking refuge in the body is often dramatised in the masturbatory scenes which punctuate the text. Early on in the novel, she caresses herself to sleep to escape the sounds of the night but, later on, when she is involved in sexual relationships with men, descriptions of these sexual encounters are often preceded by descriptions of Xuela fondling herself. So her involvement with Monsieur LaBatte begins when he sees her caressing herself in the garden at twilight:

> This scene of me placing my hand between my legs and then enjoying the smell of myself and Monsieur LaBatte watching me lasted until the usual falling of the dark.[41]

Similarly, just before she has sex with Philip, the English doctor, whom she eventually marries, she is sitting on the floor caressing herself 'in an absentminded way', with her fingers trapped in the hair between her legs. Kincaid describes these sexual encounters in some detail, exploiting well the ambivalent forces and unbalanced power relationships entailed when the fifteen year old Xuela has sex with the much older, Monsieur LaBatte or with the culturally/socially/historically powerful Philip. The bluntness in the telling of these encounters and the patient recounting of the various ways in which the narrator asserts her sexuality (she makes Philip 'eat' her as a way of silencing him when he waxes lyrical about England), both confirms the sense of Xuela's powerful physical and sexual agency *and* the very limited parameters within which she can demonstrate such agency.

The reader is given brief respite from the sterility and lovelessness of these sexual relationships when Xuela falls in love with Roland[42], the stevedore whose 'mouth was like an island in the sea'.[43] He is introduced as the lover, 'Philip's opposite', whom she thinks of when 'Philip was inside me, in those moments when the pleasure of his thrusts and withdrawals waned'.[44] But even this relationship, despite the lyricism surrounding its beginning, is doomed by history, 'he did not have a history; he was a small event in someone else's history';[45] and later, 'He did not sail the seas, he did not cross the oceans, he only worked in the bottom of vessels that had done so'. So, as if to compensate for his irrelevance to history, Roland accumulates women who will provide him with offspring to assure him of status of some kind. Xuela refuses to be added to such a list but acknowledges his disappointment:

Why did I not bear his children? [...] — I felt much sorrow for him, for his life was reduced to a list of names that were not countries, and to the number of times he brought the monthly flow of blood to a halt; his life was reduced to women.[46]

The relationship ends but Xuela does not have children with Philip either; instead, the regularity of her menstrual cycle is a source of pleasure and power throughout the text, a symbol of her ability to 'carry her life in her own hands'. Having undergone a painful abortion very early in her life, her refusal of further pregnancies is given strange and dramatic expression in a passage in the novel where, having declared her categorical refusal of motherhood, she imagines bearing children and destroying them in variously macabre ways:

> I would condemn them to live in an empty space frozen in the same posture in which they had been born. I would throw them from a great height; every bone in their body would never be properly set, healing in the way they were broken, healing never at all.[47]

By so vehemently rejecting motherhood, the narrator seeks to short-circuit history, to refuse to project herself into a future which such offspring would symbolise. When her step-sister has an unwanted pregnancy to deal with, it is Xuela who forcibly removes it by putting her hand into her womb:

> Her body shrank and crumpled up with pain. She did not die. I had become such an expert at being ruler of my own life *in this one limited regard* that I could extend such power to any other woman who asked me for it.[48]

In another scene, Xuela ponders on why she is unable to feel 'even a tiny bit of sympathy' for Philip's wife, Moira, who, like her, has a 'broken womb' but concludes that such an alliance is impossible because of the crucial distinction between them:

> she was a lad
> y, I was a woman, [...] I was a woman and as that I had a brief definition: two breasts, a small opening between my legs, one womb; it never varies and they are always in the same place.[49]

It is the 'self-possession' which the acceptance of such a truncated subjectivity allows which renders the narrator so formidable and which prohibits any relationship from flourishing. Xuela eventually marries Philip (after Moira dies) and they live high above the mountains away from Roseau. Though Philip devotes himself to her, the narrator does not flinch from exposing the self-delusions which such a love rests upon, 'He thought I made him forget the past'[50] a past full of 'conquests, [and] the successful disruption of other peoples' worlds', while she recognises that she has married him because:

It allowed me to make a romance of my life. [...]Romance is the refuge of the defeated; the defeated need songs to soothe themselves,[...] for when they are awake it is a nightmare, the dream of sleep is their reality.[51]

In response to their mutual entrapment in the legacy of colonial history, 'He and I lived in the spell of history'. Xuela retreats further into herself — and embraces silence. While Philip busies himself with his shelves of 'noisy' books, drawing on 'the noisiness of the world into which he was born' and craves the sound of Xuela's footsteps or laughter or voice, she wilfully denies him those sounds:

He grew to live for the sound of my footsteps, so often I would walk without making a sound; he loved the sound of my voice, so for days I would not utter a word.[52]

Recognising that Philip lives in a world in which he does not speak the language (patois), Xuela translates for him but distorts it so that she blocks his entrance into her world. It is in this world of mutual 'untranslatability' that the novel ends:

He spoke to me, I spoke to him; he spoke to me in English, I spoke to him in patois. We understood each other better that way, speaking to each other in the language of our thoughts.[53]

Elsewhere, the narrator explains Philip's refusal of silence in the context of his cultural and historical heritage:

Philip belonged to that restless people unable to leave the world alone, unable to look at anything for too long without becoming troubled by its very existence; *silence is alien to them.*[54]

While earlier on in the novel, looking at the houses in Roseau, Xuela observes:

In this sort of house lived people whose skin glistened with exhaustion and whose faces were sad even when they had a reason to be happy, people for whom history had been a big, dark room, *which made them hate silence.*[55]

Here, Kincaid's narrator affirms silence as a strategy which allows history to be contemplated and confronted while speech suggests a noisy escapism which results in an elision of the problems generated by that history. Silence is also the necessary corollary of Xuela's carefully honed self-reliance, a self-reliance forged at an early age out of the need to protect herself. So, Xuela doesn't speak until she's four and when she does, she prefers speaking to herself, finding that her own voice makes her loneliness less. Or, on the road she walks to school, she enjoys the tongue-tying effect of eating cashews because 'I found this, the difficulty of speaking, the possibility that it might be a struggle for me ever to speak again, delicious'.[56] She and Madame LaBatte — one of the few people in the text with whom Xuela seems able to communicate — speak to each other in silence:

To communicate so intimately with someone, to be spoken to silently by someone and yet understand more clearly than if she had shouted at the top of her voice, was something I did not experience with anyone ever again in my life.[57]

While the trope of silence figures most explicitly in *Autobiography*, it is there in each of the novels in the quality of silence which pervades these texts. Now, this is partly the effect of Kincaid's elegantly spare writing style but it is also the result of an absence of direct speech — conversations *do* happen in Kincaid's texts but they are *reported* to the reader and are always already filtered through the caustic gaze of the narrative 'I'. There are no attempts, in these texts, as is the case with Olive Senior's stories, for instance, of handing over substantial parts of the text to the voices of the people. Neither is there the attempt to fragment the body of the text with the use of a variety of linguistic registers, including proverbs, as Merle Collins does in *Angel* in her literary retelling of the history of the Grenadian revolution. Erna Brodber's novels, *Jane and Louisa Will Soon Come Home, Myal*, and *Louisiana* all similarly insist on the centrality of *the voice* as a textual strategy for responding to the damaging legacy of colonial history. Brodber's texts perhaps make the most interesting contrast with Kincaid's œuvre because Brodber's constant shifting between narrative subjectivities and her insistence on incorporating the spoken word at every turn combine with the ideological thrust of her novels towards an affirmation of Creole speech as symbol of survivalism and medium for change.

Kincaid, by comparison, acknowledges that patois exists but avoids representing it on the page, so in *Annie John*, we are told that her mother calls her a slut but the word slut — in patois — is not revealed, 'The word 'slut' (in patois) was repeated over and over...';[58] *Lucy*, accused by the maid of speaking 'like a nun', bursts into a calypso but we are not given the lyrics. In *Autobiography*, we are told that English is spoken at school and French patois at home, and, when Xuela and Madame LaBatte are alone they speak to each other in 'French patois, the language of the captive, the illegitimate',[59] but the communication they have about the coffee (which precedes the above quote) is rendered in English. The young Xuela interprets her step-mother's insistence on speaking to her in patois as an attempt to 'make an illegitimate of me'.[60] In the scene in which Roland's wife confronts Xuela in the street, a scene which many other writers might have exploited for its operatic, comic potential, Kincaid simply presents a list of the invectives the wife uses. In the autobiographical piece, 'My Brother', she first reports what her brother says and then renders it in creole in brackets, while in an interview in *Wasafiri*, she says, 'I don't even know how to speak creole any more'.[61] While there may well be truth in this with regard to her own *spoken* Creole, I would prefer to read the refusal to *write* Creole as indicative of a literary choice which necessitates the bracketing of Creole in the pursuit of a narrative voice which can contain and shape the anger which the confrontation with History produces. The precisely correct, (deceptively) simple, almost mannered English which characterises the narrative voices of Kincaid's three novels makes the rage which fuels these texts manageable. Where many Caribbean women writers from Louise Bennett on have seen in the linguistic amplitude of Creole — its *slackness* — an opportunity for the positive assertion of identity, Kincaid deliberately and self-consciously *avoids* such excesses.

Instead, the reader is isolated within the confines of a first-person narrative voice which gets its strength and clarity of vision by asserting a knowing *distance* between itself and the *community*. This distance is partly the result of Kincaid's insistence on individual responsibility; there is no refuge to be taken in group identity or easy self-forgiving. But it is also a distance which Kincaid's texts, in a variety of implicit and explicit ways, often suggest is the necessary requirement for the writer/artist to produce. In *Lucy*, while recognising that artists were invariably men and never from 'the place where I came from', she still admires their aloofness from the everyday. 'And I thought, I am not an artist, but I shall always like to be with the people who stand apart'.[62] For Kincaid, 'standing apart' from the orthodoxies of Caribbean women's writing, or Caribbean writing in general, includes the forging of a distinctive literary voice which eschews any form of Creole in favour of the precise correctness of 'Standard English'; a choice which allows her to — precisely — fine-tune the anger generated by the recognition of her historically determined placelessness and voicelessness, 'but I, Xuela, am not in a position to make my feeling have any meaning'.[63] In response to Gayatri Spivak's famous question, 'Can the subaltern speak?', many critics have posited Creole as the most appropriate medium for the subaltern to speak in — and be *heard*[64] Kincaid, on the other hand, deliberately and successfully exploits the tension of manoeuvring within the literary straitjacket of Standard English, '(For isn't it odd that the only language I have to speak of this crime is the language of the criminal who committed the crime?)'[65] This also raises questions about who Kincaid's texts speak to and certainly there is an increasing sense that the primary targets of her texts are metropolitanly-based Mariah-like readers. In an interview with Frank Birbalsingh, Kincaid says:

> but I think I'm drifting that way — to now tell the people who used to own me a few things about themselves. They invented a life for me. I cannot do that. I know the danger of invention. I will tell them the truth about them-selves'.[66]

I began this paper with quotes from Derek Walcott and Jamaica Kincaid which suggested a difference in their professed responses to history. By way of conclusion I'd like to use parallel quotes again from Walcott and Kincaid to suggest similarities in their perceptions of the role of the writer. Here is the final stanza from Walcott's 'Mass Man':

> Upon your penitential morning
> some skull must rub its memory with ashes,
> some mind must squat down howling in your dust,
> some hand must crawl and recollect your rubbish,
> someone must write your poems.[67]

And this is Kincaid's Xuela reflecting on the imprisonment — of the conquerors and defeated alike — in the spell of history:

> And I learned, too, that no one can truly judge himself; to describe your own transgressions is to forgive yourself for them; to confess your bad deeds is also at once to forgive yourself, and so silence becomes the only form of self-punishment: to live forever locked up in an iron cage made of your own silence, *and then, from time to time, to*

have that silence broken by a designated crier, someone who repeats over and over, in broken or complete sentences, a list of the violations, the bad deeds committed.[68]

It is this role of 'designated crier' which Kincaid claims for herself in *Autobiography*. The detailed intimacy of Annie's and Lucy's battle for control over their own memories, their own histories, and their own bodies is replaced by the monumental rage of Xuela and her silent scream in the face of the immovable weight of colonial history. This avenging 'angel' — the 'Lucifer' embraced by Lucy — recalls the image of 'the angel of history' in Walter Benjamin's 'Theses on the Philosophy of History':

His face is turned towards the past. Where we perceive a chain of events, he sees one single catastrophe which keeps piling up wreckage upon wreckage and hurls it in front of his feet. The angel would like to stay, awaken the dead, and make whole what has been smashed. But a storm is blowing from Paradise; it has got caught in his wings with such violence that the angel can no longer close them. This storm irresistibly propels him into the future to which his back is turned, while the pile of debris before him grows skyward. This storm is what we call progress.[69]

Kincaid's vision is a bleakly uncompromising and sobering one which seriously questions the possibility of *progress* at all. In the context of the literary output of Caribbean women writers such a sharply defined vision — however bleak — is very welcome.

Notes

1. Derek Walcott, *The Antilles, Fragments of Epic Memory*, New York: Farrar, Straus & Giroux, 1992.
2. Jamaica Kincaid, *A Small Place*, London: Virago, 1988, p.31.
3. Kamau Brathwaite, *The Arrivants*, Oxford: Oxford University Press, 1967; *A History of the Voice*, London: New Beacon, 1984.

4. There are numerous examples of texts by Caribbean women in which poetic and narrative voices are rendered in Creole; two recent examples would include Ifeona Fulani, *Seasons of Dust*, New York: Harlem River Press, 1997; Dionne Brand, *In Another Place, Not Here*, London: The Women's Press, 1997.

5. Jamaica Kincaid, *Annie John*, London: Picador, 1985; *Lucy*, London: Plume, 1991; *The Autobiography of My Mother*, London: Vintage, 1996.

6. In the short story, 'Girl', in *At The Bottom Of The River*, the mother's advice to her daughter is punctuated with the phrase 'and not like the slut you are so bent on becoming'.

7. Kincaid, 1985, p.21.

8. Ibid., p.24.

9. Ibid., p.70.

10. Ibid., p.127.

11. I am reminded here of Margaret Atwood's poem 'You Fit into Me', 'you fit into me/ like a hook into an eye/ a fish hook/ an open eye'; see A.W. Allison et al, eds., *The Norton Anthology of Poetry*, New York, 1983, p.1375.

12. Kincaid, 1991, p.90.

13. Ibid., p.20.

14. Ibid., p.31, my emphasis.

15. Ibid., pp.81-2.

16. Kincaid, 1985, p.67.

17. Kincaid, 1991, p.105.

18. Ibid., p.23.

19. 'Jamaica Kincaid talks to Gerhard Dilger' in *Wasafiri*, 16, (Autumn, 1992), 21-5.

20. Jamaica Kincaid, 'My Brother', in *Transition*, 72, (Winter, 1996), 4-34.

21. Ibid.

22. Grace Nichols, *I Is a Long Memoried Woman*, London: Karnak House, 1983.

23. Kincaid, 1991, p.134.

24. And here it is her real mother being quoted — or is it?

25. Kincaid, 1991, p.19.

26. Ibid. p.95.

27. Kincaid, 1985, p.78.

28. Kincaid, 1991, p.30.
29. Ibid., p.135.
30. Ibid., p.164.
31. Kincaid, 1996, p.228.
32. E.K. Brathwaite, *The Arrivants: A New World Tragedy*, London: OUP, 1975, pp.269-70.
33. Jamaica Kincaid, *A Small Place*, New York: Farrar, 1988; London: Virago, 1988.
34. Kincaid, 1996, p.10.
35. Ibid., p.29.
36. Ibid., p.83.
37. Ibid., p.48, my emphasis.
38. Ibid., p.57.
39. Ibid., pp.32-3.
40. Ibid., p.100.
41. Ibid, p.70.
42. Roland had made an appearance in *Lucy* as the man in the camera shop with whom she has sex.
43. Kincaid, 1996, p.163.
44. Ibid.
45. Ibid., p.167.
46. Ibid., pp.175-6.
47. Ibid., p.97-8.
48. Ibid., p.115, my emphasis.
49. Ibid., p.158-9.
50. Ibid., p.221.
51. Ibid., p.216.
52. Ibid., p.217-8.
53. Ibid., p.219.
54. Ibid., p.209, my emphasis.
55. Ibid., p.61-2, my emphasis.
56. Ibid., p.51.
57. Ibid., p.69.
58. Kincaid, 1985, p.102.
59. Kincaid, 1996, p.74.
60. Ibid., p.30.
61. See 'Jamaica Kincaid Talks to Gerhard Dilger' in *Wasafiri*, 16, (Autumn, 1992) 21-25.
62. Kincaid, 1991, p.98.

63. Kincaid, 1996, p.137.

64. See, for example, Carolyn Cooper *Noises in the Blood*, London: Macmillan, 1993; Ketu Katrak 'Decolonizing Culture: Toward a Theory for Postcolonial Women's Texts', in *Modern Fiction Studies*, 35(1) (Spring, 1989).

65. Kincaid, 1998, p.31.

66. Frank Birbalsingh (ed.), *Frontiers of Caribbean Literature in English*, London: Macmillan, 1996, p.150.

67. Derek Walcott, 'Mass Man' in *Derek Walcott: Collected Poems 1948-1984*, Toronto: Harper & Collins, 1986, p.99.

68. Kincaid, 1996, p.60, my emphasis.

69. Walter Benjamin, in Arendt, H. (ed.), *Illuminations*, trans. H. Zohn, London: Fontana, 1973, p.281.

Re-memorying, Decolonialising and Translating in Jamaica Kincaid's *The Autobiography of My Mother*

GIOVANNA COVI

Jamaica Kincaid's continuous rewriting of her own life in terms of a conflictual confrontation with her mother and country certainly goes beyond the personal claiming of her rights to independence and emancipation: her individual struggle for liberation from economic and cultural restrictions vindicates not only a history of gender discrimination, racial oppression, and colonial subjugation, but also persistently dismantles the ideological foundations that have allowed for the imposition of sexual, racial, and imperial hierarchies in modern times. Kincaid indeed contributes to the creation of a new culture which resists former as well as present forms of domination. In Toni Morrison's terms, she participates in a process of 're-memory', which allows for former oppression to shape present liberation and resistance and to conceive subjectivities that, however temporary and changeable, are fully conscious of the forces of power that threaten to reduce them to subaltern positions, precisely because they are grounded on those facts of history — personal and collective — which cannot and should not be erased.

   In a way more complex and comprehensive than, for instance *A Small Place*, *The Autobiography of My Mother: A*

Novel [1] forcefully subverts the colonial writing of the discovery
and possession of the 'other'/'new' world: its stance not only
goes beyond a simple reversal of the imperial point of view; it
also voices the implications of a rewriting of history that
liberates the subject from colonial and patriarchal as well as
from cultural domination. It does so by promoting an identity
which Adrienne Rich would describe as never resting on the
newly-found place, never turning it into a monumental,
promised land[2] — a migrant identity which keeps passing from
place to place, through time and places, and is in turn passed
through, interrupted by her encounters with difference so that
she can mimetically pass for another identity in a certain
context. In the process, such identity echoes Toni Morrison's
act of re-memorying, working with the transformative power of
the waters of a river, thus turning its past oppression into
knowledge and empowerment to fight present discrimination.[3]
By necessity and not for promoting a certain feminist ideology,
this identity thus casts a gaze on its own past, into its own
origin instead of aiming at an ideal goal in the future: it accepts
the challenge of looking into the mystery of 'who' it is rather
than resting on a given definition of 'what' it should be — the
same challenge Xuela accepts in *The Autobiography* when she
states: 'Who you are is a mystery no one can answer, not even
you. And why not, why not!'[4] The exclamation mark after the
repeated 'why not' makes Xuela's a liberatory cry for a
subjectivity committed to the pursual of relations rather than
the discovery of origins and mysteries.

Through this self-consciousness, the subject achieves its
liberation from a subaltern position. This is why *The
Autobiography* takes us on a more difficult and unfamiliar
path than, for example, *Lucy*.[5] While Lucy accepts/transforms/
re-memories her own name, the narrator in *The Autobiography*
tackles the question of coming to terms with history from a
theoretical point of view while asking herself, who am I in
relation to others? It does so by explicitly redefining history as
discourse: at the end of what she aptly calls her 'sermonette',[6]
the narrator offers us more than a picture with commentary of
a specific socio-cultural reality; in fact, she gives us also the
theory that makes that picture so devastating when she says:

...for me history was not a large stage filled with commemorations...with the sounds of victory. For me history was not only the past: it was the past and it was also the present.[7]

Conceiving history as discourse has broad implications for this text's portrayal of the world and for subjectivity in general. *The Autobiography* provides an exemplary model of Gayatri Spivak's concept of 'cultural translation' — a concept I extend to include a definition of feminist theory, which is always also practice. As translated subjectivity, a self is conceived as a passing entity, circulating among different contexts and never frozen into the transcendental icon of an identity. Like history, subjectivity is discursive. As such, it retains the rhetoricity of language and it works in the silent spaces between and around words. 'The jagged relation between rhetoric and logic', Spivak points out, 'as condition and effect of knowing, allows the world to be made of an agent who acts in it in an ethical, a political, a day-to-day way'. This is why translated thinking 'forces us to say things for which no language previously existed'.[8] Kincaid can be said to write as a translator when she declares:

For me writing is a revelation. If I knew what it would be then it would be of no interest for me to do it...I know how it works, but I haven't quite said it yet. The minute that I'm conscious of it then it's of no interest.[9]

This effort to say the yet-unsaid participates in the 'decolonialisation of language and thought', a 'slow process', which Angela Carter has theorised[10] and which helps me clarify the significance of the role played by language/rhetoric in the production of social agency and of subjectivity.[11] Carter points out that 'it has nothing to do with being a legislator of humankind';[12] rather, it works towards bringing affiliations within a particular historical context through risking language and questioning logic. In *The Autobiography*, this radically translated thinking takes apart the structuring features of Modernity — namely, the colonisation and genderisation of culture[13] — by uprooting its conceptions of history. It is from this perspective that I disagree with most of the reviewers of *The Autobiography* — even the sympathetic ones — who constantly foreground a tone of 'desolation', 'despair',[14] and 'contempt'[15] in its pages. I find that Kincaid's writing compellingly demands not to be taken at face value, otherwise even John Skow's irritated attack judging the novel an 'irritating navel-contemplation'[16] and Schine's unappealing judgement that it is full of 'inhuman narcissism'[17] should be taken into consideration.

Reading, for example, *The Autobiography* as a discursive articulation of a feminist subjectivity in a specific cultural and socio-historical context, rather than as the account of a personal life, allows me to foreground not only its historical value — Xuela as a metaphorical representation of the experience of the African diaspora and of the genocide of the Carib Indians[18] — but also its epistemological impact, its positive propositional force. Rather than the despair of the narrator's life, in Xuela I am driven to read the rejection of an Americanised cultural viewpoint that sentimentally forces happy endings upon the common hardships of life. Kincaid invites this reading, when she states that her existential view is 'fierce' rather than 'desolate', because it accounts for the fact that life is always hard and complicated[19] and when she criticises the part about 'the pursuit of happiness' in the American *Declaration of Independence* by calling it a meaningless, 'bad little sentence', because, she observes, happiness cannot be willingly pursued.[20]

Explicitly and from the beginning, *The Autobiography* demands that we rid ourselves of the structuring dichotomy governing the prose narratives of Modernity — the opposition between fact and fiction. One of the initial paragraphs in the book, in which the narrator tells us 'I was not afraid, because my mother had already died', ends with the parenthetical observation: 'it is not really true that I was not afraid then'. The next paragraph begins with the following meta-narrative comment:

If I speak now of those first days with clarity and insight, it is not an invention...at the time, each thing as it took place stood out in my mind with a sharpness that I now take for granted; it did not then have a meaning, it did not have a context, I did not yet know the history of events...[21]

Clearly, the narration is governed by the deep awareness of a historian about the relationship between 'truth' and 'invention' — it is thus a discursive elaboration of personal experience into political, theoretical knowledge, which questions the separation between fact and fiction imposed upon literature by Modern culture.[22] It is a process of 're-memory' aimed at attributing political significance to personal experience, as the long passage introducing the Speaking-I and its indissoluble relation with her mother makes clear:

My days were spent in a schoolhouse. This education I was receiving had never offered me the satisfaction I was told it would; it only filled me with questions that were not answered, it only filled me with anger. I could not like what it lead to: a humiliation so permanent that it would replace your own skin. And your own name, whatever it might be, eventually was not the gateway to who you really were, and you could not ever say to yourself, 'My name is Xuela Claudette Desvarieux'. This was my mother's name, but I cannot say it was her real name, for in a life like hers, as in mine, what is a real name? My own name is her name, Xuela Claudette, and in the place of the Desvarieux is Richardson, which is my father's name; but who are those people, Claudette, Desvarieux, and Richardson? To look into it, to look at it, could only fill you with despair; the humiliation could only make you intoxicated with self-hatred. For the name of any one person is at once her history recapitulated and abbreviated, and on declaring it, that person holds herself high or low, and the person hearing it holds the declarer high or low. My mother was placed outside the gates of a convent when she was perhaps a day old by a woman believed to be her own mother; she was wrapped in pieces of clean old cloth, and the name Xuela was written on these pieces of cloth; it was written in an ink whose colour was indigo, a dye rendered from a plant. She was not discovered because she had been crying; even as a newborn she did not draw attention to herself. She was found by a woman, a nun who was on her way to wreak more havoc in the lives of the remnants of a vanishing people; her name was Claudette Desvarieaux. She named my mother after herself, she called my mother after herself; how the name Xuela survived I do not know, but my father gave it to me when she died, just after I was born.[23]

The cover page tells us that Xuela's story is a mixture of truth and invention, a description which inscribes its own understanding: 'the autobiography' is called 'a novel'; it is 'of my mother'; and it is 'by Jamaica Kincaid', as if to show that things are even more complicated than in Gertrude Stein's *Autobiography of Alice B. Toklas*.[24] The cover shows two photos: of a woman on the front and of the author on the back cover. Jamaica Kincaid's black and white photo is copyrighted by Marianne Cook in 1992, the same photographer who authored *Generations of Women: In Their Own Words* (1998), a collection of photos in black and white of grandmothers, mothers and daughters and their own self-descriptions, with an Introduction by Kincaid.[25] In Cook's volume, next to the picture of Kincaid with her mother and daughter, we read that grandmother Annie Drew from Dominica was raised by her father, which made her 'rough', and she says about her own daughter: 'Even if sometimes she may say one or two things that are fiction, I'm never vexed. As a writer, what she will write is just fiction'.[26] Conversely, mother Jamaica Kincaid — after acknowledging 'powerful feelings of despair, dislike and even sometimes revulsion for (her) mother' but also the impossibility of 'constructing a world without her', observes: 'what's interesting about her story is that she's made a romance of her life'.[27] Finally, Kincaid's daughter Annie Shawn, named after her grandmother, points out that 'sometimes (her) mother acts like her grandmother'.[28] The photo shows this connection through young Annie: it intensifies the intellectual effort to understand the relational meaning of these three different lives and the subjectivities they have shaped. It is a mixture of 'truth' and 'invention'.

On the front cover of the novel *The Autobiography* there is a sepia picture, which is repeated in the text where, building up from what looks like ripped photos into a final full portrait, marks seven otherwise untitled, unnumbered chapters. This photo is not given copyright acknowledgment. We assume it is the mother of the title until the narrator tells us her mother died before she knew her, and the narrator never even saw a picture of her face. Xuela's mother — herself named Xuela is a cloth with her name written on,[29] heels sticking out of a white gown,[30] the hem of a long dress[31] — she is all this in her daughter's dreams, and nothing else. She remains a dress even when the daughter tries to imagine her:

...a dress made of nankeen, a loose-fitting dress, a shroud; it covered her arms, her knees, it fell all the way down to her ankles. She wore a matching piece of cloth on her head that covered all her beautiful hair completely...she carried a bundle on the top of her head...[32]

The 'bundle' on her head takes us back to the initial scene where the speaking Xuela is a 'bundle', indistinguishable from the 'bundle' of her father's 'soiled clothes' given to Eunice, her foster mother, to wash.[33] The 'dress made of nankeen', instead, reminds us of the cloth used by Eunice to fold the washed and ironed clothes of Xuela's father.[34] The same material marks the steps of Xuela's growth: the drawers of a dead man she wears during the androgynous phase in her life,[35] and the nightgown her father gave her which she wears during her first sexual encounter with Philip.[36] This fabric figuratively seals the relation between the two women, even though Xuela never gets to know her homonymous mother and wonders: 'And this woman whose face I have never seen, not even in a dream — what did she think?' [37] Nevertheless, in the end she acknowledges:

This account of my life has been an account of my mother's life as much as it has been an account of mine, and even so, again it is an account of the life of the children I did not have, as it is their account of me. In me is the voice I never heard, the face I never saw, the being I came from. In me are the voices that should have come out of me, the faces I never allowed to form, the eyes I never allowed to see me. This account is an account of the person who was never allowed to be and an account of the person I did not allow myself to become.[38]

This remark allows me to interpret the cover photo as that of the narrator in her mother's clothes — i.e., as the intimate cultural translation (neither the myth of origin, nor the belief in a goddess), but the translation of her own historical mother. Indeed, this novel is throughout a self-reflexive discourse aimed at foregrounding the political function of rhetoric (photographs and clothes capture characters just like translated words attempt to render the human experience) in the social constitution of subjectivity. Sidonie Smith theorises that women's autobiographies are not written against one's own mother[39] rather, they parallel the life of one's mother. In Caribbean words, Kincaid's *The Autobiography* is the autobiography of a woman who is becoming her own mother — in order to become herself, birth herself, re-invent herself; in other words, as Lorna Goodison's *I Am Becoming My Mother* fully implies, to celebrate the creativity and continuity of birth as the creative potential to re-define yourself.[40] Jamaica Kincaid repeatedly insists that writing is drawn from her need to investigate her own life whose origin, she fully acknowledges, is in her own mother.[41]

This is why the cover photo becomes the appropriate referent of a self-referential meditation: this subjectivity states her own identity by retaining a sense of another, a consciousness underlined by the author's photograph meant to indicate the theoretical and thus political value of Xuela's personal account. It is thus not surprising that this novel, whose subject matter is so explicitly personal, is dedicated to Derek Walcott rather than, say, to Kincaid's own Dominican mother and Carib

Indian grandmother. The dedication takes autobiography out of the personal boundaries and into the realm of cultural production, so that the insistence on the Dominican setting and the detailed descriptions of the island carry also an echo of Jean Rhys. More compellingly than being a tribute to the Caribbean cultural and literary heritage to which Kincaid's philosophical and international discourse wants to and does belong — suffice it to mention the intensity with which the loss of one's mother reverberates with the unspeakable suffering of slavery and massacre — these references dismantle the idea of Otherness and of the Caribbean as the Other of Europe, proposing — rather — the Caribbean as the Other America.[42]

Knowledge as cultural elaboration of reality is underlined by the widespread use of clothes as a figure for socio-psychological descriptions. The father who is said to have chosen 'the mantle of [the victor], always [the victor]' [43] over that of the vanquished is, rather than wears, a jailer's uniform.[44] The frustrated great aspiration in his life is reduced to owning an English suit, which is all he has to offer to his own son as a model of his personality.[45] The dramatic incidents in the life of Xuela — a 'bundle' at the beginning — are all marked by her possession and refusal of certain dresses. Most significant is the episode in which Xuela and Madame La Batte communicate perfectly without words: by putting Lise's clothes on and taking them off[46] and always refusing to wear them. Xuela understands her imposed function in the LaBatte's household and rebels against it — she opposes it, by imposing her erotic will when unclothed[47] and by renouncing her child in a dead man's clothes.[48]

She exposes the misery and the pretence of the 'simple',[49] 'reduced'[50] truths of the colonial order by exposing the falseness of the clothes of the people who represent such order — teachers, father, stepmother and sister, husband, not to mention the school uniforms whose 'colors and styles [mimick] the colors and style of a school somewhere else'.[51] For instance, Xuela's husband, Philip, although he is the only person who says he loves her, is reduced to 'a book', 'a blue shirt',[52] and a pair of beige linen trousers when he accepts her seduction.[53] His clothes, like his passion for the classifications in natural science, always leave out something and transform the truth, which 'is always so full of uncertainty',[54] into a 'pretty picture' — like that of the congregation in front of the church, which must leave Lazarus out.[55] Xuela does not buy into this 'Enlightened' epistemological frame which has supported the imposition of racial, sexual, and national discrimination over the world. Xuela fully understands the subjugation that occurs when female beings are divided into 'women' and 'ladies',[56] when humanity is separated into 'men' and 'people'.[57] For this reason, she marries but neither in order to become a wife (a man's lady) nor a mother (how can she, having been denied one herself ?); she marries, on the contrary, only after having recognised that Romance (the kingdom of love) is 'the refuge of the defeated' and after having observed: 'I believe my life was without love'.[58] And yet she marries and works out a respectable relationship with Philip. Her whole existence vindicates the subordinate role to which the Other is confined by the supremacy of Reason and Individualism by dismantling such order and claiming 'fiercely' for a different set of values.[59]

Xuela's experience brings her to realise that 'love' is indistinguishable from its opposite;[60] she fights her oppression by learning to love what she is told to hate.[61] Education will soon bring her the awareness that love cannot inhabit a history of humiliation, enslavement and mistrust.[62] Thus she will learn to love 'in defiance', a love which 'will do but only do'[63] and taste 'rancid',[64] as the milk of her foster mother tasted 'sour',[65] although better than the 'bitter' tea, 'moldy' food[66] and 'poisonous' necklace[67] of her fairy tale-like wicked stepmother. Even her love 'beyond words'[68] for a man whose mouth looked 'like an island',[69] Roland, must come to an end, because it is deceitful and 'dangerous'.[70] However, this is neither a desperate choice, nor the sign of defeat: in a way comparable to the realisation reached by Sethe in Morrison's Beloved,[71] under circumstances that are possibly even more extreme, Xuela does not believe herself to be 'nothing'[72] because of it. Rather, she shows us the significance of a difficult existence lived by refusing to rely on myths, ideologies, and beliefs. Her subjectivity is never an identity, not even when she sternly states, 'I was myself',[73] because as a child she shatters Eunice's platter fully aware that the English countryside cannot represent Heaven;[74] and, as an adult, she self-consciously calls 'an identity' — the choice to 'belong to a race' and to 'accept a nation' — a 'crime'.[75] She pays the price of not bearing children for this, but certainly not that of reducing her self to desolation. Mcguire laments that there is 'no resurrection'[76] in *The Autobiography*, and Moses complains that the book offers 'no redemption' for Xuela and 'no catharsis' for the readers.[77] On the contrary, I would rather applaud the absence of resurrection, redemption and catharsis as evidence that Kincaid's discourse moves within other parameters than those offered by the Western metaphysical tradition to explore the possibilities offered to a thinking which is poetic and historical at the same time and risks not telling us always what we would like to hear because, like Wilson Harris's 'epic voice of arrival', it accepts the challenge to live without the need to conquer death.[78] When memory engages the slow process of re-memorying and decolonialising, when it risks language and identity in order to explore new epistemic possibilities, the hope for a world no longer ruled by the impulse to conquer and control death, through conquest, rape and inquisitions starts taking shape.

Notes

1. Jamaica Kincaid, *The Autobiography of My Mother: A Novel*, New York: Farrar, Straus & Giroux, 1996.
2. See Adrienne Rich, *What Is Found There, Notebooks on Poetry and Politics*, New York: Norton, 1993.
3. See Toni Morrison, *Playing in the Dark*, New York: Vintage, 1992.
4. Kincaid, 1996, p.202.
5. Jamaica Kincaid, *Lucy*, New York: Farrar, Straus & Giroux, 1990.
6. Kincaid, pp.132-8.
7. Ibid., pp.138-9.
8. Gayatri C. Spivak, 'The Politics of Translation', Barret, Michelle and Phillips, Anne (eds.), *Destablizing Theory: Contemporary Feminist Debates*, Palo Alto, CA: Stanford University Press, 1992, pp.177-200, p.192.
9. Jamaica Kincaid, Interview with Allan Vorda. *The Mississippi Review* , 2(4), (April, 1996) located at <http://sushi.st.usm. edu/mrw/9604/kincaid.html>.

10. Angela Carter, 'Notes from the Frontline', in Michelene Wandor (ed.) *On Gender and Writing*, London: Pandora, 1993, pp.69-77. I have discussed Carter's fundamental influence on feminist theories of subjectivity in Giovanna Covi, 'Decolonialized Feminist Subjects', *Critical Studies on the Feminist Subject*, Trento: Dipartimento di Scienze Filologiche e Storiche-Università di Trento, (1998), pp.19-56.

11. Giovanna Covi, 'Decolonialized Feminist Subjects', 1998.

12. Carter, p.75.

13. See Nancy Armstrong, *Desire and Domestic Fiction: A Political History of the Novel*, New York: Oxford University Press, 1987.

14. Eavan Boland, 'Desolation Angel', Review of *The Autobiography of My Mother: A Novel*, *Voice Literary Supplement*, 11 (Feb., 1996).

15. Richard Eder, (1996) Review of *The Autobiography of My Mother: A Novel*, *Newsday* (1996, Jan 14) located at: <http://www.newsday.com/books/bkautobi.htm>

16. John Skow, 'Family Ties', Review of *The Autobiography of My Mother: A Novel*, *Time Magazine*, 150(20) (1997, November 10) located at: <http//mouth.pathfinder.com/time/magazine/1997/dom/9/the-arts-book.family-ties-htm>.

17. Catherine Schine, 'A World as Cruel as Job's, Review of *The Autobiography of My Mother: a Novel*', *New York Times* Book Review (4 February, 1996) p.5.

18. See Felicia Lee, 'A Writer Who Illuminates Her Own Dark Words', Review of *The Autobiography of My Mother: A Novel*, *New York Times* (25 January, 1996) B1, and Steve Horowitz, 'The Autobiography of My Mother', Review, *Icon*, Iowa City (1996, Feb. 8) located at: <http://www.iowacity.com/icon/backs/1996/02-08-96/books.htm>

19. Jamaica Kincaid, Interview with Eleanor Wachtel. CBC Radio 'Writers & Company' (July, 1993/January, 1996).

20. Jamaica Kincaid, Interview with Marilyn Snell 1996. 'Jamaica Kincaid Hates Happy Endings'. *Mother Jones* (Sept./Oct) located at: <http://www.mojones.com/mother-jones/SO97/snell.html>

21. Kincaid, 1996, p.15.

22. Lennard Davis, *Factual Fictions: The Origins of the English Novel*, Philadelphia: University of Pennsylvania Press, 1983.

23. Kincaid, 1996, pp.78-80.

24. Gertrude Stein, *Autobiography of Alice B. Toklas*, Harmondsworth: Penguin, 1977.

25. Marianne Cook, *Generations of Women: In Their Own Words*, San Francisco: Chronicle Books, 1998.
26. Ibid., p.20.
27. Ibid.
28. Ibid.
29. Kincaid, 1996, p.79.
30. Ibid., p.18.
31. Ibid., p.31.
32. Ibid., p.200.
33. Ibid., p.4.
34. Ibid., p.6.
35. Ibid., p.98.
36. Ibid., p.151.
37. Ibid., p.201.
38. Ibid., p.227-28.
39. Sidonie Smith, *A Poetics of Women's Autobiography: Marginality and the Fictions of Self-Representation*, Bloomington: Indiana University Press, 1987.
40. Lorna Goodison, *I Am Becoming My Mother*, London: New Beacon, 1986.
41. See for example, Jamaica Kincaid, Interview with Dwight Garner, *Salon Magazine*, (13 January, 1996) located at <http://www.salon1999.com/05/features/kincaid.html> and Jamaica Kincaid, Interview with Kay Bonetti, *Missouri Review*, located at <http://webdelsol.com/Missouri Review/interviews/kincaid.html>
42. See Michael Dash, *The Other America*, Charlottesville: University Press of Virginia, 1998.
43. Kincaid, 1996, p.192.
44. Ibid., pp.39, 50, 90.
45. Ibid., p.54.
46. Ibid., p.69.
47. Ibid.
48. Ibid., p.98.
49. Ibid., p.67.
50. Ibid., p.223.
51. Ibid., p.12.
52. Ibid., p.149.
53. Ibid., p.151.
54. Ibid., p.223.

55. Ibid., p.142.
56. Ibid., p.159.
57. Ibid., p.226.
58. Ibid., p.216.
59. Jamaica Kincaid, Interview with Eleanor Wachtel. CBC Radio 'Writers & Company' (July, 1993/January, 1996).
60. Kincaid, 1996, p.22.
61. Ibid., p.32.
62. Ibid., p.48.
63. Ibid., p.56.
64. Ibid., p.57.
65. Ibid., p.5.
66. Ibid., p.29.
67. Ibid., p.33.
68. Ibid., p.176.
69. Ibid., p.164.
70. Ibid., p.178.
71. Toni Morrison, *Beloved*, New York: Knopf, 1987, p.226.
72. Kincaid, 1996, p.226.
73. Ibid., p.167.
74. Ibid., pp.8-9.
75. Ibid., p.226.
76. K.T. Mcguire, Review of *The Autobiography of My Mother: A Novel*, located at: <http://www.desires.com/2.1/Word.Reviews/Docs/kincaid.html>
77. Tai Moses, 'A Motherless Child Rages in Jamaica Kincaid's Searing Autobiography, Review of *The Autobiography of My Mother: A Novel*', *Metro* (February 1996) pp.15-21, located at: <http://www.metroactive.com/papers/metro/02.15.96/kincaid-9607.html>.
78. Wilson Harris, 'Quetzalcoatl and the Smoking Mirror (Reflections on Originality and Tradition)' (Address to Temenos Academy, London, 7 February 1994), *The Review of Contemporary Fiction*, 17(2) (Summer, 1997), 12-23.

Here and There in the Work

of Olive Senior

Relocating diaspora discourses in relation to Caribbean women's writing

ALISON DONNELL

This paper is concerned to explore the recent theorising of Caribbean women's writing around ideas of diaspora, migration and exile, and will draw on the work of Olive Senior in order to offer alternative ways of reading Caribbean women's writing which is written 'elsewhere'. Diaspora discourses, both theoretical and literary, have been important to the construction of postcolonial studies and in particular, to the attempts within this discipline to articulate a politics of identity which takes account of the mobility of peoples and cultures across a post-colonial world. Certainly, there has been a great deal of interesting and valuable work on diasporic writings and identities which is of relevance to Caribbean writing. In particular, the work of cultural theorists such as Stuart Hall and Paul Gilroy has been important in establishing the idea of cultures and subjectivities as plastic and discontinuous in enabling ways, and provides a wider lens for reading the earlier and more regionally specific work of Kamau (Edward) Brathwaite on creolisation.[1] However, the anti-foundationalist politics of postcolonialism have produced a preference for dislocation over location, rupture over continuity, and elsewhereness over hereness which appears in most contemporary postcolonial approaches to diaspora and migration. As Barbara Kirshenblatt-Gimblett points out, this emphasis has meant that diaspora theory has only been mobilised in a rather limited way by postcolonial critics, to the exclusion of other productive but more uncomfortable fields of enquiry:

Diasporic discourse in this context is strong on displacement, detachment, uprooting, and dispersion — on disarticulation. It is appealing precisely because it lends itself to a strategic disaggregation of territory, people, race, language, culture, religion, history, and sovereignty. Rearticulation — how the local is produced and what forms it takes in the space of dispersal — is trickier because of the risk of closure, essentialism, or premature pluralism.[2]

In this paper I wish to examine the ways in which this emphasis on disaggregation has influenced recent frameworks for theorising Caribbean women's writing, and to argue that, in this field too, some attention needs to be given to the 'trickier' inscription of location and the local, not only as diasporic community, but also as home community.

Two recent books which examine Caribbean women's writing, Carole Boyce Davies's *Black Women, Writing and Identity: Migrations of the Subject*[3] and Myriam J.A. Chancy's *Searching for Safe Spaces: Afro-Caribbean Women Writers in Exile,*[4] employ migrant writing as a defining paradigm for a reading of selected Caribbean women's writing. Both books work towards: 'centralising the Black women's experience across the diaspora in ways that remove her from the place of marginalisation in a variety of cultures'.[5] Indeed, by working across a range of cultural contexts, both Boyce Davies and Chancy are able to draw our attention to the ways in which Black women writers and their work intersect with each other. This centripetal model of criticism helps to provide a valuable overarching framework other than the dominant critical paradigm of postcolonial theory or the reading pathway prescribed by national literary (sub)traditions (such as African American or Black British). Nevertheless, I think that we need to be aware of what might be lost, as well as gained, by the privileging of the migrant black woman as the subject of enquiry.

The critical paradigm through which Caribbean women's writing is read and constructed in Carole Boyce Davies's work is clearly informed by careful research and scholarly expertise in the field. Set against the auto/biographical 'Migration horror stories', this book's theoretical apparatus powerfully invokes an intellectual, almost utopian, diasporic space to which writing by Black women can come 'home'. Boyce Davies comments that:

> Black women's writing...should be read as a series of boundary crossings and not as a fixed, geographical, ethnically or nationally bound category of writing. In cross-cultural, transnational, translocal, diasporic perspectives, this reworking of the grounds of 'Black Women's Writing' redefines identity away from exclusion and marginality. Black women's writing/existence, marginalised in the terms of majority-minority discourses, within the Euro-American male or female canon or Black male canon...redefines its identity as it re-connects and re-members, brings together black women dis-located by space and time.[6]

Her work here deliberately casts its net across a vast sea and does not seek to offer a way of reading particular to Caribbean women's writing. Nevertheless, Caribbean women writers are a substantial part of her 'catch' and the heavily front-loaded theoretical apparatus assembled to read their 'migrations of the subject' does bid for interrogation.

Despite attention to the 'complicating locations of these multiple and variable subject positions in later chapters,[7] the complex pathways established by black women's cross-cultural, transnational, translocal, diasporic lives and writings, as well as the sense of mobility, difference and mediation, feed ultimately into a stable, albeit problematised, collective identity of 'black women' as the end of this book takes us back to its beginning. The emphasis upon acts of crossing rather than the specific locations where crossing start from and go to, within the theoretical underpinnings of the book, serves to foreground the conceptual sameness rather than the geographical or cultural or gendered distinctiveness of these crossings, driving towards consensus rather than discensus amongst writings. Deployed in such an embracing way, there is a danger that 'the routing of diaspora discourses in specific maps/histories', which James Clifford views as so crucial to theorisations of diasporic movements, is lost and, as Clifford warns, the concept 'slips easily into theoretical discourses informed by poststructuralism and notions of the multiply-positioned subject...[as] a master trope or 'figure' for modern, complex, or positional identities, crosscut and displaced by race, sex, gender, class and culture'.[8]

Furthermore, this tendency to stabilise diasporic identity (even though it is stabilised as radical) seems to have important consequences for how we think about Caribbean women's writing, as does the model of black subjectivity which Boyce Davies proposes through her theorising of these migrating subjects:

Black female subjectivity then can be conceived not primarily in terms of domination, subordination or 'subalternisation', but in terms of slipperiness, elsewhereness...Black female subjectivity asserts agency as it crosses the borders, journeys, migrates and so re-claims as it re-asserts .[9]

In Chancy's book too, acts of crossing and the achievement of a positive female subjectivity are linked, with the condition of exile functioning almost as a prerequisite to self-determination:

Women within the Caribbean are also speaking out, but their voices are often lost to the cause of nationalism (more or less male-defined) or coopted to service male versions of women's identity. In exile, Caribbean women can ironically politicise their discourse...resist assimilation.[10]

It is my argument that this emphasis on empowerment becomes troubling when it is presented as the dominant function of exile or migration, and when journeying becomes an assumed route to agency. For Chancy, the enabling effects of exile are similarly to be seen in the literature, which she describes as:

A tapestry of sounds and perspectives on what it has meant for Afro-Caribbean women to take control of their bodies, their lives, and, in order to do so, to have removed themselves from their roots.[11]

Indeed, this emphasis on migration and exile as the most rewarding areas of enquiry becomes problematic at the point that it defines itself against a homeland which is both undifferentiated and undervalued. While the freedom to travel and to settle elsewhere has doubtless been enabling to many Caribbean women, writers and academics included, there is an increasing body of work from within the Caribbean documenting a long history of women's agency, activism and writing which cannot be written off.[12] Moreover, the focus on migrant subjects becomes of particular concern given that increasingly little attention is being given to the Caribbean region as site of possibility. In Boyce Davies's account, the Caribbean reality and people so epitomise the theories of hybridisation that the region almost slips off the world map:

Caribbean identities then are products of numerous processes of migration. As a result, many conclude that the Caribbean is not so much a geographical location but a cultural construction based on a series of mixtures, languages, communities of people.[13]

Despite the fact that we must acknowledge the extraordinary cultural admixture which constitutes the

Caribbean region and its long history of creolisation, as well as the many Caribbean diasporic communities which extend globally, the erasure of territory in favour of cultural forms seems extreme. The displacement of 'geographical location' by 'cultural construction' further shifts debates away from the demands of hereness and of the settling process which are also significant to migration and diaspora.

Indeed, the denial of place, and the dismantling of geographical belonging, is not necessarily the source of radical cultural reconfigurations. With regards to the Caribbean, the politics which often operate through the emphasis on dislocation can be attested to in the phrases used to describe the best known writers and intellectuals from the region. Derek Walcott is often championed in the mainstream media as 'the best poet writing in the English language' and C.L.R. James is introduced as a 'world-class Marxist theorist' — in both cases the Caribbean is eclipsed as a location in an act of appropriation into Western traditions. Centres and margins are not being destabilised by these acts of crossing.

Although the greater power and profile exerted by publishing houses, the media and academic institutions in Western metropolitan centres may well mean that many of the struggles and debates associated with Caribbean identities and societies are taking place outside the region, it would be both misleading and unfortunate if we allowed the discourse of diaspora to move us away from the Caribbean as a real location. Furthermore, we should not be persuaded that acts of crossing are the only acts of agency available to or asserted by black or Caribbean women writers, nor should we accept that migrating subjects are always empowered.

Indeed, I wish to argue that if we look to the Caribbean, in all its regional complexity and diversity, it might help us to re-think our ways of theorising diasporic movements and the writings which engage with these. With a national narrative very much involved with the African and South Asian diasporas, as well as with European colonial migration, the Caribbean is a particularly interesting location for discussions about 'here' and 'there'. In a region repopulated by absentee landlords, African slaves and Indian indentured labourers ideas of homeland have always held the trace of other places and the idea of return. Claims to belonging were and are not based on a common point of origin and, although the Amerindian population in Guyana is gaining political and social profile, diasporic identifications do not generally take place against autochthonous claims. Instead, identifications with 'here' and 'there' remain more mobile and provisional even within a fixed place and time. An individual, may in different contexts and for different purposes, identify themselves as Trinidadian, as Indo-Caribbean, as Muslim, as Caribbean. Although all identities function as a series of roll-calls, the multiple calls of Caribbean identities are often more pronounced. The hyphenated identities which we have come to associate with diasporic metropolitan communities (African-American, Black British) are also important to Caribbean peoples who wish to retain their connections to a historical homeland and a contemporary community which survives, at least partially, through cultural, religious and domestic practices, as well as through narrative. Although I am unable to explore the ethnic and cultural diversity of Caribbean writers and writings fully in this article, I am interested to think about the extent to which it may be possible to argue that travelling between islands, and even between different cultural communities within an island may open up questions concerning 'migrating subjects' not foregrounded by the focus on metropolitan migration. Certainly, it seems important to point out that the Caribbean has a far greater scattering and discensus in terms of cultures, beliefs and communities than is suggested by the roll-call 'black women'.

My own work on Senior's writing, therefore, attempts to offer an alternative way of approaching migration and diaspora in relation to Caribbean women's writing. It functions as a supplement to the work carried out by Boyce Davies and Chancy, and aims to offer a glimpse of those dimensions of diasporic experience that the current focus on dislocation and disaggregation too often occlude. As one of the few creative writers who remained in the Caribbean even after her work received critical acclaim, Olive Senior has acknowledged her commitment to 'a literature that is being written from the inside out instead of the outside looking in'.[14] Although she now divides her time between Jamaica and Canada, Senior's work is virtually always located in the Caribbean, more specifically in rural Jamaica and I want to argue that paradoxically it is the locatedness of her work which enables us to think about the diaspora paradigm in new and interesting ways.

Many of the short stories in Senior's three collections to date, *Summer Lightning*,[15] *Arrival of the Snake Woman*[16] and *Discerner of Hearts*[17] address the issues of migration and relocation which are so much part of the Caribbean reality. Nevertheless, her texts do not tread the familiar literary footsteps to harbours or airports with their protagonists' journeys to a metropolitan centre, but rather retain a close and interested focus on rural Jamaica. It is often within this tighter locational frame that Senior is able to explore those journeys which take place within the island,[18] as well as the experience of returning home and what that means both for those who have left and those who have stayed, thereby addressing an often neglected dimension of the migration story.[19]

Senior's poetry is not as well known or as critically acclaimed as her short fiction, but her second collection, *Gardening in the Tropics* (1994), is an interesting text for a discussion of diasporic writing.[20] Described by her publishers, McClelland and Stewart, as Senior's 'first Canadian publication', *Gardening in the Tropics*, although the least 'rooted' in terms of literary locale, is more complex in its cultural orientation than this description would seem to suggest. Indeed, as the publisher's own back-cover description suggests, the claim for *Gardening in the Tropics* as a Canadian publication is not so easily articulated in other ways:

> *Gardening in the Tropics* contains a rich Caribbean world in poems offered to readers everywhere, but with an especial nod to Canadian readers. This Caribbean world thrives in a Canada that is felt only briefly in the volume (as an image of colourful shoes against snow), just enough to suggest a potential meeting between northern and tropical climates and ways.[21]

This claim for *Gardening in the Tropics* as a bi-locale volume is so tenuous that it seems to speak more about the need to yoke Senior's poetry back to Canada and to a Canadian readership than it does of the work itself, a need which in itself is symptomatic of the desire for so-called 'diasporic' writings to somehow display their multipositionality. Unlike the more prominent Caribbean-Canadian women writers, such as Dionne Brand, Nourbese Philip and Makeda Silvera, Olive Senior does not critically engage with Canada's national rhetoric of inclusivity or its hidden history of racist oppression and exploitation, but rather maintains Jamaica as the centre of emotional energy and interrogation in her work.

Indeed, the single image of the rainbow shoes against the snow, in the poem 'My father's Blue Plantation', which is seen as so significant to the Canadianness of the volume, actually signifies a failed attempt to reconnect to a Caribbean landscape of primary colours and of emotional belonging, more than it confirms a multicultural presence in a new home. Having reflected on the enclosed geography of her childhood home and the careful balancing of economic and moral values in the selling of bananas and the buying of shoes for church, the second part of this poem crosses into a description of contemporary adult life in the Western metropolis:

> But this was ages ago.
> We children fled the blue for northern
> light where we buy up all the shoes
> in sight. My closet filled - finally-
> with a rainbow of shoes in Hot Tropical
> Colours (which look marvellous against
> the snow.) My father's house (I'm told)
> is visible from all directions now...
> Alone fanning sand and stoning breeze,
> my father lets in all that air, lets that
> Hot Tropical Sun pour down to fill his
> blue lungs and warm his old and vegetating
> bones.[22]

Although the image of the rainbow shoes is one of agency, as the poetic persona asserts her right to buy the brightly coloured shoes shunned by her father, there is a strong sense that the act of crossing entails loss as well as gain. The distancing of the two parts across the space of the page (with left and then right margin alignment) further illustrates the difficulty of bridging a stretch of water which also marks a threshold between generations, lifestyles and values. While she connects to her siblings, as other migrants she has disconnected from her father whose life, although the off-centre focus of the poem, is now only a reported image. If her journey to the shoe shops of Canada is one which asserts agency it is perhaps an uncomfortable reminder of how empowerment too can be slippery, taking us elsewhere than we had intended, and of how individual journeys take place across a global political terrain with full closets and barren plantations.

It is interesting that Senior favours the motif of marooning and being marooned in this volume which explores the experiences of migration and diaspora across 500 years of Caribbean history. In one sense this term has everything to do with Senior's own location, as she grew up near Cockpit Country in Jamaica which was home to the Maroons. However, the fact that the Maroon (a runaway slave) is the *leitmotif* of this volume seems important for two other reasons. First, because it signals a rooting of discourse in a specific place and history and second, because it allows Senior, somewhat typically, to leapfrog the plethora of ready-made discourses which James Clifford has described as:

An unruly crowd of descriptive/interpretive terms now jostle and converse in an effort to characterise the contact zones of nations, cultures and regions: terms such as *border, travel, creolization, transculturation, hybridity, and diaspora* (as well as the looser *diasporic*).[23]

I would argue that by side-stepping this crowd, Senior is able to allow us to look afresh at the movements which take place between nations and cultures and, crucially, to draw attention via this particular motif to the tension between agency and hegemony, between gain and loss, and between strength and vulnerability which each crossing involves.

In Senior's poetry, acts of running away and abandonment are always historically situated and often speak of the way in which migration and diaspora have been gendered differently at different times. In 'Gardening on the Run', which chronicles the life of the first runaway in Hispanola in 1502, inscribing women's experiences into this narrative, the emphasis is again bi-focated with the courage and empowerment of the Maroons acknowledged alongside the recognition that the inability to settle, to cultivate and to nurture was a real cost:

The brave ones abandoned plantation
for hinterland, including women
with children and others waiting
to be born right there in the
forest (many mixed with Indian),
born to know nothing but warfare
and gardening on the run.[24]

Her work also draws attention to the less comfortable images of migration, with poems on an illegal immigrant and a stowaway. In 'Hurricane Story 1951', the imperatives of economic migration drive a mother to maroon herself in a cold England for a nursing career designed to support the son she eventually abandons by default. Ostensibly the most conventional representation of migration within this volume, the scattering of a family across the US, the Caribbean and Britain is a recognisable postcolonial diasporic tale. It is a tale in which parents seek out a better life in the colonial and neo-colonial motherlands, a tale in which political mothers also abandon their children, and ultimately a tale in which disconnection and dispossession are the markers of crossing.

Here also, the dating of the poem (at the beginning of the era of mass migration to Britain initiated by the recruitment of workers into the service industries) offers a specific location in time and place and helps to anchor the distinctiveness of the crossing. The poem opens with a close constellation of promise:

Margaret and her man Delbert
such a fine young couple
everybody said
so full of ambition
so striving
their little boy so bright
so handsome
so thriving.[25]

However, it is an image of familial strength and cohesion which breaks down after the hurricane as Margaret travels to England to nurse, and Delbert moves to America to farm, and the unnamed boy passes from father to grandmother to stepmother. But the accustomed tale of migrating subjects is defamiliarised here by the boy's strange withdrawal from language and the social world of struggling 'new' citizens. Throwing 'sounds across the ocean', he finally communicates with his mother but the two only connect through an act of drowning at distant shores — an ambivalent act in which the evocation of an amniotic ocean and the entanglement of emotions and memories sits rather powerfully, if soberly, alongside a familiar narrative of diaspora.

If the volume explores the different imperatives to journey, then it also examines a less obvious but significant aspect of the gendering of diaspora — the fact that it was often the women who were left behind. In 'All Clear 1928', set during a period of severe economic decline when a large number of men left the Caribbean to work in Central America, the female narrator rememories how:

All, all the men went with our dreams,
our hopes, our prayers. And he
with a guinea from Mass Dolphy
the schoolteacher who said that boy
had so much ambition he was bound

to go far. And he had. Gathering
to himself worlds of experience

which allowed him to ride over us
with a clear conscience. I never

told anyone. For I would have had
to tell his children why he hadn't

sent money for bread, why his fine
leather boots, why his saddle,

his grey mare, his three-piece suit,
his bowler hat, his diamond tie-pin...²⁶

Again the empowerment of self and the expression of agency
is achieved at the cost of dislocation not just from place but
from a community, a family, a sense of belonging substituted
by spectacle and the visible acquisition of success.
Nevertheless, what is interesting is that although the poem
describes how the male traveller gathers experiences and
possessions to himself, in this poem, as in others in the
volume, what Senior allows us to perceive is that the tale of
diaspora cannot be owned by the traveller alone, but also
belongs to those whose land they occupy and to those they
have left behind. By concentrating on the journey rather than
the landings or leave-takings, theories of migration and
diaspora may have created intellectual spaces for the
achievement of agency, but they also may have omitted to
mention that just as each place is home to many different
histories, so is each journey.

The 'Nature Studies' section of the volume addresses the
issue of multi-positionality in a very rooted way, as lost plants
and an abandoned cosmology are restored to a contemporary
Caribbean which is too often unaware of what was saved in
the cultural crucible of colonisation. Indeed, 'Anatto and
Guinep', one of a series of poems on Caribbean fruits and
flora, opens with the observation that:

No one today regards anatto and guinep
as anything special

No one puts them on stamps or
chooses them

for praise-songs or any kind
of festival.²⁷

These poems which explicitly address the lack of recognition and appreciation shown to a Caribbean landscape, connect Senior's work of the 1990s, to earlier Caribbean writings (particularly of the 1930s and the 1970s) concerned with the nationalisation of literature and consciousness. With these connections in mind, it is interesting to consider the cultural politics of the Caribbean in the 1990s, and the recent tendency to read the Caribbean through outside eyes and an externalising gaze fostered by the neo-colonial demands of overseas landlords, of tourists and of satellite television.

It is my argument here that we should not allow contemporary theoretical discourses around diaspora and cultural crossings to be added to the list of dislocating influences. Perhaps then, Senior's work reminds us that the fact that cultural nationalism is less easy to define in the 1990s may not mean that it is less urgent. I would argue that when we read Caribbean women's writing we need to consider both here and there, to pay attention to location as well as migration, to settling as well as journeying, and perhaps most importantly to the Caribbean, as well as to metropolitan centres, as a place where acts of reading and writing take place.

Notes

1. See for example, Stuart Hall, 'Cultural Identity and Diaspora' in J. Rutherford (ed.), *Identity: Community, Culture and Difference*, London: Lawrence and Wishart, 1990, pp.222-37; Paul Gilroy, *Small Acts: Thoughts on the Politics of Black Cultures*, London: Serpent's Tail, 1993; Paul Gilroy, *The Black Atlantic: Modernity and Double Consciousness*, London: Verso, 1993; Kamau (Edward) Brathwaite, 'Timehri', *Savacou*, 2, (1970) 35-44; Kamau (Edward) Brathwaite, *The Development of Creole Society in Jamaica 1770-1820*, Oxford: Oxford University Press, 1978.

2. Barbara Kirshenblatt-Gimblett, 'Spaces of Dispersal', *Cultural Anthropology*, 9(3), (1994), 339.

3. Carole Boyce Davies, *Black Women, Writing and Identity: Migrations of the Subject*, London: Routledge, 1994.

4. Myriam J.A. Chancy, *Searching for Safe Spaces: Afro-Caribbean Women Writers in Exile*, Temple University Press: Philadelphia, 1997.

ldойirшdアир

5. Ibid., p.14.
6. Boyce Davies, p.4.
7. Ibid, p.8.
8. James Clifford, 'Diasporas', *Cultural Anthropology*, 9(3), (1994), 319.
9. Boyce Davies, 1994, pp.36-37.
10. Chancy, 1997, p.5.
11. Ibid., pp.6-7.
12. See for example, Verene Shepherd, Bridget Brereton and Barbara Bailey (eds.), *Engendering History: Caribbean Women in Historical Perspective*, London: James Currey; Janet H. Momsen (ed.), *Women and Change in the Caribbean*, London: James Currey, 1993.
13. Boyce Davies, 1994, p.13.
14. Charles Rowell, 'An Interview with Olive Senior', *Callaloo*, 11(3) (1998) 486.
15. Olive Senior, *Summer Lightning*, London: Longman, 1986.
16. Olive Senior, *Arrival of the Snake Woman*, London: Longman, 1989.
17. Olive Senior, *Discerner of Hearts*, Toronto: McClelland and Stewart, 1995.
18. See 'Arrival of the Snake-Woman' and 'The Two Grandmothers' in *Arrival of the Snake-Woman*.
19. See 'Ascot' in *Summer Lightning* or 'The Case Against the Queen' in *Discerner of Hearts*.
20. Olive Senior, *Gardening in the Tropics*, Toronto: McClelland and Stewart, 1994.
21. Ibid., back cover.
22. Ibid., p.84.
23. Clifford, 1993, p.303.
24. Senior, 1994, pp.105-106.
25. Ibid., p.34.
26. Ibid., pp.56-57.
27. Ibid., p.74.

Remembering the Contemporary:

Lady Mary Wroth

and Erna Brodber

MARIA CRISTINA FUMAGALLI

In the last thirty years or so it has been pointed out that we have neither total, objectively real history, nor total and objectively real literary history that contains the literal sum of past life or past literature. What we have instead is the product of a cultural selection of events or works selected by convention of emphasis and omission. In order to enrich our knowledge of the past (both historical and literary) and consequently of the 'contemporary' we must explore the unemphasised, consider the omitted and, when it is the case, include them in our cultural mnemonic archive.

The two authors I want to put side by side at first sight seem to have in common only the fact that they are women. Erna Brodber was born in Jamaica in 1940. She is a poet, a fiction-writer and a respected sociologist who has been working in the Institute of Social and Economic research in Mona for a long time. Lady Mary Wroth was (probably) born in 1587 and died around 1651. Her home was the Sidney's estate, celebrated in Ben Jonson's *To Penshurst*. She grew up surrounded by writers and patrons of literature: her uncle was Sir Philip Sidney, and her aunt was Mary Sidney Herbert, countess of Pembroke, an important patron of writers and a poet and translator herself. Lady Mary's father, Sir Robert Sidney, also wrote poetry as did her first cousin and lover, William Herbert, Earl of Pembroke.

Lady Mary Wroth is perhaps the most accomplished woman writer in English before Aphra Behn.[1] She wrote *Pamphilia to Amphilantus* (the first Petrarchan sequence in English by a woman), *Love's Victory* (one of the first plays by a woman), and *The Countesse of Montgomerie Urania* (a long and intriguing romance of almost 590,000 words and the first secular romance by a woman). Most importantly, she is one of the first women writers who clearly saw herself as having the vocation of a writer. Nonetheless, since in her works the habitually submerged female voice does emerge and a female identity starts to find written expression, we can assume that she might have found very appropriate also for herself the self-definition that Brodber adopts in a recent essay:

Am I a writer? An artist? I do not know. I know though, that if tomorrow someone managed to convince me that all is hunky-dory with those who look like me, I would indulge myself in long Fieldingesque works because I love to play with words and to use my imagination, and with that before me and behind me, I would call myself a writer. Right now, I feel the term *intellectual* worker [...] best describes me.[2]

It is interesting that both Lady Mary Wroth and Erna Brodber *deliberately* choose to resort to fiction in order to articulate their experience of what it means to be a woman (and in the case of Brodber, a black woman) in Renaissance England or in contemporary Jamaica. Through fiction, or better, through a specific type of fiction, they manage to present a case history, to convey a whole range of social issues and to access their characters' interiority.

In terms of education, both Erna and Mary enjoyed a rather privileged milieu. Nevertheless their *status* as privileged women has not made their predicament as women writers an easy one. As late as 1988, when the *First International*

Conference on Women Writers of the English-Speaking Caribbean was held in Wellesley, Massachusetts, attended by most Caribbean women writing at the time (including Erna Brodber), many works had already been written by Caribbean women but these authors had never come together as a group to discuss their writings and, as Lorna Goodison remarked at the conference, it was about time that critics began to take women writers seriously and to give their works the respect they deserve.[3] The meeting contributed to 'rescue' and give expression to voices that had not always been heard as loudly and as clearly as they should have been'.[4]

Eight years earlier, then, when she published her first novel, *Jane and Louisa Will Soon Come Home*, Erna Brodber found herself in a situation not totally dissimilar from that of Mary Wroth in 1621, when she wrote *The Countess of Montgomery Urania*, the first secular English romance written by a woman. In *Silent but for the Word*, Mary Ellen Lamb argues that during the so-called Renaissance, 'the professed [public] goals of a humanistic education were perverted when they were applied to women'. For women learning was a way of 'keeping them busy, much like [...] sewing'. They were denied the rhetorical training deemed necessary for original writing and were encouraged to translate suitable works by men because such activity 'did not threaten the male establishment as the expression of personal viewpoints might'.[5] In 'Did Women have a Renaissance?', Joan Kelly-Gadol radicalises this position by arguing that there was no Renaissance at all for women — at least during the Renaissance.[6] Betty Travitsky, in 'Placing Women in the English Renaissance', claims instead that 'some women did experience a Renaissance, although it was an uneven one [...] writings expressing approved values were enshrined and newer, less reverential writings were shunted aside as the canon developed'. In consequence, she continues, 'the experience of the Renaissance for women has not yet been as fully evaluated as possible'.[7] What Travitsky suggests, therefore, is the existence of a sort of Alter Renaissance whose texts have become known only in the twentieth century, particularly since the Seventies.

In a lecture entitled 'Caliban's Guarden', in a similar attempt to 'revise' (in his case from a Caribbean point of view) the complex phenomenon of the European Renaissance, Edward Kamau Brathwaite highlights the existence of a different type of Alter Renaissance that is a perversion of the Renaissance spirit of 'Da Vinci, of Michelangelo, of Rabelais, the renaissance that', he says, 'you inherit so beautifully and creatively'. Indeed, he terms *Alter Renaissance* the effect of that 'alteration of consciousness' which took place when Europe entered the Caribbean, destroyed the Amer-Indians and later established slavery. In his words, this *Alter Renaissance* is 'an altered state of consciousness which establishes the plantation, the garden, the world in which Caliban has to grow and function'.[8] Caribbean authors, he continues, need to restore a cosmos that includes Caliban, his children and his mother Sycorax in order to counteract the *Alter Renaissance* and to subvert Prospero's world.[9] Likewise, Lady Mary Wroth and the other women writing during the Renaissance — when women were usually taught handwriting (being active) considerably after they were taught reading (being passive)[10] can be seen as struggling to give more space and dignity or better, a 'voice' not only to Miranda, who repeatedly and consciously disobeys her father's will in Act III, Scene i, of *The Tempest*[11], but possibly also to her long forgotten and, so to say, 'omitted' mother, Susanna.

When *The Countess of Montgomery Urania* was published in 1621, Lord Edward Denny harshly reprimanded Mary for attempting such an unfeminine work and admonished her to follow the 'pious example of [her] virtuous and learned aunt [Mary Sidney], who translated so many godly books and especially the holy Psalms of David'.[12] In a society in which it was considered dangerous for a Lady's reputation, to even read romances, we can imagine what a scandal Wroth must have created when she used the 'matter of romance' in order to write about women's feelings, thoughts and sexuality.[13] Moreover, when Wroth wrote her romance, romances were actually out of vogue. The fact that she chose to write one shows both her independence and the deliberateness of her purpose, especially if we consider that Sidney's *Arcadia* had redefined the romance as a serious genre which could convey a whole range of moral and spiritual issues 'underneath the prettie tales of wolves and sheeps'.[14]

The Countess of Montgomery Urania opens in traditional romance fashion with a pastoral character in lamentation. Wroth's character, though, does not mourn for the absence of (or rejection from) her beloved, but is a shepherdess named Urania preoccupied by the mystery of her own identity. Urania has just discovered that the shepherds who raised her are not her real parents and that her origins are unknown, so she cries to herself:

Of any misery that can befall woman, is not this the most and greatest which thou art faln into?[15]

Urania's lament establishes at the very beginning of Wroth's romance the importance of the knowledge of one's past, of one's re-membrance of it, as a starting point for the construction of one's identity.

In 1621 *The Countess of Montgomery Urania* was published together with a sonnet sequence entitled *Pamphilia to Amphilantus*, where Wroth subverts the established tradition by giving to her sonneteer, the noble Queen Pamphilia, the voice of a woman. The fictionality of Pamphilia, a major character in *Urania*, is debatable: Wroth's romance, in fact, is full of allusions both to her own life and to the members of her society. In the heroine Pamphilia ('the all loving') Wroth's contemporaries could not fail to recognise Wroth herself; besides, Amphilantus ('the lover of two') was unequivocally her lover and married cousin William Herbert while the Queen of Naples represented Mary of Pembroke, Wroth's aunt and, probably, her literary mentor.[16]

Hence, we could argue that *The Countess of Montgomery Urania* is a case history in the sense that Wroth offers us the first extended 'fictional' portrait of a 'real' woman by a woman.

Curiously enough, Erna Brodber's *Jane and Louisa Will Soon Come Home* not only constitutes, but was originally *meant* to be, a case history for her sociology students. It was her sister, Velma Pollard, who found a publisher for the novel.

Despite its scientific intent, *Jane and Louisa Will Soon Come Home* is a very personal piece of work, as Erna Brodber herself declares:

I felt that my examination of Jamaican society could not be written from the stand-point of the objective outside observer communicating to disinterested scholars. It had to incorporate my 'I' and to be presented in such a way that the social workers I was training saw their own 'I' in the work [...] had to have space in which people could do their own dreaming, their own thinking, and their own planning. These considerations account for the format, content, and style of this piece.[17]

Jane and Louisa Will Soon Come Home is the title of a Caribbean song for ring games. The lyrics of the song are used by Brodber as social commentary and as emblems of Caribbean experience. The story of the protagonist, named Nellie, begins in a 'beautiful garden', an idyllic, pastoral setting similar to the Garden of Eden and to the place where Urania finds herself at the beginning of Wroth's romance. In that garden, Nellie says, 'mountains ring us round and cover us, banana leaves shelter and sustain us'.[18] Nellie's first words in the book, though, refer to the colour and class division in her own family:

'Papa's grandfather and Mama's mother were the upper reaches of our world. So we were brown, intellectual, better and apart [...] The cream of the earth, isolated, quadroon, mulatto, Anglican'.[19]

Nellie is brought up by her fair-skinned Aunt Becca who emphasises this sense of isolation and dismembers Nellie's sense of self by teaching her 'to make a distinction' between herself and those others (including some members of her own family) who represent her peasant past. If she does not comply, Aunt Becca threatens Nellie, these others 'will drag [her] down'.[20] With these words strongly impressed on her mind, Nellie goes to college, receives a good education, becomes politically active and joins a group of pseudo-radical intellectuals. Despite all that, though, she remains extremely vulnerable and finally, she breaks down.

What kept Nellie going for almost twenty-five years is the fact that she had been constantly living in the 'kumbla' of respectability that Aunt Becca showed her 'where to find and how to wear'.[21] Staying 'eena kumbla' for a short time might have a beneficial effect but, as Nellie says, 'if you dwell too long in it, it makes you delicate'.[22] The trouble with the kumbla, she realises, is precisely escaping from it, leaving the protective camouflage. Yet, at the same time, this is a necessary move if she wants to recover her health and wholeness. This step, though, frightens Nellie to the point that she decides to wait until she can find somebody who can help her to 'test her feet outside the kumbla'.[23]

The first person who tries to help Nellie in her quest for a whole selfhood is her childhood friend, Baba. Under his guidance she realises that her 'path lay [...] through the aliens' who surrounded [her],[24] that is, the 'folks' that her Aunt Becca advised her to avoid and consider different from herself. 'It is one thing', she says, 'to wander into their quarters, to put on a show for them and quite another to live from day to day with them'.[25] Nellie, therefore, refuses the protective 'camouflage' of the kumbla in a sense like Erna Brodber when she wrote *Jane and Louisa Will Soon Come Home*. In her own words:

...boredom with a social science methodology devoted to objectivity and therefore distancing the researcher from the people and spurning the affective interaction between the researcher and researched led me into fiction.[26]

In a similar way, Lady Mary Wroth's decision to write fiction and not a treatise on women such as, for instance, Jane Anger's *Her Protection of Women* (1589),[27] might have been due to the fact that she wanted to explore women's interiority from *within* their subjective feelings. In *The Countess of Montgomery Urania*, in fact, Pamphilia underlines the difference between 'true feelers' who, like herself, are 'wrapped in distempers and only know how to beare' and detached 'actors' who know 'when to speak, when to sign, when to end'. Actors are camouflaged people *par excellence* and they do not interest Wroth who is instead determined to get as close as possible to the core of the inner truth of her characters. Her endeavour is consistent with the fact that Wroth never resorts to the stratagem of camouflaging her female characters in a male disguise in order to allow them to speak their mind, a device frequently used in the Renaissance (for example, Portia and Nerissa in Shakespeare's *The Merchant of Venice*). Urania, Pamphilia, (and Wroth herself) are women who speak with and about women and who do not 'go eena kumbla' to exist and function.

Nellie's journey to become what she is continues under the guidance of her dead Aunt Alice, another woman who never lived in the protective cocoon of the 'kumbla'. Never having been bothered by colour and class differences, she introduces Nellie to her dead ancestors and to her past, formerly dismembered by Aunt Becca. Nellie, like Urania at the beginning of Wroth's romance, finally recognises that to know 'all her kin' is the first step to know 'what [she is] about'.[28] Aunt Alice's function, then, is to counterbalance Aunt Becca's repressive education and to help Nellie to piece together the fragments of her ancestry, to finally get out of Aunt Becca's 'kumbla' and to remember her past and her own identity.

It has been pointed out that Aunt Alice, 'the spirit/ancestor, [...] is not regarded by Nellie as a divine or omnipotent being whose words are to be heeded with reverence. Rather, she is an individual with whom Nellie matter-of-factly converses and even challenges'.[29] In fact, it is through their dialogues that Nellie matures and remembers her identity. Similarly, in *The Countess of Montgomery Urania*, Wroth resorts to the introduction of dramatic elements in her romance in order to explore her heroine's interiority. While, most of the time, other romances [written by men] commit the accounts of conversations between their characters to long summaries, Wroth includes in her work extensive excerpts of spoken dialogues that confer a far greater immediacy to her characters. It is by means of these exchanges that Wroth's characters mature, establish their identity and learn how to give voice to it instead of simply being 'wrapped in distemper' and bear their suffering in silence as they were doing at the beginning of the romance. In fact, at the end of the unpublished continuation of the romance, the characters are presented while they 'truly tell' one another about their experiences of lovers and the suffering related to them.[32] Moreover, Urania, after maturing through her initial quest for her true identity, becomes a reference point of the romance for the other characters who are striving to find their voices.

Jane and Louisa Will Soon Come Home ends with a similarly optimistic note about Nellie's (and her people's) capacity to articulate her own experience as a woman and as a black West-Indian. Nellie, in fact, dreams of carrying a big fish in her belly which is so big that, even if she can see the tail where the nurse has prepared her, no amount of bearing down can give birth to it. 'Strangely enough', she continues:

> I felt neither sadness nor frustration nor even pain that the fish couldn't come for afterall I could see it.
>
> It will come.
> [...]
> We are getting ready.[30]

This dream is not the only one described in Brodber's *Jane and Louisa Will Soon Come Home*. The novel broadly forages on the oneiric experiences of the protagonist. In fact, an event as decisive as Nellie's first meeting with her Aunt Alice, with her dead ancestors and through them with her people, takes place precisely in a dream: 'Last night', Nellie recalls:

> I let myself into a new world. [...] I travelled with her, my Aunt Alice [...]. Things began to take shape [...] I saw [...] the myriad pieces [...] in the kaleidoscope. I saw them standing still. They were people [...] Aunt Alice said she'd show me later.[31]

Dreams have a crucial importance in Wroth's work as well: for instance, the first sonnet of the sonnet-sequence *Pamphilia to Amphilantus* which describes the very moment in which Pamphilia fell in love with her beloved, is in fact the account of a dream. Wroth's heroine falls in love *in absentia Amphilanti*, as it were: it is night, she is asleep in her room when Venus appears to her and puts in her breast a 'flaming heart' for her son Cupid to 'martyre'. 'Since', Pamphilia/Wroth says, 'a Lover I have beene'.[32]

Following the convention of the genre at various points in Wroth's romance, some of her characters find themselves imprisoned in different Towers (the Tower of Love, of Chastity, of Desire) from which they are liberated by 'the valientest Knight' and the 'loyallest Lady' — that is, Amphilantus and Pamphilia. In a similar way, in Brodber's novel — but would not it be more appropriate, at this point, to call it a romance, or better a West-Indian romance? — the protagonist Nellie is liberated from the prison (the kumbla) in which her daimonic (from the Greek 'daímön' — related to 'daíesthai' — dividing, separating) Aunt Becca has locked her by an *obeah man* who finally disappears into an electric bulb (Baba) and by her spirit/ancestors (especially her Aunt Alice).

Wroth's and Brodber's works also present similarities as far as their structure is concerned. Wroth's *The Countesse of Montgomery Urania* is organised around a very loose design with a dozen secondary plots, puzzling events, dreams and enchantments, and characters who appear in the story as suddenly as they disappear from it. *Jane and Louisa Will Soon Come Home* is built on a structure not dependent on linear development but mostly on flash backs into the life of the protagonist and on the effect that her dreams or the presence of different, sometimes mysterious, characters, have on her life and on her attempt at finding out who she really is. Most importantly, both works are characterised by a symbiotic presence of prose and poetry and are open-ended.

To conclude, I do not want my reading of Erna Brodber's *Jane and Louisa Will Soon Come Home* alongside Lady Mary Wroth's romance to be a display of athletic criticism or even funambulism nor an attempt to judge Caribbean writings by

European (feminist) standards in order to deny them their intrinsic originality. Unearthing common aesthetic strategies shared by these two writers belonging to dissimilar historical, social, political and geographical backgrounds is a way to explore (at least one of) those 'multiple series of relationships' that, according to Edouard Glissant, Caribbean culture maintains within and *without* the Caribbean Sea.[33] Moreover, underlining the affinities between *Jane and Louisa Will Soon Come Home* and *The Countesse of Montgomerie Urania* contributes to reading the history of Caribbean people — or rather, in this case the *her-story* of Caribbean women — highlighting, again in Glissant's words, 'the history they shared (experiencing it as nonhistory) with other communities, with whom the link is becoming apparent today'.[34] As we have seen, in order to subvert Prospero's world, Brathwaite asserts that Caribbean writers need to restore a cosmos that includes Sycorax, Caliban and his children. I hope to have shown that the voice of the 'omitted' and forgotten Susanna — which is articulated not too dissimilarly from those of Sycorax and Caliban's children — might also play an important role in the restoration of this cosmos. As both Urania and Nellie show us, 're-membering' a 'dis-membered' past is the only way to construct identities and to understand the complex contemporary world in which we all have to live and function.

Notes

1. There is also some evidence that Behn might have been Wroth's own great granddaughter. See Sharon Valiant, 'Sidney's Sister, Pembroke's Mother ... and Aphra Behn's Great-Grandmother?', paper, American Society for Eighteenth Century Studies Conference in New Orelans (1989).

2. Erna Brodber, 'Fiction in the Scientific Procedure' in Cudjoe, S. (ed.) *Caribbean Women Writers: Essays from the First International Conference*, Wellesley: Calaloux, 1990, pp.164-168, p.168.

3. Cudjoe, Ibid., 'Introduction', pp.5-6.

4. Ibid., p.7.

5. Mary Ellen Lamb, 'The Cooke Sisters: Attitudes Towards Learned Women in the Renaissance' in Hannay, M. (ed.) *Silent*

but for the Word: Tudor Women as Patrons, Translators, and Writers of Religious Works, Kent, Ohio: The Kent State University Press, 1985, pp.107-125, pp.116, 124.

6. Joan Kelly-Gadol, 'Did Women have a Renaissance?' in Bridenthal, R. and Koonz, C. (eds.), *Becoming Visible*, Boston: Houghton Mifflin, 1977, pp.139-164.

7. Betty Travitsky, 'Placing Women in the English Renaissance', in *The Renaissance Englishwoman in Print: Counterbalancing the Canon*, Amherst: University of Massachusetts Press, 1990, pp.3-41, pp.5, 7.

8. Edward Kamau Brathwaite, 'Caliban's Guarden', *Wasafiri*, 16 (1992), 2-6.

9. Ibid., p.4.

10. Mary Ellen Lamb, 'Introduction', in *Gender and Authorship in the Sidney Circle*, Madison: University of Wisconsin Press, 1990, pp.3-27, p.25.

11. In fact, even if she is doing what her father secretly wants her to do, that is to fall in love with Ferdinando, she is not aware of Prospero's intentions. She knows that her father has forbidden her to spend time with Ferdinando and to treat him with kindness, let alone to fall in love with him.

12. Lord Edward Denny to Lady Mary Wroth, Salisbury MSS. 130/ 118-19, Feb. 26, 1621/22. The correspondence between Wroth and Denny is printed in Roberts, J.A. (ed.), *The Poems of Lady Mary Wroth*, Baton Rouge: Louisiana State University Press, 1993, pp.237-41.

13. It is unclear if Lady Mary Wroth really meant to have her work published or if she wanted it to remain in manuscript. Cfr Roberts, J.A. (ed.) *The Poems of Lady Mary Wroth*, Baton Rouge: Louisiana State University Press, 1993, p.70; Swift, C.R. 'Feminine Identity in Lady Mary Wroth's Romance Urania', *English Literary Renaissance*, 14 (1984) 329-340 and Witten-Hannah, M.A., 'Sleeping with Monsters: Lady Mary Wroth's Complete Urania, The Book and Manuscript Continuation in *Aulla XX: Proceedings and Papers of the Twentieth Congress of Australasian Universities Language and Literature Association* (1980) p.239. The first part of the romance, published in London 1621 was withdrawn from sale only six months after publication and only twenty-eight copies of it survive today

together with one copy of her unpublished continuation which is in Chicago, Newberry Library, Case MS fY 1565 W 95. For a discussion of the reasons behind the withdrawal, see cfr. Miller, N.J. and Waller, G. 'Introduction: Reading as Revision' in Miller, N.J. and Waller, G. (eds.), *Reading Mary Wroth: Representing Alternatives in Early Modern England*, Knoxville: University of Tennessee Press, 1991, pp.1-14, pp.6-7.

14. Sidney, P., 'The Defence of Poesie', in Feuillerat, A. (ed.), *Works*. Volume Three, Cambridge: Cambridge UP, 1965, p.22.

15. Wroth, Lady M. *The Countesse of Montgomerie Urania*, London, 1621, p.1.

16. Cfr. Margaret P. Hannay, 'Your vertuous and learned Aunt': The Countesse of Pembroke as Mentor to Mary Wroth' in Miller, N.J. and Waller, G. (eds.), *Reading Mary Wroth: Representing Alternatives in Early Modern England*, Knoxville: University of Tennessee Press, 1991, pp.15-34.

17. Cudjoe, p.166.

18. Erna Brodber, *Jane and Louisa Will Soon Come Home*, London: New Beacon, 1980, p.9.

19. Ibid., p.1.

20. Ibid., p.16 and p.142.

21. Ibid, p.142.

22. Ibid., p.130. For a full discussion of the image of the Kumbla in Brodber's novel see Carolyn Cooper, 'Afro-Jamaican folk elements in Brodber's *Jane and Louisa Will Soon Come Home*', in C. Boyce-Davies and E. Fido Savory (eds.), *Out of the Kumbla*, Trenton, NJ: Africa World Press, 1990, pp.279-288.

23. Brodber, 1980, p.70.

24. Ibid.

25. Ibid.

26. Cudjoe, 1990, p.165.

27. 'Jane Anger, *Her Protection of Women* (1589), is reproduced in Ferguson, M., *First Feminists: British Women Writers, 1578-1799*, Bloomington: Indiana University Press, 1985. See also Betty Travitsky, 'The Lady Doth Protest: Protest in the Popular Writings of Renaissance Englishwomen', *English Literary Renaissance*, 14 (1984), 255-83, a study on the works of Jane Anger, Rachel Speght, Ester Sowernam and Constantia Munda.

28. Brodber, 1980, p.80.

29. Daryl Cumber Dance, 'Go Eena Kumbla: A Comparison of Erna Brodber's *Jane and Louisa Will Soon Come Home* and Toni Cade Bambara's *The Salt Eaters*', in Cudjoe (ed.), 1990, pp.169-184 (p.179).

30. Brodber, 1980, p.147.

31. Ibid, pp.75-77.

32. Waller, G.F. (ed.), Lady Mary Wroth, *Pamphilia to Amphilantus*, Salzburg: University of Salzburg, 1977, p.24.

33. Edouard Glissant, *Caribbean Discourse: Selected Essays*, M. Dash, trans, Charlottesville: University Press of Virginia, 1989, p.139.

34. Ibid.

'In the Blood':

Performing Memory

in Paule Marshall's

Praisesong for the Widow[1]

PAULETTE BROWN-HINDS

And it was clear from his tone that he wasn't thinking of the
forgotten backwater it had become, a place where lepers and
goats freely roamed the sun-baked street, but the city as he
remembered it from memories that had come down to him *in the
blood*: as Juba, the heart of the equatoria.
Paule Marshall, *Praisesong for the Widow*

Once a great wrong has been done, it never dies. People speak
words of peace, but their hearts do not forgive. Generations
perform ceremonies of reconciliation but there is no end.
Paule Marshall, *The Chosen Place The Timeless People*[2]

dance/and dare to remember
Edward Brathwaite, *Rites of Passage*[3]

In his book *Ride Out The Wilderness: Geography and Identity
in Afro-American Literature* (1987), Melvin Dixon explores the
liberating nature of specific geographic sites in African-
American narrative. He argues that the wilderness, the

underground, and the mountain top are broad geographical metaphors for the search, discovery, and achievement of self. He contends:

More than merely describing place, Afro-American writers have vigorously analyzed what kinds of behavior or performance occurs in alternative spaces and leads to control over self and environment. They shape Afro-American literary history from texts that locate places for physical and spiritual freedom.[4]

As Dixon and others have noted, since the major geographical dislocation of Blacks from Africa to the Americas, issues of home, shelter, and freedom have loomed paramount in the Black imagination.[5] Although Dixon's project identifies three specific sites as places for physical and spiritual freedom, his treatment can cogently extend to other discussions of geography in African-American literature. Inspired by Dixon's monumental work, this essay explores the Caribbean as a site of liberation and diasporic memory in Paule Marshall's novel *Praisesong for the Widow* (1983). I argue that not only does the Caribbean geography function as a way of reclaiming and re-writing a history of liberation which has been distorted, silenced, and forgotten in narratives of America, it ultimately becomes a site of 'rememory'[6] — to borrow from Toni Morrison — connecting African diasporic cultures through the performance of the West African circle dance. As critics of Marshall's work have argued, not only does she evoke a sense of 'place' in her novels, but her exploration of the Caribbean topography seeks to enlarge the frame of cultural reference for those of the African diaspora by anchoring that experience in memory — a memory that ultimately rewrites history.[7]

Born in Brooklyn the daughter of Barbadian immigrants, Marshall grew-up in a tightly structured Caribbean-American community constantly hearing stories of her parents' Caribbean 'home/land'. Before her tenth birthday she made the first of many visits to Barbados and recorded her impressions in the form of poetry. As Marshall scholar Dorothy Denniston has suggested, 'that visit may well have been significant for instilling within her the value of her Barbadian ethnicity as different from her African-American identity in New York. That visit also may have informed, if only subliminally, her sense of the immediacy of her African heritage.'[8] As many scholars have noted about her fiction as a whole, Marshall attempts to identify, analyze and resolve the conflict between displacement and cultural loss and the hegemony of the dominant culture.[9]

Paule Marshall's project, laid out in her novels, has been described by Kamau Brathwaite as one of reconnection and reconciliation.[10] As such, her work centers on the continuation of African culture in the contemporary diaspora. In her work reconnection is often achieved through African-influenced cultural expressions, mainly storytelling, music, and dance. *Praisesong for the Widow*, Marshall's third novel, tells the story of Avey Johnson, an elderly widow whose comfortable life begins to unravel during a Caribbean cruise. Haunted by memories of the past and suffering from a type of cultural amnesia which leads to an 'impoverished spirit,' Avey abandons her travelling companions and embarks on a spiritual journey which challenges the limits of time and place. While in Carriacou, it is through the Big Drum ritual and its diasporic link to the Ring Shout that Avey remembers a history she had long forgotten.

While most literary critics discuss how Avey's fragmented memories remain disembodied until she can make coherent sense of them,[11] I examine how her body remembers the past, even after her mind has chosen to forget it. I would like to suggest that sacred dance, allegorically employed by Marshall to illustrate a conjunctive diasporic experience, provides historical connection through a form of what I have termed 'kinesthetic memory'. As historian Sterling Stuckey explains in his work on the tradition of Black dance in the Americas:

Dance was the most difficult of all art forms to erase from the slave's memory in part because it could be practiced in the silence of aloneness where motor habits could be initiated with enough speed *to seem* autonomous. In that lightening fast process, the body *very nearly* was memory and helped the mind recall the form of dance to come. For in dance, such is the speed with which the mind can work, and the body respond to it, that *the time between thought and action all but disappears*. In a sense, then, the body is mind, and is capable of inscribing in space the language of the human spirit. When the tempo slows, of course, the body configures what the mind more easily recalls.[12]

As Stuckey notes, the language of dance is not expressed in words, but instead utilizes rhythm, movement, tempo, form, and symbol. For Marshall, dance functions as a form of non-verbal communication which crosses the boundaries of spoken language, culture, and history.[13] What I find particularly interesting is how the dancing body performs in the drama of the West and the creation of the 'New World.' Western philosophy, symbolized here as the Cartesian mind/body split, is an inadequate marker of humanity as 'the dance' relies on the synchronicity of thought and action. Dance reconfigures the role of the body, then, in conceptions of humanity.

The inscription of humanity for Africans in the 'New World' considered chattel — mere property by law — is made possible in that space of kinesthetic memory the 'lightening fast process' when 'the time between thought and action all but disappears'. This process, scientifically termed metakinesis, relies on the belief that there is psychic accompaniment to bodily movement which grows from the theory that the physical and the psychic are merely two aspects of a single underlying reality.[14] With this in mind, we cannot forget the history of the Black body in the discourse of the West. The attention to 'the body' goes back to the slave economy of the Americas when Black bodies were prized simply for their 'use value'. The commodification and transportation of human flesh across the Atlantic Ocean produced generations of 'humanless' humans in which every bodily action had economic consequences. This was true especially for females when pregnant slaves, for instance, did not give birth to their own children, but instead supplied parts for the plantation labor machine. Dance subsequently became one of the many ways in which the slave could empower the Black body. Dance served several functions: African slaves communicated with the spirit world through spirit possession; dance strengthened community solidarity; and as a form of worship, dance functioned as a means of achieving union with God. Dance, at various levels, then, allowed for the performance of humanity which countered the inhumanity of forced labor and chattel status.

Much like Morrison's 'rememory,' Marshall offers a concept of memory which functions in a timeless space. History, then, is a product of multiple memories which — whether or not we choose to remember them — reside and remain in the body. The Black tradition of dance speaks to a different history of the Americas: a living memory, inscribed not in what Pierre Nora calls the 'places of memory' but instead recorded in the gestures, movements, and dances of the people.[15] Or, as Nora argues, 'true memory' is obvious in gestures and habits, '...passed down by *unspoken* traditions, in the body's inherent self-knowledge, in unstudied reflexes and ingrained memories'. Similar to Nora, Paul Connerton argues that the practice of memory is 'amassed in the body'.[16] And, Joseph Roach drawing on the work of both Nora and Connerton as well as that of dance historians, develops what he calls the 'kinesthetic imagination'. He offers this concept as a faculty of memory which flourishes in that mental space where imagination and memory converge as a way of thinking through movements 'at once remembered and reinvented — the otherwise unthinkable, just as dance is often said to be a way of expressing the unspeakable'.[17] Taken together, these theorists offer a type of memory which relies on performance as the primary mode of inscription. Dance, then, is not simply mnemonic, it does more than just assist memory; the dancing body, in a sense, becomes memory.

For instance, Marshall invokes dance ceremonies that 'perform' the collective memories of generations. This becomes particularly obvious when *Praisesong* is read intertextually with Marshall's first novel *Brown Girl Brownstones* (1959) as both attempt to address the dynamic of cultural memory and dance performance. Clearly, for both Selina Boyce and Avey Johnson — Marshall's youngest and oldest protagonists —

reconnection to an ancestral past is achieved kinesthetically. In these texts, dance becomes what spiritualist Noris Binet describes in a different context as 'an expression which builds bridges to connect seemingly unconnectable spaces'.[18] In *Brown Girl*, as Selina's mother dances the 'Little Island' dance at Agatha Steed's wedding with other members of the New York 'bajan' community, Selina watches closely and begins to imagine her mother as a young girl dancing on the island pasture. The image is so vivid that Selina's fascination leads to a revelation. For the first time, Selina sees her mother Silla as more than the oppressive tyrant she battles at home: 'suddenly she yearned to know the mother then, in her innocence. Above all, she longed to understand the mother, she knew obscurely, that she would never really understand anything until she did'.[19] The dance allows her to stretch linear time to remember years before she was born and to bend geographic space to return to a place where she has never been. Silla's dancing body in this scene becomes memory, but not simply her own memory. Instead, her body functions collectively allowing different sets of memories — namely Silla's and Selina's — to encounter each other in the same discursive space. For the elderly Avey, however, this rebirth comes as a result of her performance of a past she has intentionally forgotten.

Clearly Avey Johnson's dilemma is that she has forgotten, and much of what she has forgotten slowly surfaces once she physically escapes from the cruise ship. *Praisesong's* narrative is constructed in the form of the symbolic circle, possibly the central organizing principle of the early Africans in America, and a movement which Eugenia Collier asserts is a driving force in Marshall's fiction.[20] Movement in time is cyclical, rather than chronological, as Marshall's protagonist moves from memories of the past to projections of the future. Her first memory surfaces in the form of a dream after she spends a long day in Martinique. In the dream she is literally forced by her great aunt Cuney to remember. And her initial reaction is to resist, for Avey had long forgotten her Tatem, South Carolina vacations to her family home. And had long forgotten her ritual journeys to two significant sites during her visits: Ibo Landing and the clearing across from the church as they watched the elderly Shouters perform the Ring Shout. Earlier, aunt Cuney had been suspended from participation in the Shouts because she had forgotten and committed the sin of crossing her feet. Unreconciled, but longing to participate, aunt Cuney made the Landing her religion, teaching Avey of its significance as a tale of resistance.

These memories of aunt Cuney and Tatem, South Carolina, are the first step to Avey's spiritual and cultural renewal. But the significance of this spiritual 'visit' reaches far beyond Avey Johnson's life, beyond even the pages of the novel, for Avey's dream of her great aunt Cuney recalls a sacred practice deeply rooted in African and African-American culture. Although the African bondsmen and women were from various cultures, among them the Ashanti, Ibo, and Akan, an important common bond was the circle dance which was associated with ancestral ceremonies that surfaced in America in the form of the Ring Shout. During the Shout, the participants, bodies positioned in the form of a ring, moved rhythmically in a counter-clockwise direction, singing spirituals. It was performed in a variety of settings, and the dancing and singing were directed toward the ancestors and gods. But, while dance plays an essential role in supplication in Africa, in the Euro-Christian tradition dancing in church is regarded as profane. Harold Courlander argues that the Ring Shout is a fusion of these two types of religious behavior.[21] Whether or not the crossing of the feet was ever a part of the circle dance, aunt Cuney's sin is clearly a momentary amnesia which 'caused her to forget and cross her feet'. The act which caused her temporary dismissal from the Shouts coupled with her decision to never return, created an unreconciled longing to participate in the ceremony. Avey's participation in aunt Cuney's nostalgic imaginings is that of silent accomplice. As a child at her great aunt's side, Avey would quietly watch the shouters from across the road. Although she desired to join the participants in their 'non-dance' ritual, she stayed at her aunt's side at their post across from the church. While neither women perform the 'little rhythmic trudge' with the elderly Tatem shouters, Avey's participation in the Big Drum decades later allows for a completion of the circle aunt Cuney had left open.

During this journey Avey also begins to remember the early years of her marriage to Jay and the sacred rituals and cultural performances which sustained them amidst the despair of the Halsey Street environment; the night she recalls as 'that Tuesday in 1945' when he spiritually died without mention or ceremony; and finally their move to White Plains, where for a while she re-enacts the rituals alone in her own desperate attempt of re-membering. Once again, memories imbue the narrative as Avey remembers her past life with Jay on Halsey Street. For Jay, dance and music, especially the blues, are magical and serve purposes beyond entertainment.[22] She recalls those evenings when Jay would return home from working 'two jobs for the salary of one' and listen to the blues of Ma Rainey and Big Bill Broonzy, with his head bowed in front of the phonograph as if in prayer at the altar. His reverence for the blues functioned much like the evenings the couple spent dancing to 'Flying Home', 'Take the A-Train', and 'Stompin' at the Savoy'. The blues rituals, as well as the dances he staged for Avey in the livingroom, had the power to make the poverty and despair Halsey Street symbolized vanish, or least be forgotten for an evening.

Memories of this past life culminate with Avey's realization of the moment her life changed when 'Jay had simply ceased to be'. While women are often considered the 'bearers of the culture' and 'transmitters of history' in cultural discourse, Avey's body — pregnant with her third child — projects a bleak future which 'speaks' subordination and poverty. When a pregnant and hysterical Avey confronts Jay on 'that Tuesday night in '45' accusing him of infidelity, her 'fierce' and 'defiant' threat, 'Goddamn you, nigger, I'll take my babies and go!'(106), spiritually kills Jay and the marriage. His response, 'Do you know who you look like...who you even sound like?' (106), places Avey outside the sanctity of their 'home' and casts her into the hell of the other Halsey Street tenements.[23] The sacred space of the livingroom finally succumbs to the despair of their urban surroundings as Avey's declaration echoes the chorus of their fellow Halsey Street tenants: 'It appeared finally that the street had won' (111). At that moment, without mention or ceremony Jay became 'Jerome.' Marshall explains, 'And in leaving he had taken with him the little private rituals and pleasures, the playfulness and wit of those early years, the host of feelings and passions that had defined them in a special way back then, and the music which had been their nourishment'(136). Those same rites, part of a 'vast unknown lineage that made their being possible,' are fragments or scattered memories which function as diasporic links in an unwritten history. The rituals also disappear, and the dances which once made them feel 'like new' are distant memories which Avey re-enacts alone condemned by feelings of guilt and betrayal. Once Avey and Jerome move from Halsey Street to White Plains, a critical division is created and dance no longer signifies the sacred but now belongs in the realm of the profane. As Jerome exclaims to their new friends, 'If it was left to me I'd close down every dancehall in Harlem and burn every drum!'(132) Eventually she succumbs to a type of cultural amnesia and personal memory loss. Avey's silence over time becomes amnesia.[24] This amnesia, the unwritten history, lies dormant until it is articulated through the body.

However, it is through the cruise ship — the *Bianca Pride* — that Marshall places Avey's personal amnesia within the matrix of a larger culture of forgetting by suggesting that there is a cultural amnesia attached to Avey's touristic proclivities. Her daughter Marion, who functions as her 'diasporic memory,' and her only daughter to oppose the trip asks, 'Why go on some meaningless cruise with a bunch of white folks anyway, I keep asking you? What's that about?...Last summer I begged you to go on that tour to Brazil, and on the one, the year before that to Ghana...Yet here you are willing and eager to go off on some ridiculous cruise' (14). But, whatever doubts Marion had managed to sow in Avey Johnson's mind vanished the moment she saw the *Bianca Pride*: 'All the dazzling white steel! The ship's turbines, she had to read in the brochure they had sent her before sailing, produced enough heat and light to run a city the size of Albany! Her group had stood awestruck and reverent before the console with its array of keyboards, switches and closed-circuit television screens' (15). In fact, the *Bianca Pride* functions much like what Michael Rogin calls 'spectacles of amnesia' covertly linking the history of slavery with the imperial present. According to Rogin, this historicizing concept of amnesia suggests that the forgotten link in spectacle is the visible tie to the past.[25] The ship, described as 'huge, sleek, imperial' and its 'Versailles' Dining Room function as metaphoric representations of slavery and the colonial enterprise. Avey's inability to eat the parfait, made from one of the major exports of the slave trade, further serves to connect the ship to a history of exploitation. By invoking the 'sugar crop' and Treaty of Versailles, Marshall joins writers like Jamaica Kincaid and Audre Lorde who compel us to connect Caribbean tourism to a larger history of imperialism by remembering the history of conquest, annexation, acquisition, invasion, and political engineering. We see this as well in her choice of Grenada as setting which in America is remembered as a contested site of invasion. Even the title of the first section 'Runagate' — alluding to Robert Hayden's poem 'Runagate, Runagate' about runaway slaves — connects the cruise ship to a history of oppression and slavery.

At the next port-of-call in Grenada, Avey continues to remember and recall. While on the docks, the Grenadian patois reminds her of Tatem. And much like the cruise ship, the luxury hotel provides no relief from her growing discomfort. Her memories also begin to intensify — no longer limited to her dreams — she is instead visited by her dead husband while awake. But it is not until she meets Lebert Joseph in his rum shop and agrees to join other 'outlanders' on their annual migration to the tiny island of Carriacou that the significance of her journey begins to take shape. In contrast to the *Bianca Pride*, Avey must 'cross over' to Carriacou on the small schooner *Emanuel C*. Unlike the spectacle of the cruise ship, Avey is conscious of the historical weight which surrounds her: 'Yet she had the impression as her mind flickered on, briefly of other bodies lying crowded in with her in the hot, airless dark. A multitude it felt like lay packed around her in the filth and stench of themselves, just as she was. Their moans, rising and falling with each rise and plunge of the schooner, enlarged upon the one filling her head. Their suffering — the depth of it, the weight of it in the cramped space — made hers of no consequence' (209). Avey's, 'middle passage back'[26] allows her to connect her own personal memory to a larger collective experience. The violent purging she experiences on the *Emanuel C* not only mirrors the pain, suffering and violence of the slave ship, but also prepares her body for the performance of the circle dance.

Not only is the Caribbean setting significant in Marshall's construction of an African diasporic memory, but the performance enacted on its soil contributes to the mastery of self and recollection of a larger community. Paul Gilroy in his discussion of the expressive cultures of the Black Atlantic concurs when he argues that particular elements of 'musical performance serve a mnemonic function directing the consciousness of the group back to significant nodal points in its common history and its social memory'.[27] In Carriacou, the fragments of memory which Avey experiences while on the cruise, begin to provide a type of 'map' of reconnection. First, there is Avey's remembrance of the tale of Tatem's Ibo Landing which aids her flight from the cruise. The myth, also called 'Flying Africans' or 'The Gift of Flight,' is also recounted in songs heard on Petite Martinique, a dependency of Carriacou. It has been argued that this 'gift of flight' is also an underlying theme of the Big Drum. Lorna McDaniels posits that the slave danced not only for entertainment, but to define his/her individual system of escape — of flight.[28] This also accentuates the historical significance of Avey's flight.

Second, there is the common circle dance, the 'rhythmic trudge' practised in a loose circle in honor of the ancestors. Like the Ring Shouts of Tatem, the Big Drum ritual, initially performed by Blacks prior to emancipation, was developed from common African traditions. Both rituals can be linked to the circle dance, which was associated with ancestral ceremonies found in various West African cultures. The ritual, usually held in a yard which is considered a spiritual place by those of African descent throughout the West Indies, is symbolically linked to the community. For Marshall, the community is a global one, which links the Carriacou Islanders with the 'shouters' of Tatem.

At the height of the ceremony, Avey hears Lebert's high-pitched voice send off another song, 'Plewe mwe Lide'. Translated, the Patois sung by Lebert means 'lament, lament for me, weep...' 'Hele,' a mode of bawling or wailing, is normally performed at funerals in Carriacou. The phrase, part of the Bongo that Lebert speaks of when he first meets Avey, tells the story of a family separated during slavery and dispersed throughout the Caribbean. According to the song, when they came to take the wife away she begged her friend Lide to grieve for her and console her children. The Bongo is a dance style/song customarily performed at funerals in the West Indies. The dance — Derek Walcott refers to as foot-asserting, earth-asserting, and life-asserting — is performed at wakes and considered a spiritual celebration at death.[29] The dance ritual becomes a type of 'internal migration' which allows Avey to resolve and connect the past with the present — and Africa with the Americas. By participating in this Bongo, Avey also joins the islanders in mourning the physical and spiritual displacement, separation and loss caused by the African slave trade, as well as renews her own memory of that history of the diaspora.

Third, there is Lebert Joseph who functions as another diasporic link as well as Avey's spiritual 'tour' guide. Lebert can be viewed as one of the Ibos whose attempt to make the voyage back to Africa lands him in the 'borderland' of the Caribbean. Or, like the African deity Legba, the trickster figure and guardian of the crossroads, as he performs the Beg Pardon and becomes Avey's mediator between the spirits of the old world — the ancestors — and the promise of a renewed future. Marshall explains, 'Nevertheless those in charge remained the elderly folk, and chief among them Lebert Joseph...He was constantly darting over to her...with a sly smile, his head performing its trickster dance' (242-43). I believe Lebert as trickster also hearkens to the role of the trickster in burial ceremonies throughout the African Diaspora. According to Sterling Stuckey, in Suriname, for instance, the Anansi trickster tale was told to amuse the deceased during burial.[30]

Lebert also functions as a conjurer, communicating with the dead and healing the living. When Avey first meets him in his rum shop, she notices his 'lame' walk, but it is not until they reach Carriacou and prepare for the Big Drum that she notices his walking stick. The stick, described as 'the wand of a metronome' or 'a hypnotist's finger,' also brings to mind Tatem's Mr. Golla Mack, who fashioned walking sticks shaped like Ibo Landing, and offers another connection to Africa, Tatem, and Carriacou. In West Africa and the southern United States, known conjurers were said to have possessed intricately embellished walking sticks, also known as conjure sticks, which fashioned carvings of various reptiles. These healers were believed to have cured their patients by presenting them with the cause of their illness and their fears in tangible reptilian form.[31] Avey's illness — marked by her uneasiness on the cruise ship, her inability to eat the decadent foods of the Versailles Room, her purging on the small *Emanuel C*, her forgetting of the past — are all connected to the amnesia that has come to control her life.

During slavery, both in the United States and the Caribbean, dance and music became unifying cultural elements for the transported Africans and their descendants. As McDaniels explains, 'those that lost personal nationhood or tradition could reclaim it through an affinity to a particular drum beat that possessed the power to reassign one to a nation'.[32] Consequently, a 'nationless' Avey, who explains that she does not have one, and only acknowledges herself as a 'visitor' or 'tourist' when asked by Lebert, is finally assigned to a 'nation' through her performance of the circle dance. Avey's participation is sparked by a series of memories seemingly invoked by the dancing bodies of the elderly folk. The final memory fragment, Jay's declaration that he would 'close down every dancehall,' spurs her body into motion. And it is her body that remembers, once the collective participants provide assistance. But this encouragement is not verbal. The 'encouragement' instead takes the form of the collective body: 'what seemed an arm made up of many arms reached out from the circle to draw her in...'(247). Avey's 'single declarative step', along with the throng of dancers, ignites the kinesthetic memory which characterizes the dance and allows her body to re-member. At first she closely follows the other dancers and then 'her feet of their own accord began to glide forward'. As the body continues to remember the Ring Shouts of Tatem, 'her hips under the linen shirtdress slowly began to weave from side to side on their own' (248-49). Her aged limbs, stiff muscles, unrehearsed movements are transformed 'with a vigor and passion she hadn't felt in years', infusing her deadened spirit with new life.

Lebert is able to assign her to a specific group through her bodily movement. After Lebert watches Avey participate in the Big Drum he says, 'You know...I watched you good last night at the fete and I can't say for sure but I feels you's an Arada, oui. Something about the way you was doing the Carriacou Tramp there toward the end put me in mind of people from that nation'(252). The body, then, is privileged as the site of memory. It can be read, much like a written text, with the unwritten, undocumented, and often unacknowledged history of African dispersal.

Avey's 'conversion' and restoration of her memory through the performance of the Carriacou Big Drum ritual disrupts the prevailing neo-colonial narrative of tourism. Her 'meaningless cruises' to the region gain a new significance. Her initial flight from the cruise ship to Grenada and then to the island of Carriacou is part of the 'middle passage back' that Avey must experience to recover the memories of a heritage she has suppressed. Clearly, Marshall's narrative does not indulge in a romanticized return to a mythical 'motherland' — although the island is referred to as 'more a mirage rather than an actual place' — but offers the Caribbean as a mediating space between Africa and the Americas. Marshall also offers the Caribbean as a 'sacred space' of renewal for Black Americans. Popular tourism slogans take on a new significance: 'Come back to Jamaica' is replaced by 'Come/Won't you come...?' in a diasporic plea of unity to those seeking spiritual escape, or cultural 'holiday'.

On one hand, participation in the Big Drum ceremony is a necessary step for Avey because it allows her to petition her ancestors, among them aunt Cuney, for forgiveness from her spiritual and cultural transgressions. Clearly, Avey's sin is that she allowed herself to forget. Her given name, Avatara invokes the notion of an 'avatar' and in turn her spiritual mission to pass on the history of the African Diaspora. On the other hand, it also allows her to petition the ancestors for the soul of the angry aunt Cuney she encounters in her dream whose unreconciled feelings of the Tatem Ring Shouts plagued her in death. In a sense, it is also through the ritual dance that Avey is able to reconcile and mourn the 'memories of her prior life' before that Tuesday in 1945 when 'Jay' died without mention or ceremony, as well as petition the ancestors for his spirit. When Avey is finally able to join the elderly dancers in the circle on the tiny island of Carriacou, she achieves a form of reconciliation which must be repeated by each generation in an endless cycle of reconnection. This is most clearly evidenced by her participation in the dance/non-dance, her decision to return to Tatem to tell the tale of the Ibos to her grandchildren and anyone else who will listen, as well as in her decision to embrace her given name, Avatara. Finally, it is the West African Circle Dance which links the African diaspora to heal the wounds of forced migration and cultural alienation. These rituals, we then understand, perform collective memories and shared histories of separation and loss.

Notes

1.   A version of this essay was originally published as 'In the Spirit: Dance as Healing Ritual in Paule Marshall's *Praisesong for the Widow*', *Religion and Literature*, 27(1), (Spring, 1995), 107-117.
2.   From the Tiv of West Africa and Marshall's epigraph for *The Chosen Place, The Timeless People*, New York: Random House, 1969.
3.   From *Rites of Passage, The Arrivants: A New World Trilogy*, London: Oxford University Press, 1973, p.13.
4.   See Melvin Dixon, *Ride Out the Wilderness: Geography and Identity in Afro-American Literature*, Urbana: University of Illinois Press, 1987, pp.4-5.
5.   Ibid., p.2.
6.   In *Beloved*, Toni Morrison defines her concept of memory through the voice of Sethe. Rememory, unlike Marshall's concept is 'site specific'. Rememories, Sethe explains, are tied closely to 'place'. Both writers, however, develop memory as a timeless concept. See Morrison's *Beloved*, New York: Alfred Knopf, 1987.

7. Joyce Pettis, *Toward Wholeness in Paule Marshall's Fiction*, Charlottesville: University of Virginia Press, 1996, p.13.
8. See Dorothy Denniston, *Reconstructions of History, Culture and Gender*, Knoxville: University of Tennessee Press, 1995.
9. See Denniston, Pettis and Abena Busia, 'What Is Your Nation/ Reconnecting African and Her Diaspora through Paule Marshall's *Praisesong for the Widow*, in Cheryl Wall (ed.), *Changing Our Own Words: Essays on Criticism, Theory, and Writing by Black Women*, New Brunswick: Rutgers University Press, 1989, pp.196-211.
10. Notably, Caribbean historian, poet and literary critic Edward Kamau Brathwaite categorises Marshall's work with other writers who explore the African presence in Caribbean literature. See his 'African Presence in Caribbean Literature', in *Daedalus*, 103(2), (Spring, 1974), 73-109.
11. See, for instance, Helen Locke's 'Building Up From Fragments': The Oral Memory Process in Some Recent African-American Written Narratives' in *College Literature*, 22(3), (October, 1995), 109-119.
12. From P. Sterling Stuckey's essay 'Christian Conversion and the Challenge of Dance', in Susan L. Foster (ed.), *Choreographing History*, Bloomington: Indiana Press, 1995, p.55.
13. This is extremely significant in a region like the Caribbean which has a history of various languages due to colonialism and even different forms of the same language. For example, see Edward Kamau Brathwaite's historical work, *The Development of Creole Society in Jamaica (1770-1820)*, Oxford: Clarendon Press, 1971.
14. Choreographer and dance critic John Martin considers this theory of metaphysics formidable, but one of the only terms available to express one of the vital points of the modern dance. From 'Characteristics of the Modern Dance', in Michael Huxley and Noel Witts (eds.), *The Twentieth Century Performance Reader*, New York: Routledge, 1996, pp.255-62.
15. Pierre Nora develops a distinction between 'places of memory' as artificial sites to store history, and the primarily oral 'environments of memory'. See Nora's 'Between Memory and History: Les Lieux de Memoir', in Genevieve Fabre and Robert O'Meally (eds.), *History and Memory in African-American Culture*, New York: Oxford University Press, 1994.

16. Connerton's work has proven to be quite useful in supporting my ideas on the performance of memory. See his introduction in *How Societies Remember*, New York: Cambridge University Press, 1989, pp.6-40.

17. Roach's work *Cities of the Dead: Circum-Atlantic Performance*, New York: Columbia University Press, 1996, places performance within the context of the memory/history debate.

18. Noris Binet is an Afro-Caribbean artist, born and raised in the Dominican Republic whose work focuses on the interrelationship of art, healing and spirituality. In *Women on the Inner Journey*, Nashville: Winston-Derek Publishing, 1994, p.3, she argues that dance is one expression which can channel spiritual energy for the purposes of transforming the physical world.

19. From *Brown Girl Brownstones*, New York: The Feminist Press, p.145. Also at the close of *Brown Girl*, Selina chooses to escape her tight-knit community in New York to perform as a dancer on Caribbean cruise ships.

20. See Eugenia Collier, 'The Closing of the Circle: Movement from Division to Wholeness in Paule Marshall's Fiction', in Mari Evans (ed.), *Black Women Writers 1950-1980*, New York: Doubleday, 1984.

21. For a more detailed discussion of the Shout, see Courlander's *Negro Folk Music USA*, New York: Norton and Company, 1971.

22. Wilfred Cartey remarks that 'The ritual of dance and song and poetry in which (Jay) and Avey Johnson and the two young children nest, is cocooning African source of strength and renewal', in *Whispers from the Caribbean*, Los Angeles: University of California Press, 1991, p.479.

23. At this moment Avey's actions mirror her Halsey Street neighbour, she and Jay have seen outside their apartment window. 'Though the body may appear to be where we are most individual, it is also the material form of the body politic', states John Fiske in 'Offensive Bodies and Carnival Pleasures' in *Understanding Popular Culture*, New York, Routledge, 1991, p.70.

24. In his essay 'The Muse of History', in Orde Coombs (ed.), *Is Massa Day Dead?*, New York: Doubleday, 1974, Derek Walcott remarks, 'In time the slave surrendered to amnesia. That amnesia is the true history of the New World', p.11.

25. Michael Rogin, 'Make My Day! Spectacle as Amnesia in Imperial Politics' in Amy Kaplan and Donald Pease (eds.), *The Cultures of U.S. Imperialism*, North Carolina: Duke University Press, 1993, pp.496-534.

26. This term 'middle passage back' coined by Black feminist critic Mary Helen Washington, is commonly referred to in essays on *Praisesong for the Widow*. See Busia, Denniston, or Pettis.

27. See Paul Gilroy, *The Black Atlantic: Modernity and Double Consciousness*, Cambridge: Harvard University Press, 1993, p.198.

28. See Lorna McDaniels, 'Memory Songs', dissertation, University of Maryland, 1986, p.88. For more on the role of dance in Black cultures see Rex Nettleford *Inward Stretch, Outward Reach: A Voice from the Caribbean*, London: Macmillan, 1993. Also Jacqueline Malone's *Steppin' on the Blues: the Visible Rhythms of African Dance*, Urbana, University of Illinois Press, 1996.

29. See Walcott's discussion of the Bongo in 'Meanings', *Savacou*, 2, (September, 1970), 49.

30. See Stuckey's *Slave Culture*, New York: Oxford University Press, 1987, p.17. He explains, 'For the dead, it appears, were especially susceptible to humor and to exceptional occasions. This explains the prominence of the trickster tales of Anansi the Spider being used to 'amuse the spirit of the dead' in Suriname. But since the trickster, most notably the hare, pervade much of Black Africa, as does the ring ceremony honoring the ancestors, and since the trickster and the circle are associated not only in South America where Africans were enslaved but North American slavery as well, the evidence implies a wide association of the two in Black Africa and, consequently, among numerous African ethnic groups in North America'.

31. Robert Farris Thompson, 'African Influence on the Art of the United States', in Craig Foster and Donald Ogilvie (eds.), *Black Studies in the University*, New Haven and London: Yale University Press, 1969, pp.162-163. Sami Ludwig also commented on the American Medical Association's symbol of the snake as a link between 'traditional' medical doctors and folk healers.

32. See McDaniel's, 'Memory Songs'.

On Creativity, Autarchy

and Memory

BERYL GILROY

Creativity refers to the mental processes generating theories, artistic forms and ideas. It is the result of divergent thinking which encourages the use of ideas, words and objects in exceptional and surprising ways. The element of surprise is crucial to creative acts of any kind.

In this work 'creativity' should mean not only divergent thought but also divergence in the selection of topic, its context, style, plot and characterisation, if the piece is to reflect culture and give weight to the text.

Creativity, like history, like moments of existence, like every day experiences, differs according to what we strive to retrieve from the chasms of experience to record with passion and integrity. As women writers we attempt to show whether we are empowered or not by expectations, chicanery or deceptions which lurk within the parameters of group, tribe, function or nation only to forestall our self-liberation and autarchy or political coming of age.

Women worldwide share the gender consciousness, which I describe as womb-identity, with all its implications for the girl as she undergoes the passage into womanhood. Up to then most girls are so self-obsessed that political thinking is resisted everywhere except in the peer group coterie. An awareness of womb-identity affects women in crucial ways; ways that personalise their political position, and underline the politics of being in 'that place at that time'. I am certain that writers other than myself bear in mind this need to underpin a woman's search for self-definition as we give birth to our stories.

As mothers we first learn, and then pass on to youth, traditional or tribal knowledge of what must be remembered, what is taboo and what will cause harm or even death. Traditionally, women preserve their offspring, men defend them. It is up to us to focus on whatever must be kept chic and shining in the memory of the family, the clan or the tribe. Actually whatever the ecology or environment, it is the woman's duty to take care of it and of all its idiosyncracies.

Through repetition and reinforcement, memory helps by imprinting upon the brain the pathways for cultural survival. For example, facets of daily life, journeys, sacrifices and so on were recorded, as the cave paintings of Africa, Europe and other places prove. Like a good book they have never failed to surprise and delight those who were lucky enough to see them. Like memory, creativity is a whole-body act involving and combining the cerebral with the spiritual and exploring systems of need, unease and desire in order to convert the unthinkable into the believable.

To do this, we evoke memory, an individual and sometimes illusory construct that comes heavily encrusted with thoughts, feelings and experiences gleaned across the life span. When decoded and placed in context they form subjective 'memories', derived from and yet distinguishable from 'memory' per se.

To the creative writer, memory in all its guises sees more than the eye. It is held captive in every sphere of study and has been variously described as phenotypic, genetic, associative, accessible, biological, episodic, echoic, flash-bulb, short or long-term iconic, holographic, semantic, reproductive, immediate, lexical, working, integrative, de-integrative and re-deintegrative or rememory, used when writing from recall.

I grew up in a village with little visual stimulus. No posters, advertisements, or any other impediment to clear visuality. All our landmarks were of nature: trees, shrubs, flowers, the houses of neighbours, the voices that called out as one passed by, the boom of drums, jingling bells or the shouts of children at play and the twitter of birds overhead.

Consequently, children developed memory which, in some cases, was more acute than sight.

To survive was to notice and to notice was to see. If an animal was killed somebody saw who had killed it and how, when and where it was killed. They might have even heard its last moan or words. As for the griots of Africa, no part of history could be retrieved without exposing the whole.

Every now and then some new form of memory is discovered and we are offered another name for it. However in spite of that, women writers use memory to grasp consciousness and change the currency of existence. In our service to others, we are bound by labels (mother, wife, girlfriend, son, child) wrapped in expectations, habits and customs that confine us to our gender roles. Therefore we spend our lives establishing tropes that place us in dissonance with our authentic, interior feelings and neglect the communion with what drives us towards the politics of the self and autarchy.

This does not mean introducing frenzy, anarchy or lack of compromise into relationships. If we listen to and dispute with ourselves, we come to methods by which we can serve our autarchy with cornflakes and get paid for it. We would no longer forbid ourselves restoratives like affirmation, self-knowing and self-love, or ignore the power of self-respect only to put all our energies into accretion in the service of those who demand it of us.

We use our bodies as store houses of hurt and graveyards of pain, anguish or terror, but the work of many of us shows that we are aware of these self-inflicted wounds; so we displace our hurts and angers upon the characters we create. We give them our voices. We allow them to laugh, cry and hate for us. We hide our fears in them to protect our wounds. Sometimes they heal for us.

The politics underpinning creativity can be, and often is, curative. The body is as we are and also the storehouse of our memories. The more pathological of these bury themselves in us to become those diseases of the self. Those, that mutate and grow as our wounds, become more septic. Our first graveyard is our bodies. We must reclaim them through reaching out for our autarchy as women.

Elaine Scarry in *The Body in Pain* defines body memory as certain skills that cannot be eradicated, as well as certain types of behaviour of cultural significance.[1] 'Such memories distinguish knowing with and through the body from knowing about the body; and it is this tension affecting the processes through, with and about' their bodies that activates women's consciousness whether they are writers or not.[2] The presence of a learned culture permits the demanding of political concessions from women. Men, as a rule, are active in this process of denying us our political rights. Using memories to anaesthetise us, some begin, 'remember that time when'. Such flows of love talk, control talk and baby talk force memory to burrow into our organic and gullible well-being to create paradoxes. We in turn have to deprive Narcissus of his reflection by refusing to play the memories-game or games of incipient neonacy. It is the work of women writers to clarify and elucidate paradoxes by constructing associative images which can replace some forms of talk. Contemporary practitioners place memory in all the sensory systems of the brain. To the psychoanalysts, men and women, memory is phenotypic and activated at birth, to begin an autobiography of the self. There is however, some ambiguity here and we must ask — When does the present become the past? How do we construct the future? Is the past mechanistic time, events in time or the duration of the events, their dimensions and purpose?

Mircea Eliade in *Rites and Symbols of Initiation* states:

Psychoanalysis especially, has found out how to use as its chief curative method, the memory, the recollection of primordial events which could only mean one's earliest childhood. This process causes a return to archaic thought which allows the reliving of trauma. When the psyche comes to crisis, it is to infancy that the individual must return to confront once more the source or the origin of the trauma.[3]

Freud the father of Psychoanalysis introduced Judeo-Christian time and history into the equation and discovered that the earliest childhood marks the supreme beginning when all is decided. To the infant, the prenatal period is akin to paradise for weaning brings the exit from paradise, although the need to symbolise the breast would surface and resurface throughout the whole life span.

In my own work I blend several types of memory to create reality. Echoic, panoramic and de-integrative memory may mutate, double-take or fudge the recall or what has been remembered, but when associated with other forms, the stage is set for re-disintegrative memory, loosely called re-memory, to restore all the tensions of particularity and autarchy or political consciousness.

In *Frangipani House*,[4] Mama King's memories contain both generalities and particularities but, if Freud is to be believed, then generations would contain her poignant trauma. In *Totems and Taboos* he writes, 'I have supposed that an emotional process, such as might have developed in children who had been ill-treated by their father (or parents) has extended to new generations who were exempt from such treatment...'.[5]

Jung posits a collective unconsciousness, a series of psychic structures which exist as archetypes prior to the individual psyche. Since the archetypes are not formed by individual experiences like the ideas of Plato, they are impersonal and participate organically and even historically in the life of the species. When we experience 'déjà vu' we might understandably ask whether the collective unconscious is at work. Jungian psychology is complex and offers myths, dreams and psychic images. I regard all known phenomena as products of existence and use them in my work.

Toni Morrison, prolific and continuous in her use of memory, attains clarity, power, depth, and certainty in the shape and development of her characters, and maintains the insouciant tension of her text by using many kinds of memory. The term 'rememory' I take to be simplistic. It does not do justice to the robust clarity of feeling and the glowing pathos her text conveys and treats the whole concept of 'Memory as Oracle' in a secular and unpsychological way.

In Morrison's *The Bluest Eye* the child, a girl, is given a doll, an icon to the adults, for Christmas; but the child sees it as something outside her world of the 'commonplace' which in the life of a Black child means grits, watermelon and gospel songs on Sunday.[6] She is bewildered as she projects her life as a Black child into a dyadic encounter with the doll. She cannot pretend to be its mother, as she projects the present, the past and the future into the doll as transitional object. Reality begins to disintegrate. All similarities and sameness become pathology. The doll remains outside her consciousness, and she contemplatively destroys it. Morrison writes:

When I took it to bed unyielding limbs resisted my flesh...It was most uncomfortable, a patently aggressively sleeping companion. I had only one desire to dismember it...To see what it was made of...I fingered the face to discover the dearness, traced the turned up nose, poked the glassy eyeball, poked at the pearly teeth, twisted the yellow hair but I could not love it or find its loveableness. Then it gave a sweet and plaintive cry. It said 'Mama' which sounded like the bleat of a dying lamb.[7]

The grown-ups frowned at her, tongue-lashed her, judged her. She found her way into the kitchen, where she sat alone in its warmth as she peacefully listened to 'Big Papa' playing his violin just for her. She was a woman in the making — for herself, by herself and with herself individual and autarchic. Threat had been avoided and the eye of ritual closed by projection and the rebuttal of pain.

In *Boy Sandwich*[8] the icon is the album of photographs — the re-incarnation of family and friends, the scent of flowers, the sounds of nature, and picnics on the sand. It is both object and subject providing the space-fillers for the centrifugal force of memory linking past with present to determine the future. The album contains trapped emotions that could be resuscitated by language, to function as myth, as vernacular or as folklore. There are no longer any unrealities, no gathering of bones except through the unrestrained verbal creativity which links the intention of the reader to that of the writer. For the old folk, the album is the memory of life once lived with vigour but which now flows gently but inexorably towards its close. To all the others it is but a reintegration of fudged memories to form a comprehensible history.

In the novel *In Praise of Love and Children*[9] Melda's fantastic creativity identifies her brother's wife, Trudi, as the culture of colonialist poverty with all its relentless savagery. She comes home to a 'mother' no more sympathetic than the mother of her pathological childhood and Trudi becomes the receptacle for all the seepage from her wounded soul. The memories of both are kaleidoscopic, lexical and echoic, but eventually each individuates and comes to the point at which creativity, imagined and objectified, leads to autarchy, as Melda's chequered Cinderella complexes no longer erupt, and she recalls a smiling reflection at the bottom of the water barrel.

Gather the Faces[10] comes heavily coded with reaction, religion and cultural mentality, undertones of anguish, unease and flash-bulb memory. They are a young and one dimensional pair but Eros in fantasy lures Marvella to recite the Songs of Solomon. She accepts her eroticism while his remains well concealed.

Finally in *Inkle and Yarico*,[11] Inkle's life of wealth and indulgence encapsulates him in attitudes of superiority. Even when useless, his culture remains supreme and he unknowingly lives out the life of a plantation slave. Inkle is ethnocentric and racist to the end with Yarico powerless in all things and confused by a culture which is enigmatic, sociocentric and sadistic.

In *Stedman and Joanna*,[12] John Stedman who touched the skirts of the enlightenment, was selective in his ministrations. He saw no wrong in educating the heathen. He admired the industry and creativity of the slaves and helped Joanna to marginal independence. Autarchy was not an option for her. It is shown when persons are free to be creative. Slaves showed creativity in activities that improved their lives, basketmaking, weaving nets and sewing, carpentry and other life-skills.

Joanna's ability to create was limited, but to survive she had to be a selective mute, choosing when, where and how much to speak. In Stedman's journal, the recorded moments of Joanna's voice are few and far between. She could not debate with her captors or even with her husband whose mission was to convert and civilise. Like her father, he too 'put Joanna to school'. But true to the society, there would always have been the ghoul of cruelty stalking even the couple's most personal moments.

Autarchy comes when there is a bank of retrievable 'memory' that would cause the internal landscape to bloom and create an interweaving of desire for the positive, the loving and the sustainable. Autarchy flows from political and emotional literacy. It is smothered when women lack the will or the language to express their worst concerns, to recognise and resist attempts at emotional blackmail, sexual harassment, infantilisation by word or gestures such as fist or finger flagging, ridicule, guilt tripping, and all that parents and partners do to keep control of one's will to know. These are different times. The textures of the cords that bind us must be unravelled and inspected. And we could do this with our words in writing.

Notes

1.   Elaine Scarry, *The Body in Pain*, Oxford: Oxford University Press, 1980, pp.109-11.
2.   Ibid.
3.   Mircea Eliade, *Rites and Symbols of Initiation: The Mysteries of Birth and Rebirth*, trans. Willard R., Traskand, New York: Spring Publications, 1994, pp.55-7.
4.   Beryl Gilroy, *Frangipani House*, London: Heinemann, 1986.
5.   Sigmund Freud, *The Origins of Religion: Totems and Taboos, Moses and Monotheism and Other Works*, Harmondsworth: Penguin, 1990.
6.   See Toni Morrison, *The Bluest Eye* , St. Albans: Panther, 1970, pp.22-24.
7.   Ibid.
8.   Beryl Gilroy, *Boy Sandwich*, Oxford: Heinemann, 1989.
9.   Beryl Gilroy, *In Praise of Love and Children*, Leeds: Peepal Tree Press, 1996.
10.   Beryl Gilroy, *Gather the Faces*, Leeds: Peepal Tree Press, 1996.
11.   Beryl Gilroy, *Inkle and Yarico*, Leeds: Peepal Tree Press, 1996.
12.   Beryl Gilroy, *Stedman and Joanna, A Love in Bondage*, New York: Vantage Press, 1991.

Complex Identities: Caribbean

Canadian Women Fiction Writers

MARY CONDÉ

To speak of contemporary Caribbean women's fiction in English is already to have imposed five separate classifications. What further classifications might be used? The area from which the writers come, the area in which they now live, the settings which they use, their ethnic descent, the generation to which they belong, or their political agenda? A grouping under 'Guyana', for example would include Beryl Gilroy, who left 'British Guiana' for Britain over forty years ago, Grace Nichols of the next generation, Jan Shinebourne, who is of mainly Chinese descent, Narmala Shewcharan, who is of mainly Indian descent, Pauline Melville, who is of mixed Afro-Guyanese and English descent (and who looks completely white), Joan Cambridge who has set her novel *Clarise Cumberbatch Want to Go Home*[1] in New York City, and Norma DeHaarte, who lives in Canada. The group 'Trinidad' would include the African American writer Rosa Guy, and works as different as Valerie Belgrave's utopian historical romance *Ti Marie*,[2] and the socially conscious writings of the Canadians Claire Harris and Dionne Brand.

In the March 1996 issue of *Books in Canada*, George Elliott Clarke argues in 'A Primer of African-Canadian Literature' for a classification which cuts right across that of 'Caribbean'.[3] He insists on the longevity of the tradition, and refers contemptuously to 'Uninformed commentaries' which 'reduce African-Canadian literature to a matter of 'West Indian writers'. Obviously Clarke is viewing the tradition from a Canadian perspective, yet, as he himself admits, he is using the term 'Canadian' fairly loosely:

> ...indeed, Acadian literature lays claim to the American poet Henry Wadsworth Longfellow, the author of *Evangeline: A Tale of Acadia*, though he never set foot in Canada. African-Canadian literature should possess just as wide a scope.[4]

Such looseness was attacked by the poet Michael Thorpe in a letter in the October 1996 issue of *Books in Canada*; he objects, for example, to Clarke's inclusion of the Jamaican writer Olive Senior merely on the grounds of a relatively short residence in Canada, and claims that 'Canadian citizenship and subject-matter form the least contentious qualifications'.[5]

'Caribbean Canadian', it can be seen, is an essentially complex classification, but not a Canadian classification which is uniquely complex. By the year 2000 half the population of Toronto will be people of colour; Dionne Brand has said of Toronto and Trinidad, 'I live somewhere between those two places — and it's a place too — a new place we're making — a place a lot of people live in'.[6] The 'new place we're making' is under construction in the short stories of her collection *Sans Souci*, characteristic of Caribbean Canadian women's fiction in occupying a new place in literature which ironically emerges from the demolition of a number of fantasies based on place.[7]

Chief among these fantasies is the double reality of the misrepresentations of Canada to the Caribbean, and of the Caribbean to Canada. The story 'Sketches in Transit... Going Home' captures the 'new idiosyncrasies' of Trinidadians like Jasmine, flying home on a brief holiday trip for Carnival. Brand alternately records and comments on the chorus of anonymous voices from the workers who are 'Like children, eager to forget their past',[8] a chorus which keeps alive 'the myth of easiness and prosperity in the metropole' so that 'No one back home believed that things were not better out here and no one could be convinced of it'.[9] The drudgery and humiliation of office-cleaning and hospital work in Toronto, where they lead their 'tight and deceptive' lives is deliberately concealed by these immigrants, so that the tradition of distaste for the Caribbean home is maintained, and the islanders become not true inhabitants but products, 'grown for export, like sugar cane and arrowroot'.[10]

In stories like 'No Rinsed Blue Sky, No Red Flower Fences', the Caribbean is in its turn misrepresented to Canada. The title refers to the anonymous protagonist's despairing fantasies that the sea must be just outside the apartment.[11] Feeling 'claustrophobic' and 'land-locked' in Toronto, she writes desperate anonymous letters throwing herself on the mercy of the Immigration Department, and, equally illogically, derives comfort from a poster of a Caribbean landscape:

A girl in a wet T-shirt, the sea in black, the sun on her body, represented home. Home had never been like that, but she kept the poster. Its glamour shielded her from the cold outside and the dry hills back home at the same time.[12]

The poster's distortion of 'home' for tourist consumption helps her to bear the fact that her own children are growing up far away without her while she takes care of white children, losing her identity as she is obliterated into the Canadian landscape:

...holding their hands across busy streets, standing with them at corners which were incongruous to her colour, she herself incongruous to the little hands, held as if they were more precious than she, made of gold, and she just the black earth around.[13]

In Brand's stories, the characters usually perceive the solution to unhappiness as mobility: finding a new place. 'Train to Montreal' opens with the implied comparison of the jazz pianist's recital with a journey, since he will not begin until he has found his shoes.[14] It leads into the female protagonist's train journey to Montreal to see her lover, hoping that:

Perhaps there would be a better place to ask him if he would live with her. A change of venue.[15]

Finding a new place, however, is a destructive activity in Brand's terms: the opposite of making a new place, since it depends on being in transit. In the story 'Blossom, Priestess of Oya, Goddess of Winds, Storms, and Waterfalls', Blossom and her friends Peg and Betty, demonstrating against the doctor who has sexually harassed her, are ironically told by the police that 'as long as Blossom and them keep moving they wasn't committing no crime'.[16] Blossom keeps moving in this story by shifting between her existence as an alienated Trinidadian immigrant and as Oya, the goddess of turbulent movement, who takes possession of her, 'rumbling and violent like thunder'.[17] Neither she nor the anonymous protagonist of 'No Rinsed Blue Sky, No Red Flower Fences' has succeeded in making a new place which can serve as home. In this they reflect the melancholy reality of the Caribbean domestic workers in Canada interviewed in Makeda Silvera's collection *Silenced.*[18] These *Talks with Working Cass Caribbean Women About Their Lives and Struggles as Domestic Workers in Canada* movingly express the same conviction as that of Brand's fictional protagonist, that 'there was no other place to be right now' but 'out of place'.[19]

Gail from Trinidad says of her employers:

When you are living with them, they make you feel as if you really don't belong, and where the devil do you really belong? It's a funny thing to happen to us, because it makes us feel like we don't know if we coming or going.[20]

Myrtle from Dominica, supporting eight children back home, says, 'I am 54 years old. I came to Toronto 12 years ago. Sometimes it looks like I only came yesterday. What I mean is that I hardly know anywhere'.[21] Primrose from Jamaica is only a less extravagant version of Blossom's spiritual ecstasy:

I bought myself some religious tapes and when things burn me, when things hurt me, I lock myself up in the washroom with the tapes and sing and pray and cry. I have to do that or I don't know where I would end up.[22]

Molly and Irma, also from Jamaica, confirm the truth of the paranoid terror of the Immigration Department expressed in 'No Rinsed Blue Sky, No Red Flower Fences', and of the desperation of women who have no place to turn. Hyacinth from St Lucia, raped by her employer, says, 'There was times when I really felt ashamed, like a nobody, because there was nobody to tell about it'.[23] Noreen from St Vincent says she prays to the Lord because 'Who else going to listen to a woman without education? Who else going to listen to a 50-year-old servant? Tell me who?'[24]

These real-life voices are the voices to which Brand is giving a place in her fiction, despite the difficulties which Black Canadian women's fiction has itself experienced in finding a place. Claire Harris cites in her article 'Working with/out a net' the rejection of a young adult novel[25] (clearly Marlene Nourbese Philip's *Harriet's Daughter*) by several Canadian publishers and its eventual publication by Heinemann in London.[26] A review in the *Globe and Mail* described the setting as 'unpredictable'. As Harris comments, 'One can almost hear 'a black neighbourhood in *Toronto*?'[27]

Writing in 1983, the Toronto poet Lillian Allen had addressed the question: 'Why has Black women's writing been virtually excluded from the literary terrain of Canada?' Like Harris, she complains of the lack of a market for Black Canadian women's writing, and asserts, 'if you tried to count the Black Canadian women writers you know, you'd probably get stuck on your second finger'.[28]

Claire Harris claims that to be an Afro-Canadian writer is to be 'always on the verge of not-belonging. Of being un-Canadian', since 'After 200 years of black settlement an air of disbelief still surrounds the term 'Black Canadian'.[29] In her work of mixed fiction and poetry *Drawing Down a Daughter*, the Trinidadian heroine says impatiently of Canadian racism to the father of her child, 'Nobody puts up with that bullshit for very long'. He replies, 'Really, eh? We have, we Afro-Canadians, for pretty close to 300 years, which is why they expect you to put up with it too!'[30] This fictional observation is confirmed by Adrienne Shadd in her essay 'Institutionalised Racism and Canadian History: Notes of a Black Canadian'.[31] Shadd, a fifth-generation Black Canadian born and raised near Chatham, Ontario, who moved to Toronto at the age of ten, reports that:

> ...when we moved to Toronto I was made to feel different, alien, even though no one specifically referred to my racial origin. It is a feeling which has never fully left me and perhaps explains why to this day I do not feel comfortable in a group of white people.[32]

The 'new place we're making', then, although it's 'a place a lot of people live in', is not a place it is easy to create in Canada. Linda Hutcheon in *Splitting Images: Contemporary Canadian Ironies* suggests two possible reasons why this should be so: that there is nothing in Canada to which conformity can readily be urged, and that Canada already feels itself to be marginalised, both by the British colonial past and the American colonising present, making the absorption of other 'marginal' groups more difficult.[33]

Incidentally, Lillian Allen, in writing of her identity as a writer specifically as a product of 'the British colony of Jamaica' draws our attention to the usually anonymously Caribbean identity of the Caribbean-Canadian writer.[34] Dionne Brand, when asked at the Voice Box whether she would describe herself as 'Caribbean Canadian', replied that she would prefer Black Canadian' or 'African Canadian' without even mentioning that she is, specifically, from Trinidad, thus editing out, as it were, a step in history.[35] Her own collection of working-class interviews, the equivalent of Silvera's specifically Caribbean collection, is *No Burden to Carry: Narratives of Black Working Women in Ontario 1920s to 1950s*. Of the fifteen women interviewed, only three are from the Caribbean or have families from the Caribbean or at any rate mention this. But it is significant that even the intensely Caribbean text *Silenced* ends with a tribute to Rosa Parks, the African American domestic worker from Montgomery, Alabama, whose refusal to give up her seat on the bus to a white man in 1955 sparked off the US Civil Rights Movement: an important reason for aligning oneself with the larger group of 'Black Canadians' or 'African Canadians' is its political weight. Hazelle Palmer, author of the short story collection *Tales from the Gardens and Beyond* attracts this description in that book:[36]

The daughter of Caribbean immigrants, Palmer spent her childhood in Montreal in the 1960s and 70s — two decades which marked the rise of Black consciousness and the Black Power Movement.[37]

According to Walker's study of *The West Indians in Canada*, because white Canadians cannot distinguish between the different islands, Caribbean people in Canada have come to share a common identity to an extent unknown in the Caribbean.[38] Hazelle Palmer's Mrs G., writing home to her friend Tiny, confirms this common identity as a necessity: 'We all come from different islands, but it seems to me we have to stick together here'. She bleakly adds:

One thing, no matter which island we come from, we all agreed things in Canada are really different than we thought or what we wanted to believe. Although there is work here, times are tough. Every time you try to take one step forward, you're pushed two steps back. It's hard to put your finger on it, to name exactly what makes things this way. But you are reminded every moment of every day that you're in a white man's country. I tell you I have never seen so many white people in my life. I feel lost, almost invisible among them. Yet, I know they are aware of me. I am not entirely sure they want me here.[39]

The sense of a shared community, yet a shared anonymity, is poignant here. The royalties from *No Burden to Carry* go to the Immigrant Women's Job Placement Centre, presumably amongst other things to indicate Dionne Brand's sense of the 'ownership' of the book: it is logical, since Caribbean women fiction-writers both characteristically deal in memories and valorise the anonymous working woman, to tap directly into these memories as well as funnelling them through a named, owned fiction. But the Black woman writer herself often has a kind of anonymity forced upon her, asserts Lillian Allen, because:

You see, when other women get up to speak, they get to represent themselves and their own point of view, but when I get up to speak or do anything I am expected to represent my entire race.[40]

Dionne Brand in her autobiographical statement 'Bread out of Stone' puts this point more sharply when, speaking of what Black writing can accommodate, she remarks that:

There is never room, though there is always risk, but there is never the room that white writers have in never speaking for their whole race, yet speaking in the most secret and cowardly language of normalcy and affirmation, speaking for the whole race.[41]

One of the ways in which Brand makes a conscious effort to avoid the 'language of normalcy and affirmation' is by choosing narrators who are intensely conscious of the significance of their place on the map, of the geographical and historical place they occupy, like the 'woman in enemy territory' who narrates the story 'At the Lisbon Plate'.[42] The Lisbon Plate, a Portuguese bar in Toronto, is doubly enemy territory in its representation of Portuguese imperialism in a Canadian context: the narrator is irritated by her view of a statue of Christopher Columbus, 'the piss-face in the parkette',[43] and, indeed, takes it as a personal affront:

It's most appropriate that they should put his stoney arse right where I can see it. I know bitterness doesn't become me, but that son of a bitch will get his soon enough too.[44]

A statue in a park which should be prominent, but is not, is discussed very movingly in *No Burden to Carry* by the Caribbean Mrs Violet Blackman, who regrets that an anonymous black hero should not be more widely celebrated.[45]

Marlene Nourbese Philip opens *Looking for Livingstone: An Odyssey of Silence*, another mixture of fiction and poetry, with a map, 'a primitive one, scratched on animal skin', but it is a map for a fantasy journey, back in time into the European version of the history of Africa, her original home.[46] Another Canadian writer from the Caribbean, Dianne Maguire from Jamaica, who now lives in Vancouver, explores the idea of 'home' in a different way in 'Dry Land Tourist', a short story in which the word is constantly repeated.[47] The heroine Ellen, at first merely identified as the 'tall woman' at the entrance to a Jamaican crafts market, is forced to retreat back to Canada from 'the Jamaica of her childhood',[48] ironically bearing away with her the carving which speaks to her of this although she cannot cope with the human being, reduced to poverty and violence, who carved it. This perception that the 'new place we're making' is a place fraught with hostility and loss is, however, matched in *Tales from the Gardens* by the acknowledgement of the difficulties of life in Barbados. Makeda Silvera's collection of stories, *Remembering G*, works by presenting a relatively idealised picture of rural Jamaica with Canada as only a shadowy, and ironically idealised, presence.[49] Only to a limited extent does fiction by Caribbean Canadian women writers conform to a recent description of 'modern Caribbean discourse' as 'generated by a dialectical interaction between a pastoral nostalgia and a national nightmare'.[50]

Historical novels by Caribbean Canadian women writers like Norma DeHaarte's *Guyana Betrayal*[51] are still relatively rare: the main focus of their fiction is on the formation of a new identity. Yet, ironically, these writers seem now to be directed towards a heightened consciousness of 'difference'. When the canon-forming New Canadian Library series was launched in 1957 by the publishers McClelland and Stewart with Malcolm Ross as general editor, it was McClelland who suggested the title 'New Canadian Library', explaining in a letter to Ross that this was not only to avoid such 'blatant symbols' as beavers and maple leaves, but because:

...we hope these books will appeal to immigrants as an opportunity to bone up on Canadian literature.[52]

Robert Lecker in *Making It Real: The Canonization of English-Canadian Literature* comments on this concept as 'crucial to the NCL marketing plan';[53] immigrants, however, were to be exclusively pupils, not educators. Ross wrote to McClelland in reply that:

...the series title seems OK — if 'new Canadian' doesn't suggest immigrant literature and/or very *recent* literature.[54]

But by 1991, establishment attitudes and marketing plans had sufficiently shifted for the Greek Canadian writer Smaro Kamboureli to observe in a lecture:

Thou shalt be ethnic, our legislators say; thou shalt honour thy mother tongue; thou shalt celebrate thy difference in folk festivals, and thou shalt receive monies to write about thy difference.[55]

If Caribbean Canadian women writers respond to this directive, it will probably not be in the form of a nostalgic celebration of a lost homeland, but in the form of a critical appraisal of how they are constructing Canada as a new place. Dionne Brand's new novel, *In Another Place, Not Here*, combines the themes of a continuing political responsibility to the Caribbean and the making of a new life for lesbians of colour in Toronto.[56] Marlene Nourbese Philip is, apparently, also just completing a new novel: it is unlikely that this will not confront the complex identity of a Tobagonian who is simultaneously a Canadian.

Caribbean Canadian women writers are exceptionally alert to nuances of placing and naming, both historical and geographical, and this gives their fiction an exceptional richness.

Notes

1. Joan Cambridge, *Clarise Cumberbatch Want To Go Home*, London: Women's Press, 1987.
2. Valerie Belgrave, *Ti Marie*, London: Heinemann, 1988.
3. George Elliott Clarke, 'A Primer of African-Canadian Literature', *Books in Canada* (March, 1996).
4. Ibid., p.7.
5. Michael Thorpe, 'Letter', *Books in Canada* (October, 1996) p.40.
6. Dionne Brand, speaking at the Voice Box (Royal Festival Hall, London, 1992).
7. Dionne Brand, *Sans Souci*, New York: Firebrand, 1989.
8. Ibid., p.135.
9. Ibid.
10. Ibid., p.134.
11. Ibid., p.87.
12, Ibid., p.89.
13. Ibid., pp.86-7.
14. Ibid., p.15.
15. Ibid., p.19.
16. Ibid., p.34.
17. Ibid., p.41.
18. Makeda Silvera, *Silenced: Talks with Working Class Caribbean Women About Their Lives and Struggles as Domestic Workers in Canada*, Toronto: Sister Vision, 1989. Originally published by Williams-Wallace, 1983.
19. Brand, 1989, p.87.
20. Silvera, 1989, p.98.
21. Ibid., p.73.
22. Ibid., p.96.
23. Ibid., p.56.
24. Ibid., p.21.
25. Claire Harris, 'Working With/out a Net' in Davis, G. (ed.), *Crisis and Creativity in the New Literatures in English: Canada*, Amsterdam and Atlanta: Rodopi, 1990.

26. Marlene Nourbese Philip, *Harriet's Daughter*, London: Heinemann, 1988.
27. Harris, 1990, p.73.
28. Lillian Allen, 'A Writing of Resistance: Black Women's Writing in Canada' in *The Feminine: Women and Words* (Les femmes et les mots). Conference Proceedings, Edmonton: Longspoon, 1983, pp.63. 65.
29. Harris, 1990, p.71.
30. Claire Harris, *Drawing Down a Daughter*, Frederiction, B.C.: Goose Lane, 1992, p.70.
31. Adrienne Shadd, 'Institutionalized Racism and Canadian History: Notes of A Black Canadian' in McKague, O. (ed.), *Racism in Canada*, Saskatoon: Fifth House, 1991.
32. Ibid., p.4.
33. Linda Hutcheon, *Splitting Images: Contemporary Canadian Ironies*, Toronto, Oxford and New York: Oxford University Press, 1991, p.65.
34. Allen, 1983, p.66.
35. Brand, 1992 at the Voice Box, London.
36. Hazelle Palmer, *Tales from the Gardens and Beyond*, Toronto: Sister Vision, 1995.
37. Ibid.
38. James W. St. G. Walker, *The West Indians in Canada*, Ottawa: Canadian Historical Association, 1984, p.20.
39. Palmer, 1995, pp.43-4.
40. Allen, 1983, p.63.
41. Dionne Brand 'Bread Out of Stone' in Schcier, L., Sheard, S. and Wachtel, E., (eds.), *Language in Her Eye: Views on Writing and Gender by Canadian Women Writing in English*, Toronto: Coach House, 1990, p.53.
42. Brand, 1989, p.97.
43. Ibid., p.101.
44. Ibid., p.99.
45. Brand, 1991, pp.46-7.
46. Marlene Nourbese Philip, *Looking for Livingstone: An Odyssey of Silence*, Stratford, Ontario: Mercury, 1991, p.7.
47. Dianne Maguire, 'Dry Lane Tourist' in *Dry Land Tourist and Other Stories*, Toronto: Sister Vision, 1991.
48. Ibid., p.8.

49. Makeda Silvera, *Remembering G and Other Stories*, Toronto: Sister Vision, 1991.
50. P.S. Chuahan, 'Caribbean Writing in English: Intimations of a Historical Nightmare' in *English Postcoloniality: Literatures from Around the World*, Westport, Conn., and London: Greenwood, 1996, p.45.
51. Norma DeHaarte, *Guyana Betrayal*, Toronto: Sister Vision, 1991.
52. Robert Lecker, *Making It Real: The Canonization of English-Canadian Literature*, Concord, Ontario: House of Anansi, P, 1995, p.161.
53. Ibid., p.161.
54. Ibid.
55. Smaro Kamboureli, 'Of Black Angels and Melancholy Lovers: Ethnicity and Writing in Canada' in Collier, G. (ed.) *Us/Them: Translation, Transcription and Identity in Post-Colonial Literary Cultures*, Amsterdam and Atlanta: Rodopi, 1992, p.53. (First delivered as the Caroline Heath Lecture at the Saskatchewan Writers' Guild annual literary congress, November 1991).
56. Dionne Brand, *In Another Place, Not Here*, Toronto: Knopf Canada, 1996.

'Out from Under the Shadow of Jean'

Critical bias and critical neglect in the construction of a tradition of Caribbean women's writing: the case of Elma Napier

SARAH LAWSON WELSH

The 1980s were crucial in seeing a number of important recuperations by academics and reissued editions by publishing houses of early Caribbean women's texts — Allfrey's *The Orchid House*[1] and certain of Eliott Bliss's novels among them. In a critical context, Elaine Campbell (1990) and Evelyn O'Callaghan's (1984) research into white Creole women writers and early women's writing more generally, as well as critical re-evaluations such as Alison Donnell's reappraisal of the poetry of Una Marson and of other early writers (Donnell, 1995, 1996) have been extremely important.[2]

However, many of these primary texts (for example, Marson's poetry, Allfrey's short stories) are not in print or easily accessed and even some otherwise important woman-centred scholarship on this early period has its weaknesses. Whilst such research is promising and 'the positive move towards woman-centred scholarship in the field of Caribbean literature during the last two decades has ensured both recognition and serious critical attention for contemporary Caribbean women writers, there remains a notable dearth of research and academic attention on women's writing in the region which predates the 1970s', both in terms of making a wider range of early women's texts available and in improving the quality and coverage of the critical response to them.[3]

One of the writers who is frequently neglected and virtually unknown, is Elma Napier. Napier came to Dominica in 1932 and remained there until her death in 1973. She was born in Britain, and, like Rhys, had part Scottish ancestry. She lived in Australia for a period, where her first writing, a collection of travel stories, entitled *Nothing So Blue* was published in 1928.[4] She published two novels *Duet in Discord* (1936)[5] and *A Flying Fish Whispered* (1938)[6] and also two autobiographical works in the 1940s, which interestingly fail to include her Dominican experience: *Youth Is a Blunder* (1948)[7] and *Winter Is in July* (1948).[8] In the 1950s she published a series of short stories in English journals and Caribbean little magazines, the most interesting of which are 'Carnival in Martinique' and 'No Voyage for a Little Barque'.

Napier's first novel written in Dominica, *Duet in Discord*, was published in London in 1936 under the pseudonym Elizabeth Garner.[9] *Duet in Discord* is a rather crudely drawn and self-conscious romantic fiction, narrated in the first person by the novel's protagonist Carol to her sometime and much younger Australian-born lover Tony. Carol is a white European interloper whose 'grandmother on my mother's side owned slaves'[10] and who settled on the island with her son after the death of her husband in the First World War. Unlike the considerably more well-to-do protagonist of Napier's second novel, *A Flying Fish Whispered*, Carol is apparently an impoverished white, although wealthy enough to send her son away to school. Her contentment on the island and personal belief in its healing powers, has none of the subtlety or complexity of Rhys's alienated heroines. She professes:

> ...I do not altogether understand these people. I do not know their language. But they look to me for help; impose upon me, like me, I think, a good deal. It would have been absurd if I had allowed an alien influence such as yours [Tony] to spoil for me the contented existence that is mine. It is the love of the people and their simplicity, coupled with an unrivalled beauty of sea and land, that has brought me back to sanity when for a while my world rocked in disorder'.[11]

and earlier in the novel, she reflects:

...of all the white women in the island — there are perhaps fifty — I think that I alone live here because I like it. And 'like' is of all words the most ridiculous with which to express the love that I have for this place, love that has something almost physical about it'...[12]

Interestingly, in the first extract Carol perceives the white Australian interloper Tony as the 'alien' influence, but not herself and she refuses to accept the view of the insufferably 'colonial' Buntings that this was 'a place so forsaken by God and the best people'.[13]

There are few interesting vignettes in *Duet in Discord:* the marvellously fiery Ma De' who summons the Breton Priest five miles on horseback under pretence of being on her deathbed and meets him with the words:

Dying!...Who told you that I was dying? Last week you climbed the ridge to see the wife of my brother. It was hightime you took the trouble to come and see me'.[14]

She also bequeaths land to Carol and casts an obeah spell over it, so that her children will be able to sell the produce grown on their neighbouring land to Carol at an advantageous price.

However, overall the few interventions into discussions of race, politics and identity are superficial and awkwardly staged, such as Carol's discussion of the Abyssinian crisis and of the 'loosening...bond[s]' of empire over dinner with the 'coloured road engineer', Lester Warren. Moreover, the West Indian setting, despite its considerable accuracies, the shifting and unpredictable movements of land and the effects of the elements, is exactly that — a backdrop to the narrative's romantic machinations. Thus the ruins of an old sugar works, Hodges' works, is enshrouded in mystery: 'Nobody knows who lived in this house, not who, nor what was Hodges'[15] and elicits nothing more from the narrator than a comment that this was 'a good place, it seemed, in which to ponder upon the impermanence of human relationships'.[16]

The later *A Flying Fish Whispered*, published under the same pseudonym in London in 1938, is a longer, denser, more complex text. Here, social realism gradually gains sway over the more understated romance plot, the crucial turning point being Teresa's realisation that her attraction for the white interloper Derek Morell from nearby Parham Island, who has recently purchased the island of Neva, cannot be maintained in the light of knowledge of his outmoded aspirations, his hardened racial attitudes, and his shoddy treatment of the islanders on his land.

As the delusions of romance give way to a grittier portrait of Derek and, by implication, the ailing, outmoded and increasingly isolated colonial mentality with which he is identified as trying to rehabilitate, so Teresa is figured as an increasingly resistant and resourceful subject. Derek comes to Neva 'driven by the lust of possession, wanting a place of his own'[17] and with 'sugar in my heart and in my brain'.[18] Derek has been disinherited not only from a sense of belonging on and in the land but also from a particular social niche as he is forced to work for eighteen years as a Civil Servant after the bankruptcy of his father and the subsequent sale of the substantial family estates in a land settlement scheme. However, his will to possess both Teresa and the island are both doomed to failure. As Teresa observes early on: 'He didn't look like a planter, nor a man suited to the wilderness'.[19]

Indeed, Teresa's refusal to submit to Derek's sexual designs is traced in parallel to his failure to achieve his dream of establishing productive sugar plantations on the island. One passage in particular makes explicit the yoked idealism of his designs on both:

It didn't seem real to Derek that she should have come. Slim and graceful and dressed in green, she was the living spirit of his cane-field...but Teresa was too essentially female to be kept on an ideal plane...the woman he wanted [was] no myth of the cane-fields but a breathing, hot-blooded creature...Derek had his cane-fields where he wanted them. But merely planting sugar couldn't make St Celia look like Parham Island...Derek would never get sugar from his canes, only juice out of which rum would be made. And the canes themselves had refused to submit to the uniform monotony of more conventional fields, but were sprawling out of line in an unrestrained St Celian fashion that made them strangely ornamental.[20]

What Derek can never see in 'green cane-fields billowing like the sea'[21] (declaring 'Sugar is to be my toy, my gambling game'[22]) is realised by Teresa: the social and historical realities of 'a people groaning under their burden', a burden with contemporary as well as historical inflections.[23]

Teresa's sexual resistance is in turn politicised by her involvement in a popular campaign to challenge Derek's ruling prohibiting the islanders from using his land to moor their boats, fish and graze their livestock. Napier gives Teresa an impeccable if rather obvious pedigree in a suffragette mother. As she comments:

So, long ago, her mother had fought for the rights of women. So, now, must her daughter fight for the rights of negro fishermen.[24]

At the close of the novel, with the very real possibility of popular insurgence imminent, Teresa and her brother Tommy are clearly aligned with the island poor and against the colonial administration. As Teresa puts it:

For or against nations we individuals can do nothing therefore, isn't it all the more our duty to strive for the tiny bit of justice that we can see, and perhaps control?[25]

However, this too-easy optimism and the realignment of Teresa and Tommy on the islanders' side is muted by Teresa's recognition that 'she had failed to do anything for the people of Ville Rousse' and that the appeal against Morell's ruling could be interminable and unproductive.[26]

A *Flying Fish* does represent a development in terms of Napier's treatment of a fictionalised Dominica not merely as backdrop but as subject. Thus for example, the largely reductive and unfavourable comparisons of the Caribbean landscape to that of Scotland or England which are found in *Duet in Discord* give way to a deeper sense of identification in *A Flying Fish*. However, the sense 'that you could make one place become another, because you wanted to'[27] is still represented in Janet's yearnings to return to farm turnips in Fife, Scotland,[28] in some of Teresa and Derek's framings of the Caribbean landscape in terms of the Devon, Brittany or Ligurian coastlines and in Colonel Grace and the doctor's 'indifference to the landscape'.[29]

Likewise the social divisions and attitudes to race which are barely commented on in *Duet* are interrogated and examined in greater detail in *A Flying Fish*. Among the issues *A Flying Fish* engages with are the lot of the poor whites, cultural differences in attitudes to naming, childbirth, childrearing and death, landrights, education and differing approaches to healing. The middle section, entitled 'Interlude', deals seriously and in some detail with the problems of the landless poor squatting on crown lands on neighbouring Parham Island. Not only does this section problematise Derek's earlier claim that the people are simply too 'independent' and wilful to submit to waged work and introduces the issue of a genuinely popular politics of resistance, 'the giving of votes to, and the using of them by, a peasant people'[30] but it also begs to be contrasted with the less progressive state of affairs on Neva/St Celia. As Teresa remarks of Parham: 'It isn't like that in our island...it isn't like that at all'.[31]

Napier satirises a range of colonial figures and figures of authority. The Legislative councillors are regarded by Teresa as having 'only the power of prefects. The headmaster is always in his study'.[32] Against this perception of compromised power Napier portrays the pompousness, niceties and affectations of a self-regarding colonial administration. Throughout both of Napier's novels, absenteeism, literal and metaphorical, is explored. It is seen not just amongst the departing 'Graces [who] left St Celia in a cloud of pretty speeches, and, shaking the dust of it from their feet, straightaway forgot the island...'[33] but through a range of characters. Napier also depicts a wider range of indigenous characters, many in greater depth in this second novel.

Napier has been described as representing 'the meeting of expatriate writer and native-born writer',[34] in itself a contentious and under-researched area in Caribbean women's writing which deserves further critical attention. I would suggest that the geographical and taxonomic positioning of Napier as a writer located, somewhat ambivalently, on the cusp of different 'belongings' and different traditions of writing on and in the Caribbean, make her work a fascinating subject for exploration.

Clearly Napier's writing can be located in relation to the better known Creole women writers of her generation such as Rhys (*Wide Sargasso Sea*, 1966), Allfrey (*The Orchid House*, 1953) and Bliss (*Luminous Isle*, 1934). Certainly her writing bears comparison with these writers. For example, *A Flying Fish Whispered* shares with Allfrey's *The Orchid House* an examination of what O' Callaghan terms 'transitional politics' and employs the same metaphors of overblown decadence, disease and decay inherent in the flora of the island, to signal the waning of colonial dominance. As I've suggested, in Napier's text, the colonial administrators and officials who reside or visit the island are satirised unsparingly and are seen to represent the continued spirit of absenteeism par excellence. In some respects, Derek Morell in *A Flying Fish* represents a last failed attempt at revivifying 'what Allfrey depicts (in *The Orchid House*): the gradual disappearance of the last of the West Indian colonising fathers'.[35]

The independent, liberal socialist protagonist of *A Flying Fish Whispered* also bears resemblance to Joan in Allfrey's novel, the one campaigning for better working conditions for the islanders, the other for landrights against the restrictive directives of the landowner Derek Morell. This parallel is carried over to the respective writers themselves, for both Allfrey and Napier were white women who combined a political career with a literary one. Indeed, Elaine Campbell argues that Napier was one of the important models for Allfrey in her decision to pursue a political career.[36]

Both *A Flying Fish Whispered* and the earlier — and slighter — *Duet in Discord* deal with 'the ambivalent nature of ties between colony and metropole'[37] but in Napier's texts, the perspective is not so much one of the white Creole but of the expatriate woman. Napier's own diasporic trajectory to Dominica, rather than away from it, inverts the more familiar route taken by Rhys and thus sets up a series of interesting points of connection regarding the role of the Caribbean writer as expatriate.

Both of her female protagonists, Teresa and Carol, come to the Caribbean as widows and are thus interestingly positioned vis-à-vis the island society. Indeed, Napier is especially interested in the outsider or interloper figure and both of her novels examine the relationships between a 'settled outsider' and a newly arrived interloper. Thus the novels might be read not simply as romantic fiction, or merely as interesting cultural documents but as explorations of the social, sexual and cultural connotations of white 'outsidership' in West Indian society. Like Rhys's Antoinette, Teresa realises after the tragic death by fire of her servant Tilly, that: 'This wasn't her party any more. Tilly was among her own people and their ways were not hers'.[38]

Napier's work raises the issue of how Caribbean women's writing is to be defined and where the boundaries are to be drawn. It raises the question: What makes certain literary foremothers more valid than others? Napier was born in Britain, lived in Australia but spent most of her adult life in Dominica, and a third generation of Napiers continue to live and write there, including her grandson, Lennox Honychurch who has written a well-known and well-respected history of Dominica.[39] Is there a need to guard against a slippery slope of all-inclusiveness in configuring a tradition of Caribbean Literature (as Brathwaite clearly felt when he famously framed Rhys as a bone fide Caribbean writer) or are there dangers in omitting the expatriate writer from the otherwise currently critically fashionable category of migrant writer?

Is there a need, moreover, in the light of the critical discourses proliferating around the migrant writer, to theorise these kinds of in-between or hybridised identities also? Napier wrote under two names and in several guises: romantic fiction as Elizabeth Garner, autobiographical, travel and short stories as Elma Napier. She also provides different glosses of culturally specific terms in different texts, suggesting perhaps different intended audiences. In *A Flying Fish Whispered*, her protagonist Teresa reflects on the peculiarities of being 'in-between' and on the unfixed and unfinished nature of expatriate subjectivities:

> ...sometimes she wondered — being now blasé about bananas and impervious to glamour — whether familiarity did not take altogether too much of the kick out of life, whether the pleasure of despising a tourist was quite equal to the thrill of still being one... she consoled herself with the realisation that her won ignorance could offer everlastingly brave new worlds to conquer. For who was she to despise a tourist, who could not look at a bunch on a banana tree and tell at a glance whether it had seven hands...who could patter only the bare jargon of a trade that half the island lived on'...[40]

The fact that writing such as Napier's and that of many other women writers of the first half of this century remains inaccessible and virtually unknown, testifies to the enduring critical hegemony of an androcentric Caribbean canon and a blindspot in the critical privileging of contemporary Caribbean women's writing in the 1990s. There is still an urgent need for archival research if such fascinating early voices as Napier's are not to be consigned to a perpetual 'b-list' of critical neglect, regrettable ellipses in our understanding of the enormously rich and diverse tradition of women writing in the Caribbean.

Notes

1. Phyllis Shand Allfrey, *The Orchid House*, first published London: Constable, 1953.
2. See for example, Elaine Campbell, 'Afterword' to P.S. Allfrey, *The Orchid House*, London: Virago, 1982; Alison Donnell, 'Contradictory (W)omen's Gender Consciousness in the Poetry

of Una Marson', *Kunapipi*, XVII(3) (1995) 43-58; and Alison Donnell, 'Writing for Resistance: Nationalism and Narratives of Liberation' in Joan Anim-Addo (ed.) *Framing the Word: Gender and Genre in Caribbean Women's Writing*, London: Whiting and Birch, 1996, pp.12-27.

3. Alison Donnell and Sarah Lawson Welsh (eds.), *The Routledge Reader in Caribbean Literature*, London: Routledge, 1996, p.17.
4. Elma Napier, *Nothing So Blue*, London, 1928.
5. Elizabeth Garner, *Duet in Discord*, London: Arthur Barker, 1936.
6. Elizabeth Garner, *A Flying Fish Whispered*, London: Arthur Barker, 1938.
7. Elma Napier, *Youth Is a Blunder*, London: Jonathan Cape, 1948.
8. Elizabeth Garner, *Winter Is in July*, London, Jonathan Cape, 1948.
9. Elizabeth Garner, *Duet in Discord*, London: Arthur Barker, 1936.
10. Ibid., p.203.
11. Ibid., p.228.
12. Ibid., p.10.
13. Ibid., p.167.
14. Ibid., p.183.
15. Ibid., p.6.
16. Ibid.
17. Garner, 1938, p.203.
18. Ibid., p.52.
19. Ibid., p.12.
20. Ibid., pp.240-1.
21. Ibid., p.161.
22. Ibid., p.54.
23. Ibid., p.161.
24. Ibid., p.258.
25. Ibid.
26. Ibid., p.247.
27. Ibid., p.44.
28. Ibid., p.61.
29. Ibid., p.259.
30. Ibid., p.150.

31. Ibid., p.153.
32. Ibid., p.158.
33. Ibid., p.261.
34. Evelyn O'Callaghan 'Literature and Transitional Politics in Dominica', *World Literature Written in English*, 24(2) (1984) 349-359.
35. Campbell, 1990, p.240.
36. Ibid., p.242-43.
37. O'Callaghan, 1984, pp.349-59.
38. Garner, 1938.
39. Lennox Honychurch, *The Dominica Story - A History of the Island*, London and Basingstoke: Macmillan, 1975.
40. Garner, 1938, p.263.

TEXTUAL SPACE AND
REMEMBRANCE

Merle Hodge's

Revolutionary Dougla Poetics

A reading of *Crick Crack Monkey* and *For the Life of Laetitia*

SHEILA RAMPERSAD

'Dougla' is a Hindi word that in parts of India is used to describe the offspring of inter-religious or inter-caste sexual unions. In many parts of the English-speaking Caribbean[1] it identifies the children of Indian and African parents; the mixed race child is referred to as a dougla. According to Jeremy Poynting, dougla, 'dogla' or 'dogala', is often used contemptuously by Indians. 'Since most Indians disapprove of sexual unions with Africans, persons of mixed parentage are a visible sign that racial endogamy has been breached'.[2] For the orthodox Indian community, therefore, dougla also connotes vice, idleness, mental problems and vagrancy, the stereotypically undesirable qualities of 'creolised behaviour'.[3]

The population of douglas in the Caribbean is small and the numbers seem to fluctuate depending on the state of Indian/African relations in particular countries at historically specific moments.[4] The concept of the dougla and of douglarisation has made a fairly recent entry in Caribbean theory and has been contextualised within the Caribbean discourse on mixed race ancestry. Poynting drew upon social science research into this category[5] in order to extrapolate a 'dougla sensibility' which he argued was illustrative of the complex negotiation with a mixed racial heritage in the process of identity formation in the Caribbean.[6] Roseanne Kanhai advanced this project by extending her reading to the works of Indo-Caribbean women writers published in *Creation Fire: An Anthology of Caribbean Women Writers*.[7] In investigating the extent to which these works constitute a growing feminist consciousness among Indo-Caribbean women, Kanhai identifies three cultural factors which these writers claim as the parameters of their creative imaginary. '...the heritage of indentureship and plantation labour, male domination within the Indo-Caribbean community, and relationality to the dominant Afro-Caribbean culture'.[8] Referencing the work of Joy Mahabir, Niala Maharaj, Rajandaye Ramkissoon-Chen and Ramabai Espinet, Kanhai finds that some poems by these women function in 'the zone of Afro-Caribbean folklore' and invoke myths that 'rural Indian and African women have used to explain structures that oppress them as poor women'.[9] She finds that these works 'reveal a receptivity to creative inspiration from the dominant Afro-Caribbean culture in spite of the uncongeniality of Indian-African relations'.[10]

Kanhai stops short of using the word dougla but her project illustrates a metaphorical douglarisation in the way Indo-Caribbean women writers engage with the African experience through African-derived myths and symbols. Shalini Puri has termed this engagement a 'dougla poetics' and sees a progressive politics emerging when 'dougla' is released from its biological moorings and expanded as a political concept.[11] The dougla, she feels, becomes an interesting site for 'the collision of classifications, for negotiations over the dougla's racial 'value' and place in a racially hierarchised society, and for the disruption of notions of racial purity upon which racial stereotypes depend'.[12] This is how Puri elaborates the political potential of the dougla:

Keeping in mind, then, that the original meaning of the word 'dougla' was 'bastard' or 'illegitimate', I suggest that one might think of a dougla poetics as a means for articulating potentially progressive cultural identities de-legitimised by dominant culture and the 'Mother Culture'. For first, the figure of the dougla draws attention to the reality of inter-racial unity...any egalitarian politics clearly needs to emphasise the shared histories of oppression of Afro- and Indo-Trinidadians... Moreover, any egalitarian cultural nationalism must address the problem of inter-racial violence against women... A dougla poetics thus offers a vocabulary for a political identity, not just a biological one.[13]

Puri cautions that a dougla identity is not a political panacea because first the word carries many sedimented meanings, and secondly, there is no reason to think that a dougla identity would necessarily be any less masculinist than existing racial identities.

Although I wish to cite previous work on douglarisation as the broad framework for this discussion, I hope to complicate the conceptualisation of a 'dougla poetics' and in that regard the concept of douglarisation is given a slightly different inflection here. First, in privileging feminism as a primary analytical tool, my own approach differs from Poynting's project. Second, in choosing to shift the discussion from Indo-Caribbean women's fiction to writings by Merle Hodge, an African-Caribbean writer, I infuse the term with, I hope, further potential than is realised in Kanhai's project. And thirdly, mindful of Puri's caution against a masculinist racial identity, I locate the promise of the political configuration of douglarisation in Caribbean women.

In my definition then, douglarisation refers to a cultural osmosis specifically between Indian and African communities in the Caribbean. This elaboration of douglarisation is mindful of the ways in which the literature under consideration evidences influences of African-Caribbean female resistance on Indian women's creative consciousness. Importantly, it also elaborates the ways in which African-Caribbean women writers draw from the Indian community in the creation of their fictional worlds. The Indian presence is therefore no longer anchored to the writings of Indo-Caribbean writers, but viewed within the context of a multi-ethnic literary tradition.

Twenty three years lapsed between the publication of Merle Hodge's *Crick Crack Monkey*[14] and *For the Life of Laetitia*.[15] That period witnessed significant social changes in Hodge's homeland, Trinidad and Tobago, changes that have made the Indian presence less and less avoidable in Caribbean nationalist discourses. There is an innocence and naïveté about the way Hodge sketched the Indian experience and Indian/African relations in *Crick Crack Monkey*, published in 1970, and there is a deliberateness, a measure of didacticism in the way she returns to this subject in *For the Life of Laetitia* published in 1993. The ways in which the evolving writer engages with the evolving politics of Indian/African relations and the implications of that for douglarisation as a revolutionary site within discourse and culture and society are the substantive concerns of this paper.

In a 1989 interview, Hodge outlined the political intention of her creative work as an aim to go beyond the simple mimetic representation of Caribbean realities (the contradictions and the ambivalences) to a transformation which aims at 'building of the Caribbean nation' to assume its 'cultural sovereignty'. One of the least interrogated aspects of Hodge's work is how the Indian experience functions within the 'Caribbean nation' of her political vision and how this experience is translated as the 'folk' community of her fictional worlds. Caribbean 'folk' community has its conceptual origins in the 1970s Creole society thesis[16] and much of the critical reckoning with Hodge's work has been premised on this understanding of Caribbean society.[17] But in both these novels Hodge is reconfiguring the 'folk' with the Indo-Caribbean female presence. Douglarisation then is a different lens that enables a reading of this reconfiguration of the 'folk' in the Caribbean experience. I wish to argue that the dougla poetics in her creative expressions announces itself not only in the magnanimity and intimacy with which she treats Indian figures, but in the deliberate yet delicate evolution of her novels' capacity to reach into the Indian community in Trinidad in the configuring of 'folk' community.

The Folk Barricade Against the Bitch in *Crick Crack Monkey*

In the imagined community[18] of *Crick Crack Monkey* lateral comradeships are forged on the basis of class so that the whole village, regardless of ethnicity, gender and generation, is mobilised to form a barricade against 'The Bitch': the middle class, Europeanised Aunt Beatrice who advocates an ideological movement away from folk ways. The ethnic diversity of the people who constitute this imagined community that Hodge mobilises to people the world of *Crick Crack Monkey* is significant. There is the extended family of Tantie; there are the boys on the block, among them Krishna; Neighb' Ramlaal and Neighb' Ramlaal's Wife and children. And of course there is the virtually voiceless but, I will argue, extremely important Doolarie.

In this novel of childhood, the process of identity formation is crucial and it is a point taken up by critic Renu Juneja in an extensive exploration of Hodge's work.[19] Juneja begins by asserting that chronology and gender are legitimate considerations in a study which attempts to narrativise a process of self-definition inevitably twinned with cultural alignments, where the self is reconstituted in terms of these alignments. To view the process as a form of 'becoming' (an authentic, assertive, or autonomous persona or a part of a culturally distinctive community), she suggests, is to acknowledge the possibility of stages — a before and an after:

The disjunctions between the before and the after in these childhood novels are synecdochical and metonymic images of cultural disjunctions. Finally to focus on 'becoming' in relation to cultural conditions is also to admit the relevance of the extra textual, of connections to real conditions outside the text, and to admit as well, much against the grain of the prevailing theories of the death of the subject or the author, to some relationship (however meditated) between the constructed self in the narrative and its author's experience. The self that emerges in these texts is a social construct and the journey of reconstruction involves efforts at recognition by the person of *her relationship with time, history, society and others*[20] (italics inserted).

Africans and Indians occupy a non-conflictual place in Hodge's rendering of this folk community in *Crick Crack Monkey*, and Tee's relationship with a culturally distinctive community is integral to the process of Tee's becoming. My contention here is that one of the primary factors which renders this community culturally distinctive is the organic integration of the Indian experience. Such organic integration of the Indian and African communities manifests on different levels. There is the peopling of the community already identified. Moreover, there is one seemingly throwaway line in the text which resonates with significance. In the continuing strategising against The Bitch, Tantie reckons that Toddam and Tee should be bundled away to Point d'Espoir; by the time they returned it would be time for Tee to go to school and Toddam 'they could simply lose among Neighb' Ramlaal-Wife own when there was no one at home'.[21] The impracticability of hiding an African child among Indian children only surfaces when one considers the race of both families, their biological lineage. Metaphorically this one liner is loaded in its political intent and it is this vision of organic integration that Hodge extends in the way she uses Moonie's wedding and locates the young Doolarie.

As Tee first leaves Tantie to live with Aunt Beatrice, 'The Bitch' is reminded that Tee has to return for Moonie's wedding. It is instructive that the moment of Tee's separation from her folk roots is marked by her being prevented from attending the wedding. The missed wedding occasions two related points. First, Tee's imagining of the celebration she is missing is articulated with a perspective that can only be described as external and stands as an illustration of one of the criticisms of the novel's representation of Indians. Hodge's description of Moonie's wedding is external; she describes Moonie transformed:

...into a startlingly pretty and fragile doll smothered in folds of delicate cloth and flowers and surrounded by a drove of women, vast and meagre, all shrouded in uhr'ni...babus in sparkling white dhotis squatting with their sticks and peering up myopically at the great crowd... I thought of dhalpouri and good hot pepper. The height of the festivity for Toddam and me was eating off a piece of banana leaf...[22]

This is an argument made by Patrick Taylor, looking specifically at ethnicity in Trinidad literature, to develop his point:

Hodge creates a model of colonially-imposed, racial and ethnic conflict in relation to which the young girl Cynthia must discover herself. Her Tantie links her to African traditions, her friends to Indian ones. Unable to leave Aunt Beatrice's house, she longs for salt fish and roti; she wants to attend the wedding of her Indian friend Moonie... Hodge's book is incomplete, Cynthia does not quite reach adulthood, and the perspective on Indians remains external. However the contradictions are exposed, and there are implications for the reconstruction of a community free of the manipulative values of a Europeanised middle class.[23]

However, at the level of the metatext, the representation is far from superficial and my second point is what Taylor misses in his analysis. I want to argue that what is significant here is not the descriptive rendering of the dream wedding but how the wedding functions in the text. Tee's absence from the wedding is symbolic of a promise broken and it is here that the balance tilts in favour of Aunt Beatrice's world of colonially imposed values. Hodge announces this significance when, shortly after missing the wedding, the young narrator tells us 'Since the weekend of Moonie's wedding neither Auntie Beatrice nor I had brought up the subject of my going home for a weekend'.[24]

The missed wedding and its significance are internalised and form part of Tee's dreams. In this realm she *becomes* Moonie — 'I thought that I was the bride'[25] and that fluidity of racial identities at the psychic level is, to me, a more adventurous analysis. In the process of Tee's becoming, then, one of the identities she internalises is the Indian woman's. Yet, at the very same moment, Tee's inability to attend Moonie's wedding, 'that coolie affair'[26] indentifies racial integration as a primary casualty of Tee's socialisation into Aunt Beatrice's middle class world.

In *Crick Crack Monkey*, the middle class, as represented by Aunt Beatrice, is hostile towards any semblance of racial solidarity. Aunt Beatrice labels Moonie's wedding a 'coolie affair' and her entry into the novel and Tee's life is marked by her physical separation of Toddam and Doolarie:

Aunt Beatrice separated them firmly and again bade Doolarie go home. Again she only withdrew a few feet and stood staring wide eyed and expressionless, as we went down the path with our unexpected benefactor... As Aunt Beatrice piled us into the back seat she said to him with irritation: You see how she has these coolie children running around with them? The man grunted.[27]

As Tee is encouraged to recoil from her folk community, Hodge renders her protagonist's distance in terms of racial pejoratives. Tee reflects that:

All this I was seeing again through a kind of haze of shame; and I reflected that even now Tantie and Toddan must be packed into that ridiculous truck with all those common raucous niggery people and all those coolies.[28]

The psychic disruption in Tee's life then manifests itself in her rejection of her African working class family and her Indian working class neighbours. This crystallises in Tee's rejection of Doolarie. Suddenly Tee sees Doolarie, not as a young friend of Toddam, but as a figure:

...in her yellow dress, and white shoes, and the fronts
had already been cut away to give her toes room; and
greasy paper bags announcing that they contained
polorie, anchar, roti from Neighb Ramlal Wife...[29]

Doolarie is an interesting figure in *Crick Crack Monkey*.
She is virtually voiceless but her presence is central to an
understanding of Hodge's negotiation with douglarisation. As
Tee becomes Moonie in her dream, Doolarie becomes Tee at
another level. Note how easily and quickly Toddam and Tee,
who appear at the very opening of the novel looking out the
window for the new baby, become Toddam and Doolarie. As
Tee goes off with her aunt towards another world and another
experience, 'Tantie stood in the gallery with her arms folded
while Toddam and Doolarie came down to the bottom of the
path to peer into the car'.[30] The ease with which the creative
sensibility shifts from Tee and Toddam to Toddam and
Doolarie is deliberate, I think, in Hodge's fictional elaboration
of her political vision. As Tee grows further and further away
from her community, Tantie writes to her that 'Dularie is also
fine she said Tantie I keeping you company till Cyn-Cyn come
back'.[31] Again, the ease with which the centrality of Doolarie
is being engineered and with which this Indian child is being
drawn into the organic centre of the community represented
by Tantie is significant.

Doolarie's appearance at the end of the novel deserves
analysis in the context of another insight by Juneja. Juneja
comments that:

Tee's turning away from her creole past, her internal
colonisation, is imaged as a bodily withdrawal, a physical shrinking. She hides in bathrooms; she scuttles
through back doors; she plunges into thick shrubbery.
She wants 'to shrink, to disappear'.[32]

At the beach, in a moment of climatic tension, she 'savagely
slaps' Aunt Beatrice's hand, 'Recoiling and turning' away
from human contact'.[33] Bodily functions like eating,
undertaken with relish in the past, become a cause for

shame. She eats like 'a burglar creeping over to the cupboard, surreptitiously lifting a plate...'.[34]

At the moment when Tee is furthest from her roots, a distance depicted by resistance to physical intimacy, Doolarie is physically embraced by Tantie as 'overcome with shyness, [she] buried her head in Tantie's lap'.[35] This, for me, is a climactic moment in the plot of the cultural metatext. Tantie recognises that she has lost Tee and gathers up Doolarie to leave.

Neighbourliness and Folk Community in *For the Life of Laetitia*

Twenty three years after the publication of *Crick Crack Monkey*, Hodge published her second novel, *For the Life of Laetitia*. This novel traces the development of Lacey through secondary school and affords its protagonist a more mature and less impressionable social consciousness than Tee's. The class conflict at the forefront of Tee's life survives in the background of this novel. At the centre of this text is gender relations and it is in this context that Hodge explores the positioning of the young rural Indian woman. In this novel, too, racial conflict is foregrounded so that racial accommodation is less implicit, less utopian perhaps, than in her first novel.

The integral centrality of the Indian presence here is immediately declared in the location of the novel's action in Sooklal Trace. Again, Hodge peoples this community with a representative assortment of characters — in addition to the extended family network of Ma's household, there is Rampie, the owner of a shop; Jai, the owner of a perilously old American car; Charlene, the dougla child linked biologically to Ma's household by her son Leroy who is Charlene's father; Tara, Charlene's mother; and Maharajin, Charlene's grandmother. Lacey's secondary school community is populated with figures such as Miss Hafeez, Mr Tewarie, Naushad Ali, the peripheral Persaud, and the central Anjanee Jugmohansingh.

Hodge embodies her political vision here in the dougla child, Charlene, and her understanding of racial conflict is articulated in the insertion of the word 'racial' to replace racist in the Caribbean lexicon. Her constant use of the word 'neighbour' and its derivative, neighb', in her two novels shows itself here as an attempt to name an encounter. Anjanee reminds Lacey of Lacey's neighbour Tara, so the two start a neighbourly relationship; the intimacy of the word proclaims the intimacy of the relationship. This novel, then, overtly negotiates the Caribbean creole lexicon to pay attention to the social configuration of Caribbean societies.

The random relationship developed between Laetitia/Lacey and Anjanee (random because their encounter results from having last names that start with the letter J) is Hodge's point of entry into some of the dynamics of the Indian woman's reality. Lacey and Anjanee develop a closeness based on their rural, working class background and the varying degrees of oppression they suffer under a dominant patriarchy. Anjanee's marginalisation takes another form as well — she is Indian and is ashamed of her food which is generally roti and talkarie, and she is constantly harassed by Mrs Lopez. Lacey shares in Anjanee's isolation and the friendship begins.

Anjanee's reality is determined by her oppressive brothers and father who do not support her education and who think she should be satisfied with achieving a functional level of literacy. She sells produce in the village each morning before attending school so that she could pay the bus fare. When her baby sister is ill, she withdraws from school for several days to help her mother care for the child. She is unable to afford books and travels such a long way to school that she is always tired in class. Eventually she becomes anaemic as she is unable to sustain a proper diet.

The detailed physical circumstances of Anjanee's life are sketched throughout the novel as the two girls draw closer and Anjanee increasingly confides in her friend. Despite the severe physical constraints in Anjanee's life, she continues to attend school and write exams. Her motivation is a determination not to end up like her mother. This young voice of rebellion is attempting to break free of the cycle of service to the patriarchs that determine the life of so many Indian women. Anjanee outlines the circumstances of her mother's generation:

If you see how much work my mother does have to do when the day come!... So only me to get up four o'clock in the morning and help her knead the flour so everybody could eat and get food to carry. Only me to help her bring water and bathe the little ones for school, feed the baby, wash everybody clothes, iron everybody clothes, sweep the house, sweep the yard, cook a ton load of food in the evening again.[36]

The housewife's rigorous and oppressive role may seem a touch too traditional to be believable, but ironically the strength of this portrayal derives from Hodge's attention to social realism. The circumstances of the rural Indian woman are as traditional as they are oppressive and Anjanee's determination 'not to end up like that' turns out to be prophetic: 'I not going to end up like my mother, I rather dead'.[37]

The only way out that Anjanee and her mother recognise is education. Anjanee's mother is aware of her own social entrapment:

...does just shake she head and say 'Where I will leave them and go, beti? I ain't have schooling. You want me to go by the side of the road and beg?[38]

Anjanee's determination to be educated is a fundamental need to escape her restrictive reality. Her death cannot be read as defeat but as indicative of a fundamental shift in perspective among young Indian women; she prefers death to her mother's circumstances. Resistance and agency can be read into her death.

Hodge ensures that this perspective is what lingers after Anjanee's death by articulating the cultural stereotype of the young Indian woman who commits suicide through Miss Velma who declares: 'These Indian girls so quick to take poison'.[39] However, Hodge had already prepared the reader for this by bringing Anjanee to life in the text and investing her with the fullness of human dignity and struggle. Ironically, in its invocation, the stereotype is debunked.

The fullness with which Anjanee's story is integrated into the text is manifested on another level. Her death and the start of Lacey's menstruation define the end of innocence and Lacey's passage into adulthood. Lacey becomes ill and is bedridden for days with a high fever. When she wakes, she is glad to be in the world again and her catharsis is complete. In Lacey's becoming in relation to her world, in her process of development, her encounter and relationship with her Indian friend is fundamental. In the shaping of Laetitia's consciousness by that central experience, Hodge is writing into being a promise of racial unity and of female liberation.

The promise of racial unity is named in another place in the text. The young dougla child, Charlene, is placed to symbolise that promise of racial unity. Less overtly placed is Maharajin. Maharajin, Tara and Charlene represent three successive generations of Indian womanhood. Maharajin is kept at a respectful distance away from the text but we are told that she strongly resisted the inter-racial relationship between Tara and Uncle Leroy that gave birth to Charlene. She put Tara out of the house yet when Tara managed to get a job in town, Maharajin refused to let her take Charlene with her. The language of Ma's summing up of the situation is telling:

> First she want to give up the ghost because the daughter making creole child — or kilwal child, according to she — and she want to throw the two of them in the road. Now you nearly have to full-out application form to get the kilwal child. Eh-eh!...she must be have grands till she forget they name! I can't understand why she must be so stingy with mine.[40]

The vexation in Ma's tone is the vexation of a neighbourly quarrel, not the antagonism of racial hostility. This is basically a family quarrel in Hodge's representation and this is very significant.

Hodge plays with this idea again in her engineering of a class discussion on race. Hodge shows how the innocent relationships of children are corrupted by adult prejudices.

Mr Tewarie is racial, the children contend, in the way he always lets off the Indian boys and blames the African children for all wrongdoing. His disruptive, corrupting presence in the text climaxes in a rapid exchange of racial stereotypes and a redefinition of the word 'racial'. In the children's imaginary, '...racist is like over in America, or South Africa...Like them Klu klee...Klu Klu...Klu Klux Klan and thing. We not so...'. The class agreed. 'Racist' was the word used for those wicked white people in South Africa and America. In our country we just had some people who were racial'.[41] Hodge is here arguing that our Caribbean creole lexicon reflects the dynamics of the Indian/African encounter and that our encounter is different from other hostile racial encounters in other locations in the world. It is this understanding of the Trinidad reality that gives her representations their depth in both her novels.

Hodge's rendering of the female reality, both Indian and African, is not simply diagnostic but also prescriptive. Anjanee's death and Lacey's survival beg the question: what exists in Lacey's situation that protects her from Anjanee's fate? The most identifiable factor is the opportunity for bonding by women and the capacity for resistance by African women. Ma Zelline is unmarried and childless and would want it no other way; Ma is autonomous and defies the world in protecting her extended family and likewise Miss Velma is encouraged to resist the domineering Mr Cephas. Anjanee's immediate environment does not appear to have that network to cushion her trauma and encourage an alternative developmental option.

The potential for solidarity and community across race lines is one of the achievements of Sam Selvon's *A Brighter Sun* where the relationship between Urmilla and Rita shows how women separated by ethnicity and race, but unified by male centred systems of oppression, can provide a nucleus of support through which community is constructed.[42] Hodge has written a deeper, fuller exploration of this potential in *For the Life of Laetitia*.

The promise of douglarisation in constructing communities is Hodge's overarching triumph in these works which seek to position gender issues at the point at which they intersect with class and race. The female experience here is distinctive and revolutionary in the frequent intertwining of gender conflicts with other social conflicts.

Notes

1. In Jamaica, where there is a small community of Indians comprising both the descendants of indentured labourers and recent voluntary migrants, the word is not used. The term 'coolie royale' is used in the same way that 'Chinee royal' is used to describe the children of mixed ancestry.

2. Jeremy Poynting, 'Literature and Cultural Pluralism: East Indians in the Caribbean', unpublished Ph.D thesis, School of English, University of Leeds, 1985, p.547.

3. Niels M. Sampath, 'An Evaluation of the 'Creolization' of East Indian Adolescent Masculinity', in *Trinidad Ethnicity*, Kevin Yelvington (ed.), Knoxville, Tennessee: University of Tennessee Press, 1993, pp.235-253.

4. There is no census category for douglas; they are included in the 'mixed' category. Research by Norma Abdulah on 'Structure of the Population: Demographic Developments in the Independence Years' in *Trinidad and Tobago: The Independence Experience 1962-1987*, Selwyn Ryan (ed.), St Augustine: The Institute of Social and Economic Research, 1988, show that the census category 'mixed' decreased between 1960 and 1970 by about 40,000. This was consistent with an increase in the size of the African grouping. This change can be explained by the Black Power movement and Black consciousness during this period when notions of 'pure' ancestry were mobilised.

5. For more on this see essays in *Trinidad Ethnicity*, Kevin Yelvington (ed.).

6. See Poynting's chapter, 'The Dougla Sensibility: A Study Mainly of the Fiction of Samuel Selvon' in his Ph.D thesis.

7. Ramabai Espinet (ed.), *Creation Fire: A CAFRA Anthology of Caribbean Women's Poetry*, Ontario: Sister Vision Press, 1990. Kanhai analyses the Indian women writers in the anthology in 'The Masala Stone Sings: Indo-Caribbean Women Coming into Voice' presented at the 1995 conference on Challenge and Change: The Indian Diaspora in its Historical and Contemporary Contexts held at UWI, St Augustine, Trinidad.

8. Kanhai, p.5.
9. Ibid., p.16.
10. Ibid., p.13.
11. See Shalini Puri's 'Race, Rape and Representation: Indo-Caribbean Women and Cultural Nationalism' presented at the 1995 conference on Challenge and Change: The Indian Diaspora in its Historical and Contemporary Contexts held at UWI, St Augustine, Trinidad. She first used the term 'dougla poetics' in 1994 in a paper entitled 'East Indian/West Indian: Discourses of Race and Place in Contemporary Trinidad'.
12. Ibid., pp.11-12.
13. Ibid., pp.40-41.
14. Merle Hodge, *Crick Crack Monkey*, London: Andre Deutsch, 1970, Oxford: Heinemann 1981, reprinted in 1985 (twice) and 1986. All references to this text are from the 1986 Caribbean Writers Series edition.
15. Merle Hodge, *For the Life of Laetitia*, Farrar Straus Giroux, 1993 and reprinted in 1995. All references are from the 1995 edition.
16. See O. Nigel Bolland's 'Creolization and Creole Societies: A Cultural Nationalist View of Caribbean Social History' in *Intellectuals in the Twentieth-Century Caribbean*, Volume 1, *Spectre of the New Class: the Commonwealth Caribbean*, Alistair Hennessy (ed.), London: Macmillan, 1992.
17. Jennifer Rahim's 'Laughter in Merle Hodge's *Crick Crack Monkey*', Renu Juneja's 'Intersecting Culture and Gender: Fiction by West Indian Women', Patrick Taylor's 'Ethnicity and Social Change in Trinidadian Literature', Carole Boyce Davies and Elaine Savory Fido's *Out of the Kumbla*; and Evelyn O'Callaghan's *Woman Version*.
18. I make reference here to Chandra Talpade Mohanty's use of the term in *Cartographies of Struggle: Third World Women and the Politics of Feminism*, Indiana: Indiana University Press, 1991.
19. Renu Juneja, *Caribbean Transactions: West Indian Culture in Literature*, London and Basingstoke: Macmillan, 1996, pp.21-50.
20. Ibid., p.23.
21. *Crick Crack*, p.13.
22. Ibid., pp.78-9.

23. Patrick Taylor, in Kevin Yelvington (ed.), *Trinidad Ethnicity*, Basingstoke: Macmillan, 1993, p.257.
24. *Crick Crack*, p.84.
25. Ibid., p.79.
26. Ibid., p.78.
27. Ibid., p.11.
28. Ibid., p.86.
29. Ibid., p.106.
30. Ibid., p.69.
31. Ibid., p.105.
32. Juneja, p.31., refers also to *Crick Crack*, p.97.
33. *Crick Crack*, p.33.
34. See note 32.
35. *Crick Crack*, p. 106.
36. *Laetitia*, p.64.
37. Ibid.
38. Ibid., p.65.
39. Ibid., p.202.
40. Ibid., p.146.
41. Ibid., p.95.
42. Samuel Selvon, *A Brighter Sun*, London: Wingate, 1952; London: Longman, 1971.

'To Us All Flowers Are Roses'

Writing ourselves into the literature of the Caribbean

VELMA POLLARD

'There was nothing about us at all', wrote Olive Senior, Jamaican poet and fiction writer, in the much anthologised 'Colonial Girls High School' commenting as much on the content ('borrowed images') as on the attitude to language (For our language/—'bad talking'—/detentions) in the education she describes.[1] The need to change that picture and to find a voice that represents the speech communities out of which they write has been part of the preoccupation of Caribbean creative writers certainly in the second half of this century in which the primacy of the European languages they inherited came to be debated. Different writers have met the challenge in different ways in environments where linguistic codes are associated with different levels of stratified societies. Few chose to write exclusively in the creole languages which have emerged as the popular means of expression. (Louise Bennett stands out for having written in Jamaican Creole.)[2] Most artists have written predominantly in English but have used varying means to achieve a creole flavour, to portray a creole identity.

This paper will illustrate how Jamaican women, writing predominantly in English, have written themselves, their culture, their identity into their work by exploiting the dual linguistic heritage. One of the advantages of writing in an environment where the official language is related to the popular creole is the possibility of using the same word or the same phrase to convey different meanings. The closest relationship between the languages is at the level of lexicon. Sometimes one word operates as different parts of speech in the two languages; sometimes two or more English words come together to make idiomatic expressions that are uniquely creole. The paper will elaborate on the different modes of linguistic integration which different writers have used to achieve an expression that is at once authentic, and available if to different degrees, to both insider and outsider readerships.

The language of the earliest written creative efforts of colonised peoples the world over has tended to be the language of the coloniser which is the language of Education and of all official transactions in these societies. In the former British West Indies, that language has been English. The very act of writing in another language, during the fledgling years, was revolutionary in a situation where 'Literature' invariably meant English (or at least British) Literature. In schools in the Caribbean as in other British colonies, children were learning British and European History and studying English novels, poems and plays. Merle Hodge in her novel *Crick Crack Monkey* (1970) dramatises/satirises this situation.[3]

Olive Senior's now famous words describe it succinctly: 'There was nothing about us at all':[4]

Studying: History Ancient and Modern
Kings and Queens of England
Steppes of Russia
Wheatfields of Canada

There was nothing of our landscape there
Nothing about us at all.[5]

When writers began to react negatively to being written out of the literature or to being represented entirely by English, the language of their formal but not of their intimate motions, they sought ways of including the sound of a local and authentic voice in what they wrote.

Different writers achieved this in different ways. Very few chose to write exclusively in the creoles, popular languages born of the interaction between the African languages of the slaves and the European languages of the planters. Louise Bennett of Jamaica, among the women stands out for having written in Jamaican Creole (JC), from the forties when she began, right up to the present. Today Bennett is regarded as a Performance poet which means that her verse is meant to be performed, spoken before an audience, not read in a quiet interchange between reader and text.

Other writers have written predominantly in English but have used varying means to achieve a satisfactory JC flavour. The super/subordinate relationship between English and the JC allows class distinctions to be made through the manipulation of the languages. The representation indicates that English is usually used by the upper and middle classes, JC by the others. Indeed this is the general picture. But there is nothing cut and dried about it. JC speakers speak 'up' in certain formal situations, that is, they try to speak English and though they do not always achieve it they achieve something between JC and English. And all classes relax in JC.

This paper will illustrate how Lorna Goodison and Olive Senior, Jamaican women writing predominantly in English, write themselves, their culture, their identity into their work by exploiting the dual linguistic heritage.

One of the advantages of writing in an environment where the official language is related to the popular creole is the possibility of using the same word or the same phrase with different meanings, the closest relationship between the languages being at the level of Lexicon. So for example the title of this paper 'To us all flowers are roses' which is also the title of Lorna Goodison's (1995)[6] collection of poems means in English (at a metaphorical level) that all flowers are as valuable as roses are, but in Jamaican Creole it means (at a very literal level) that the term 'rose' may be used to describe all flowers. So that a rose garden need not have any roses at all though it may have Anthuriums and Zennias. The following quotation from a farewell speech on my campus exemplifies this. The worker who was chosen to give the gift to the outgoing principal's wife said, 'Through, as we know Miss L. ... like roses we give ar this Orchid' (Because we know that Mrs. L. ... likes roses, we are presenting her with this orchid). The title of one of my own collections of short fiction is *Considering Woman* which in English has woman as object to be thought about.[7] In JC she is subject and the present participle/adjective 'considering' describes her attitude. To consider, in creole, is to think (especially if I 'consider my mind'). She is a thinking ('considering') person.

What sometimes happens is that the foreign reader who does not understand JC has access to one meaning while the JC speaker has access to two. The important point is that the JC speaker is constantly identified as an important part of the Jamaican man/woman scape even when the writing is mostly in English.

Let us examine briefly the opening lines of an exquisite short Goodison poem, 'O love you so fear the dark':

O love, you so fear the dark
you so accustomed to fighting...[8]

Line two might be read in English with a stress on 'you' making it a repetition of the form in line one. But it might also be read as a JC line with a shortened 'you' and a shortened 'so' and becomes 'yu so accustom(ed) to fighting', a version which would translate into English as 'you [who] are so accustomed to fighting'. The phonological change puts the sentence into a category of JC expression treated below, where the verb 'to be' is not used.

The brief description of the Caribbean (in this case Jamaican) language environment given above does not do justice to the complexity of the language situation. Language is closely linked to class. In the literature it is used to make distinctions in this area. Not one but several Caribbean selves are identifiable each using a code that is different in some respect from the others. I have used Lorna Goodison's 'Ocho Rios II' to illustrate this point elsewhere.[9] In that poem the voice of the Rastaman for example is distinct from the voice of the peasant farmer which in turn is distinct from that of the first person (middle-class?) narrator. I want to illustrate it here albeit less dramatically by looking at a part of one of

Olive Senior's earlier poems 'City Poem'.[10] Senior recalls an inner city street where a middle class young woman walks with some terror as young men call out to her:

hello hello. miss. psst psst.

The first person narrative voice comments:

but I cannot answer: The Age of Anxiety
alas, is still very much alive

In parenthesis there is the comment:

(And if you taught me to speak
with your words would I touch
could I reach beyond the collapse
of garbage cans in hungry streets?)

   The next movement describes a terrible day in the lives of the very citizens who people the hungry streets. A bulldozer had come to destroy homes (shacks to outsiders) to facilitate the building of lower income houses. A woman describes her own reaction and the more extreme reaction of her friend Mavis:

Wen de bulldoza come a back-a-wall
we jus pick up all we have an all
we have is chilren an we leave
Mavis doan wan leave Mavis aksin
why why why A seh Mavis
move fus aks question las
di ting out dere biggern yu
an it caan talk...

   The poem continues in English asking the rhetorical question:

Why
did you damage
the statue
of the National hero?

and responds:

> —Because I have plenty damage
> inside me.[11]

While all the selves represented here may be female (except for the sound of the male call 'psst psst'), English represents the concerned middle class; creole the suffering female self.

In spite of the use of JC which has by now been frequently mentioned in literary commentary on Caribbean writing, it is true to say that English is STILL the more widely used language in the writing not only for historical reasons but because it makes the writing accessible to a wider reading public. Language is sometimes used to give a Creole flavour to a whole poem in which case sometimes a mere word or phrase may be used. Lorna Goodison has become a genius at that. I want to look more closely first at the JC grammatical features selected when the intention is to use mostly English and then at the effect of the lexical selections that are made when this is the intention.

The verb 'to be' is perhaps the most commonly used verb in English. In JC, however, there is no equivalent for this verb in many places where the speaker of English expects it. So for example 'mi cold'/ I am cold, 'mi vex' / I am angry, 'yu tuu fuul'/ you are too stupid.

The absence of that verb 'to be' (zero-copula) does not get in the way of comprehension by the speaker of English. So for example Senior in her 'Meditation on Yellow' speaking for the historically conscious local 'I' serving tourists (modern Columbuses) comments wryly:

> So I serving them
> coffee
> tea
> cock-soup
> rum
> red-stripe beer
> sensimilla.[12]

and says of her/himself 'I not quarrelsome...I tired now...'

For one day before I die
from five hundred years of servitude
I due to move
from kitchen to front verandah.[13]

Later she suggests that tourists cannot catch the Caribbean rhythm

(for you have to born
with that).[14]

Note again also the Goodison lines quoted earlier, 'yu so accustomed to fighting'.

Next to the absence of the verb 'to be' the most obvious/ outstanding grammatical feature of all Creoles is the unmarked verb. The base form of the verb (used in English with 'to' for the infinitive) is the commonly used verb. No tense indication is contained there (some analyses make it perfect aspect). The form is the same for yesterday today and tomorrow. There are numerous discourse related ways of expressing time and of course there is the adverb or adverb phrase.

In the poem 'To us, all flowers are roses', Goodison mixes English verb and Creole verb in a characteristic sentence. She writes about the names of flowers and speaks of:

A strong young breeze that just takes
these names like blossoms and waltz
them around, turn and wheel them on the tongue.[15]

After the initial marked verb 'takes', all others are unmarked. And reinforcing the Creole sensibility is the fact that 'wheel and turn' is a phrase from a local folksong which asks:

Wha mek yu da wiil an tun mi?

Later in the same poem she writes that a cargo of slaves landed free because:

somebody sign a paper even as they
rode as cargo shackled on the high seas.[16]

Invoking the Creole sensibility with a mere word or phrase
is Lorna Goodison's special power. Sometimes she invokes a
special aspect of the landscape — the Rastafarian presence
for example. My earlier mention of 'Ocho Rios II' suggests that
Goodison is a great manager of the code-switching that is a
commonplace in Jamaican speech. Critics have commented
on this feature (see for example Baugh, Mordecai, Pollard and
most recently Chamberlin). But my comment on this occasion
is restricted to her use of the single word or phrase in the
same enterprise.

'My will' is a poem written entirely in English.[17] It is a
catalogue of wishes for important spiritual (non-material)
good things for her son. Near the end of the third of five
stanzas she writes: 'may you never know HUNGRY' (my
emphasis). It is easy to miss the fact that the naturally
expected abstract noun 'hunger' is replaced by the adjective
'hungry'. In JC the form used for the English adjective does
the function of both adjective and adverb. The substitution of
that one word for the expected other immediately raises the
wish to the level of a benediction from an old and wise woman
in a traditional community. And this is in keeping with the
image of the lines immediately before it when she wishes for
her son inter alia:

...the right to call
all older than you
Miss, mister or mistress
in the layered love of our
simplest ways.[18]

In the title poem of the recent collection, to which reference
has already been made, an unusual alternative pronunciation
appears in an environment of English. Among the Jamaican
place names listed is 'hola Mount Zion'. It invokes for those
who recognise it not simply JC but the drums of Rastafari
performing a popular song:

...It is Holy here, Mount Moses
dew falls upon Mount Nebo, south of Jordan,
Mount Nebo, rises here too hola Mount Zion high.[19]

(The 'hola' is written in lower case suggesting that a pun on it is possibly intended. The English 'whole of' becomes 'hola' in JC).

That 'hola Mount Zion' is a line from a rendition by the Mystic Revelations of Rastafari and allows the inclusion of that other theology in a string of place names invoking the Christian religion.

The final and personal affirmation of that poem introduces within an English sentence, a Jamaican word whose meaning is highly specific. If you know it you understand the pride in being a Jamaican that these words proclaim in this case a free woman, a daughter of slaves from Jamaica:

...I was born at Lineen —
Jubilee! — on the anniversary of Emancipation Day.
I recite these names in a rosary, speak them
when I pray, for Heartease, my Mecca, aye Jamaica.[20]

The public maternity hospital in Kingston, the Victoria Jubilee, named for that queen is lovingly called 'Lineen' in a euphonious pronunciation of 'lying-in' which is the state of woman waiting to give birth. The 'I' of the poem was born in that place on the anniversary of the Emancipation of slaves — the first of August. She prays for peace which for her, as it is in many other Goodison poems, is located in a physical/ literal and metaphorical place 'Heartease', a place as highly valued as Mecca was in early world history.

This title poem of Goodison's most recent collection most unashamedly speaks two languages, writes to two audiences. It begins by proclaiming the Akan ancestry to which many Jamaicans are heir 'Accompong is Ashanti'. Accompong is the name of a place, a maroon settlement as the poem goes on to tell:

...maroons dwell in dense places
deep mountainous, well-sealed
strangers unwelcome. Me no send you no come.[21]

That last is a place name too, 'Me no send you no come'. It means the same thing as 'strangers unwelcome' of the preceding sentence. At least the sense is the same for it translates 'If I don't send for you, do not come'. The one who is inside will determine when the other, who is outside should arrive, 'Do not come until I send for you.'

And everywhere in this poem, insider information is interspersed with general information, the former indicated by carefully selected, heavily weighted JC sounds.

Barbara Lalla in the chapter 'Re-Membering the Marooned Consciousness' in her recent critical work *Defining Jamaican Fiction — Marronage and the Discourse of Survival* writes of the 'secret encoding of Creole epistemes under guise of conformity (and with all the advantages of international 'legibility' and labels it 'the most subtle of the linguistic transgressions that constitute the verbal dimension of marronage'.[22] This is one way of describing the doublespeak throughout this particular Goodison poem. It is one of the less obvious/more subtle characteristics of the English/Creole code-mixing that is a natural part of Caribbean speech and more recently Caribbean writing. It is an extension of the pun which has been commented on in Jamaican from the beginning of this century. The lexical connection between the two codes in use makes this feature common and natural. There might be a problem where the reader from outside of the culture wishes for total comprehension. But almost any reading outside of one's culture acknowledges less than total understanding. It is only that when words are recognisable the feeling is that all meaning should be easily accessible. The speaker of English might have this feeling when she/he reads anything written in an English related creole. And there is indeed comprehension at two levels possible here:

'To us all flowers are ROses'
'To us all flowers are roSES'.[23]

Notes

1. Olive Senior, *Talking of Trees*, Kingston: Calabash Publishers, 1985.
2. See, for example, Louise Bennett, *Jamaica Labrish*, Kingston: Sangster's Book Stores, 1966.
3. Merle Hodge, *Crick Crack Monkey*, London: Andre Deutsch, 1970.
4. Senior, p.26.
5. Ibid.
6. Lorna Goodison, *To Us All Flowers Are Roses*, Urbana: University of Illinois Press, 1995.
7. Velma Pollard, *Considering Woman*, London: The Women's Press, 1989.
8. Lorna Goodison, *Heartease*, London: New Beacon Books, 1988.
9. Velma Pollard, 'Mothertongue Voices in the Writing of Olive Senior and Lorna Goodison' in Nasta, S. (ed.), *Motherlands*, London: The Women's Press, 1991.
10. Senior, p.66.
11. Ibid.
12. Olive Senior, *Gardening in the Tropics*, Toronto: McClelland and Stewart, 1994, p.15.
13. Ibid, p.16.
14. Ibid.
15. Goodison, 1995, p.69.
16. Ibid., p.70.
17. See Lorna Goodison, *I Am Becoming My Mother*, London: New Beacon Books, 1986.
18. Ibid., p.19.
19. Goodison, *To Us All Flowers Are Roses*.
20. Ibid.
21. Ibid.
22. Barbara Lalla, *Defining Jamaican Fiction*, Tuscaloosa: University of Alabama Press, 1996.
23. Goodison, *To Us All Flowers Are Roses*.

Olive Senior's Female Characters and the Expression of Cultural Duality in *Discerner of Hearts*

AIDA BAHR

Olive Senior is one of the most important Caribbean women writers whose narratives are very much concerned with the situation of women, particularly in Jamaica. All our islands share the sad history of colonial oppression which includes slavery and the merciless drainage of our natural resources; together with the imposition of European cultural patterns, regarded as civilised, while African cultural traditions, brought by the enslaved, were considered barbarous. The fact that this African-rooted culture is still alive in our countries demonstrates its power, its capacity for resistance.

It can be said that throughout the Caribbean there has been a great cultural struggle, bigger even than the political struggle which continues today. As a result, these two cultural sources are to be taken into account and have merged to become a mixed, Creole culture.

Olive Senior writes about women, and her female characters are authentic because they are taken from her own reality, her own experience. *Discerner of Hearts*,[1] Senior's first work published in Canada, comprises nine stories and only one of them, 'The Glass-bottom Boat', presents, in the narration, a male point of view. It is interesting that this man, whose thoughts form the narrative thread of the story, has been driven to occupy the position of the woman in the family. After being retired, he stays at home and waits for his partner to come back from work. This is a book of stories about common life, which does not imply there are not very dramatic situations. In fact, killings take place in two of the stories, and violence and cruelty are depicted here and there in the entire collection, because those are ordinary ingredients in the daily life of Caribbean women.

Many aspects of Jamaican society are presented in these stories. Some of them are recurrent: single mothers, the exodus to the cities, or even other countries, police abuse, educational problems and, above all, women's expectations of life, at any age. In spite of this, there is, more or less, a balance among rural and urban locations. The small village environment is, however, much more detailed and the characters are more vivid and richer in such surroundings. Something that attracts the attention of the reader is that in three of the pieces, the protagonist is the second daughter of the family. Her psychology is very similar to that of the elder sister in all three cases. Could it bear a resemblance to the author's own life? One cannot be sure, but clearly this character, called Teresa, Bridget or Sadie, is quite dear to Olive Senior, and she has developed the figure fully and convincingly.

In a society ruled and controlled by men, women are doubly subjugated. I am going to refer in this paper, however, only to the cultural duality that operates for both sexes. It is not a new subject in Olive Senior's work. One of her most delightful stories, an early one, 'Two Grandmothers', deals exactly with this matter: a girl communicates to her mother informing her how her two grandmothers are trying to educate her according to two different patterns or codes of behaviour.[2] One is black, poor, lives in a little village in the country; while the other one is wealthy, 'modern' and supposedly white. It becomes clear that the girl feels a strong pull towards the 'modern' grandmother, representing a shift in her values. The story is a remarkable exploration of the contrast between white Western culture (I refuse to call it European because

North America is nowadays the stronger model) and Black African culture.

In *Discerner of Hearts* this cultural duality is operating at a fundamental level within the conflicts presented in the stories. The imposition, through centuries of the colonisation process, and of the cultural patterns sustained by white people, have been deeply carved in (Caribbean) people's minds. A feature of this is, first of all, the overestimation of Europe and the underestimation of Africa, and, by extension, the American colony itself. The following short dialogue between two sisters in one of the stories shows clearly the differentiation in quality of elements related to the two spaces, no matter they are really the same. The girls are taking part in a fantasy game in which the elder one is crowned 'Queen of the Hyacinths', and the little one thinks her sister is referring to the water hyacinths they have at home:

'Those things are weeds, you know that. A terrible pest. Why do you think they try to kill them every year? Real hyacinths are proper flowers. They grow in *England*. People go gathering them in meadows'.
'What's 'meadows'?' Sadie asked.
'Pastures', said Muffet.
'So why can't they gather them in the pastures?'
'Because pastures are full of ticks and cow dung and cows. And meadows are full of hyacinths and daffodils and written about in books'.[3]

So, the girls' exchange is not just about words. It is about the proposal of a physical image, a strong aesthetic model. Throughout the book also, we find reinforced the importance of having long, silky hair or the terrible disadvantage of dark skin. Discrimination on this basis sets in even within the family. For example:

Except for Manuela, Desrine's children all had black shiny skin like hers and hair that was short and coarse. 'Natty head', Manuela called them all. 'Bungo pickney'. To their faces. Manuela was several shades lighter than other children, with big round eyes framed with delicate half-moon eyebrows and purplish skin like a starapple, and she had a much straighter nose, a proper nose she got from her grandmother, she proudly told Sadie, not Miss Mary, who was black and had a flat nose like the rest of them, but her father's mother who was born in Panama and had Indian blood in her.[4]

Because of Manuela's physical characteristics such as paler skin and longer, softer hair, everybody treats her as if she is someone special. Even Desrine does.

This rejection of African features gains more intensity as individuals assume a wealthier position, and in so much as they look whiter, it also involves the rejection of values related to African culture. In another example, Sadie refers to Miss Mary's medicinal heritage 'from her ol' grandfather, who was a true-true African' [...].[5]

Sadie liked to have things like that to talk about, for she knew that her boldness shocked the girls she was supposed to mix with at school. None of them would dream of admitting they knew anything about bush and Africans. Rather, they were busily preparing to go to 'high school' where their fathers would pay large fees so they could be turned into ladies who would straighten their hair and rub Ponds Vanishing Cream into their faces every night [...].[6]

So, this self-negation of African origin targets cultural traditions as well as physical images. In the world depicted by Olive Senior, respectability and social position go together with colour of skin and acceptance of white Western ways of life. Therefore, young women try very hard to 'improve' their appearance, in order to get a good marriage (which means marriage to a partner as white as possible).

In 'Window', the sick mother of the protagonist expresses: 'Black people born to be poor. Nobody expects any better of them'.[7] This woman, who has become poor herself, hopes to rescue her family from bankruptcy by getting a suitable match for her daughters. She sends the elder to Kingston for that purpose. The possibility that her second daughter might marry the Black grandson of their old maid is unthinkable, even for the boy's own grandmother, no matter he has savings through his hard work on the Panama Canal Zone and is ready to repair the house and farm the land. It also takes a very long time (it does not really happen at all in the story) for the girl to gather the courage to accept the boy's love, although she is undoubtedly attracted to him.

Another way to gain respectability is through education, if the person is decidedly poor and black. It is clear in *Discerner of Hearts* that it is almost impossible for poor parents to get their children a proper education, unless they prove to be very intelligent and win a scholarship, but sometimes, even then results can be negative. In 'The Case Against the Queen', Sonny fails to become a doctor because he is not strong enough to overcome the pressures of adapting himself to a different country, where his own culture is disregarded as non-worthy. He does, however, succeed in learning the manners of the place such as ways of speaking and dressing. In the process he becomes convinced that he has been deprived of his heart, because:

The people only understand machines. That's what I have found out about them. Want to turn us all into machines. So they can work us as they like and wear us down as they like and nobody can say one little thing. Because we are not human any more.[8]

A different scenario is presented in 'You Think I Mad, Miss?' a story in which the finest achievement is the characterisation of the mad woman: Isabella Francina Myrtella Jones. In her colourful, spontaneous language, the narrator explains to everyone she encounters how she tried very hard to become a teacher, but a love affair, and most of all her beliefs in the power of obeah, despite all her efforts to get scientific knowledge, drove her into her present state. She is the best example of this coexistence of two cultures within a person, a state holding two realities far from merged. It may be said that the character is divided between her aspirations to be an educated person, far above what she herself calls 'negromancy', and her fears of the power of negromancy, which she considers to be real. She pretends to become an intellectual, but on another level, she finds herself unable to rationalise the causes for the failure of her love relationship and promptly seeks an explanation within obeah. She is not the first to do so, but her expectations and her love affair are ruined as she descends into madness. Her cry of despair at the end of the story bears the bitterness of someone who finds herself unable to fit into the world.

I turn now to one of the main surviving elements of African culture within the region, that of religious practice. Religion became one of the strongest weapons for the slave's defence. Deprived of everything, religion came to mean for the slaves, self-assurance, their past history, their homeland. It was the equivalent of an only treasure; an only source of power. Even today, religious practice remains an important means by which poor people can have a sense of control over their lives. It is significant that the two attitudes more often observed towards such matters from educated people are either to condemn the practice, or to study it as a sign of ignorance on the part of the believers. The latter view is not untypical of scholars who take African culture as a research subject but do not really consider it a civilised culture. To illustrate, I shall offer the story of an episode which took place in Santiago de Cuba, during a recent 'Festival of Caribbean Culture'. It involves two distinguished Caribbean ladies in discussion with a Puerto Rican scholar. The scholar himself is employed at a North American university and is researching for his doctor's degree. He is also a 'santeria' believer, and an active practitioner himself. The ladies, complaining about the animal sacrifices, asked him if he thought that the practice could be stopped by means of a better education. He replied angrily that he was an educated person himself and would never accomplish a sacrifice unless it was completely necessary but, I quote his words: 'If I have to kill ten goats to save a human life, ten goats go'.

In Olive Senior's *Discerner of Hearts*, prejudice against African religion is clearly depicted. In 'Zig Zag', for example, Sadie's mother throws Manuela's guzu through the window in sheer vexation. Also, Theresa's parents consider Father

Burnham to be in an illegitimate position. They mistake him for an obeahman. When Theresa asks Cissy, her maid, about this, the answer underlines the very little knowledge her employers had about these matters:

'Father Burnham an obeahman? So yu mother say?... Father Burnham is a good man. A bush man. He only deal in growing things, things that natural — bush and root and herb and what comes from doctor-shop. He don't deal with dead thing — blood and feather and grave dirt and all them sinting. Father spend his whole time counteracting wickedness that obeahman do. If obeahman put it on, Father will take it off.[9]

Teresa will find out, at a later point in the narrative when she dares to enter the balmyard to see Father Burnham himself, that there are some commonalities between her religious practice and his. She therefore recognises the biblical scenes illustrated there but also is surprised to find all the figures of people, Jesus included, painted black.

The girl stumbles on syncretism, the assimilation of the elements of different cultures and their adaptation to a specific cultural scheme. So, she finds the two different worlds confronting each other: the world of the more or less rich, who live with Western standards and the world of the poor, who dream of achieving those standards but cannot help living in their own milieu. Some of this has nothing to do with African culture, but rather with poverty. Nevertheless, there are signs of the permanence of some cultural values: women's fertility, for instance. In 'Discerner of Hearts', within the story that names the book, Cissy, the black maid, complains to Theresa:

Theresa, you too young to understand, chile. I am nothing but a mule. Everywhere I go. I know them calling me a mule. Even my own mother start up bout it now. What good is a woman if they can't have pickney? Everybody else have baby but me poor soul. The girls my age, some of them have all two, three pickney. And me can't have even one little one. My own little sisters are all having pickney. Everybody except poor me-gal.[10]

Similarly, in 'Zig Zag' the maid Desrine, who has suffered the frustration of the possibility of her daughter not getting to school, now expresses her pleasure at the prospect of having a grandchild, something to boast about to the other women. Sadie overhears her telling the childless Cherry of her satisfaction at having her daughter 'prove' herself, that is, show she is not a mule by becoming pregnant.

This example takes us to one of the most significant groups of characters in the book: the maids. They can be considered as symbols as they represent the link between the two worlds mentioned: they live in rich houses and sometimes they imitate their employers, but they are a powerful source of knowledge about African-rooted culture for children within those families. In four of the stories, the girls are placed in the middle of the two forces: their mothers and their maids. In all of them, they are closer to the maids and have easier communication with them. Sometimes this is due to the mother's lack of attention towards the daughter, as in 'The Lizardy Man and His Lady', but most of the time this is related to the child's own temperament and affinities. In 'Window', for instance, Bridget is quite aware of how much her family depends on Ma Lou and how this has created an unbreakable link:

Without Ma Lou, Brid thought, they'd be nothing [...] Ma Lou had been with them all her life; it was unthinkable that she should not be there always. Ma Lou belonged to them as they belonged to her. Brid used to think that their lives and Ma Lou's were intertwined like the Scotchman fig which grew on to the big silk-cotton tree, twisting and embedding itself into the trunk of the other to such an extent that it was hard to figure out which was the silk cotton and which the fig.[11]

Brid shares the housework with the old maid and even the struggles of life. She also has Dev, Ma Lou's grandson, as a playmate when they were children. This creates a community among them. Her dilemma becomes that of being fair skinned and standing out or being different. Such difference promises to make her poverty all the more visible.

Everyone else around was poor, too, ate turn cornmeal and shad just like them, or worse, had houses ten times worse than theirs, without floors even, and had no nice furniture like they had — the pieces that hadn't yet been sold. But that was different.[12]

All of this explains why at the end of the story she is eager to accept Dev's love in spite of his colour. In both stories: 'Discerner of Hearts' and 'Zig Zag', both girls, Theresa and Sadie, love their mother, but they are much more inclined towards their maid. In the second case, Sadie feels strongly attracted by Desrine's life and family and she is capable of seeing them with true human understanding. Besides, she finds out, and not unpleasantly, that she is very much akin to the maid. She knows that she is racially mixed and experiences the humiliation of being scorned for her 'bad' hair. In the symbolic dream at the end of the story, Sadie seems to have chosen her own family world, but there is real sorrow for having been cut out of what could be an affectionate relationship with Desrine and her children.

In contrast, Theresa, the protagonist of 'Discerner of Hearts', takes steps to align herself with her maid, Cissy, someone who understands her far better than anyone in her family, including her mother. She states, for example:

Cissy always told the truth. Cissy said things like 'Well, is true you not pretty like them other one here, but when you turn big woman you can fix yuself up...'. She would glow under Cissy's compliments...[13]

Theresa shows the possibility of the real merging of the two worlds, the two cultures. She faces them with respect and understanding. Through her relationship with Cissy and Father Burnham, she learns that what matters most is the human being's will. So she stops hiding. She is no longer afraid to show her own self and is, therefore, ready to accept everybody else and respect their values, despite appearance. The wisdom this little girl achieves should also be the achievement of the rest of the people in the world. I believe that Olive Senior has this in mind.

Notes

1. All quotations are taken from Olive Senior, *Discerner of Hearts*, Toronto: McClelland and Stewart Inc., 1995.
2. Olive Senior, *The Arrival of the Snake Woman*, Essex: Longman, 1989.
3. Olive Senior, 1995, p.157.
4. Ibid., pp.168-69.
5. Ibid.
6. Ibid., p.161.
7. Ibid., p.61.
8. Ibid., p.53.
9. Ibid., pp.16-17.
10. Ibid., p.11.
11. Ibid., p.63.
12. Ibid., p.61.
13. Ibid., p.12.

Joan Riley and Remembrance:

A Critical Reading of *Romance*[1]

ROSHI NAIDOO

As one of the first black British women writers to be printed and circulated by a high profile press, Joan Riley was the subject of much debate about the representation of black people, and her role and responsibility as an author. Since the publication of her first novel, *The Unbelonging*[2] in 1985 there has been contention over her portrayal of black men, the representation of abuse within black families, and her depiction of black self-hatred. Her work has been described as 'depressing', and she has faced the charge of affirming racist misconceptions and stereotypes about black life.[3] Other critics though, have admired Riley's courage in confronting uncomfortable issues and read her work as confirming that there is no singular 'black women's experience', as well as presenting a strong challenge to those who would ask that women's issues be sidelined for the 'greater' good of black political solidarity.

The contentions over her novels pointed, in part, to the responsibility she was perceived to have, for writing the collective experience of African-Caribbean women in Britain. Rather than considering the role of authors or debates about 'race' and representation, I want to suggest that Riley *can* be read as contributing something important to recording that thing called 'black women's experience' in Britain as long as we recognise that this 'experience' is not homogeneous. Collective histories of black Britain have overlooked many marginalised subjects, and these are the protagonists that turn up in Riley's novels with complex relationships between the 'self', dominant white culture and black communities in Britain. Her work reminds us that subjects negotiate their place in society through particular encounters which are shaped by gender, sexuality, social class, language, region and the body. *Romance*'s focus on a fat, black woman and her relationship to mass produced commodity culture does succeed in telling us something about African-Caribbean women in Britain and does succeed in contributing to something which can be seen as a collective memory, but it does that by bringing out the complexities of the relationship between individual experiences and that wider history.

I want to pursue this point by looking at the novel *Romance*, a literary work which underlines how the complexities of African-Caribbean women's subjectivity shape political consciousness. The novel thematises black women's relationships to texts, and uses romance fiction as a register through which to reflect how the character Verona comes to critical consciousness. Verona is a perfect example of a subject marginalised and alienated not just in relation to dominant British society but also to a wider African-Caribbean community, to her family and importantly to her body. As a fat black woman, Verona battles with forms of oppression not usually at the centre of black political struggles, yet the way in which she comes to critical consciousness illustrates to perfection that old feminist adage that the 'personal is political'.

The ironic title of the novel signals the theme of black women and texts. Verona, one of the two main protagonists in *Romance*, avidly consumes romance novels, using them to enhance both her fantasy life and her personal relationships. Rather than either condemning or condoning Verona's escapist fantasies, the novel uses the romance genre as a register against which her life can be read. For example, Verona's experiences can be juxtaposed to the neat, 'happy ever after' narrative closures which typify romantic novels, thus ironically setting her dreams of true love and eternal happiness against the historical actuality of her life.

Although Riley's style appears naturalistic and has been treated as such by critics,[4] *Romance* cannot strictly be termed a naturalist text despite its accessible, linear narrative structure and its use of naturalist techniques. The people in the novel wait at bus stops, prepare food and make child care arrangements, but other textual strategies move beyond naturalism and open up different ways of reading. Importantly, the title *Romance*, as a reference to the consumption of romance fiction, self-reflexively draws attention towards the practice of reading. Therefore, despite the naturalist elements, it cannot be read as a 'slice of life', either in its narrative techniques or in how it treats dilemmas of belonging and identity. While it conveys a milieu in accurate detail, the treatment of identity within it is not naturalist in the historical sense of showing the inexorable workings of heredity and environment. Rather it shows identity in progress, and the possibility of social change and personal liberation through political action, and thus avoids the pessimism of naturalism as it is traditionally understood in literary history.

Romance opens with Verona in crisis as she arrives home to find two white men from her workplace waiting outside to frame her for a robbery she did not commit. Verona's main concern is that her sister Desiree, ill and overly protective of her younger sibling, should not find out. Verona's anxieties are figured through the physical discomfort she experiences. 'The lumpy folds of flesh on her body were damp and clammy with trapped sweat, and under her grey duffel coat the drab, unfashionable brown dress clung uncomfortably to her skin'.[5] However, her body size is also a means of protection. When she experiences the 'out-of-control feeling'[6] and the fear of defending herself, she reminds herself of the safety she has within her large body and that other invasions can never be as terrible as her experience of rape. 'She was safe in the protection of her large body — and her experience of that other night, more terrifying than this could ever be'.[7]

Verona's remembering of her rape at the moment of being interrogated by the men juxtaposes the two experiences of invasion and being silenced. 'Her hands went automatically to her belly, pressing it in remembered pain. It had hurt for so long afterwards, she had wondered if he had bored a hole in her.' Therefore when one of them touches her arm she pulls away, 'suffocating with the contact and the painful memory'.[8] The representation of Verona's body illustrates again the point Gabriele Griffin makes about Riley's earlier novel *The Unbelonging*; that the body 'becomes the source not of celebration but of permanent anxiety'.[9] Griffin traces the powerlessness of Hyacinth, the emotionally and physically abused subject of the novel, through her alienation from her body and her inability to prevent it 'spilling over', such as losing control of her bladder.[10]

Like Hyacinth, Verona too has become alienated from her body because of sexual abuse. Her problematic feelings about her body are evoked through her relationship to food, the sexual encounters she seeks, and her need for romance fiction as her primary site of pleasurable gratification. Through the romance she is able to displace herself from the reality of her body. But unlike Hyacinth, Verona has more moments of confident articulation and more options for resistance which she discovers as the novel progresses. The support of her sister establishes that Verona is not totally emotionally isolated; therefore it is significant to the narrative that Verona has not told Desiree she was raped and that the rapist was Desiree's former boyfriend, Ronnie. Although she keeps it from Desiree, she is nevertheless resentful that her sister has not guessed. Therefore Verona punishes Desiree by withholding information on her private life. It is the incident which Verona is silent about, and the consequent actions it provokes, which cause her anxieties, depression and a sense of being enclosed within her body.

Verona's addiction to comfort food surfaces at moments when she wishes to defer confronting problems, such as facing the men from her workplace. 'She longed for a sweet, something to chew on to ease her nervousness'.[11] Food can be a source of communication and creativity for women but *Romance* also points to a darker side of women's relationships to food by looking at surreptitious eating as addiction. Pleasure and escapism are represented by two things for Verona: the eating of sweets and chocolates while reading her latest romance. The first produces a physical sensation of fulfilling a craving; the second fulfils her craving for sexual and emotional gratification — suggesting they both have drug-like properties.

The sort of romance fiction that Verona prefers is signalled as the formulaic *Mills and Boon* type, and although there is very little actual textual comparison between Verona's life and the romance text itself, it acts as a comparative presence. Through romance she evades her anxieties and problems; she displaces her fat, black body in favour of inhabiting the subject position of a slim, white heroine that the romance narrative celebrates. 'The earlier trauma of the day temporarily forgotten, Verona was totally immersed in the role of the beautiful blonde heroine, her whole being transported to the French countryside and the tall, dark, handsome count'.[12] Verona has found a means to escape the troubling aspects of herself and at first, seems in danger of being overcome by the personae she adopts in her mind. The terms of romance fiction also code Verona's fantasy life and how she mentally transforms the unappealing men she dates into dashing, handsome heroes.

Verona indulges her fantasy life at every opportunity, but the resulting feelings of well-being are achieved only momentarily because of the violent intrusions of the world around her. This is achieved in the text by the comparisons between Verona's fantasy with her drab reality. 'Her spirit lifted, her mind letting go of worry and shifting to her latest fantasy. Narrowly missing a spot where a dog had relieved itself, she moved reluctantly to the winding path'.[13] This day-dream transposes her from the winter of South London to the Mediterranean: 'The green fields drowsed under the blossom-scented heat of an imagined Spanish sun'.[14] In her fantasies she is desirable and desired. She imagines in the same stylised rhetoric of romantic novels and positions herself as the object of the male gaze: 'the brooding mysterious stranger, following her with his eyes. She could almost feel him watching her, drinking in the graceful sway of her hips, the slender beauty of her legs under the wide gipsy skirt and the soft glow of her long blonde hair'.[15] Lost in her own world she wanders into the road where the dull, urban landscape refuses to be displaced. 'A man in a brown Mini had stopped inches from her and was leaning red-faced through the window, looking almost as scared as she felt, and screaming obscenities'.[16]

To escape the memory of her rape she prefers to date older, unattractive white men, in the belief that she can protect herself from it happening again. Verona feels that through such relationships it is possible to have some measure of power, reflecting her need for control in a world where she has very little. Her control comes from exploiting the distance inherent in their difference.

> She realised that men like Guy were fascinated by her skin, finding the colour and texture alien and exotic. They were flattered by her attention. With them she was in control and could indulge her fantasy. She needed that control. It was her second line of defence, along with her huge size.[17]

Verona therefore acts out a complex system of inverted power games. This requires that 'reading Riley's reading of Verona reading romance', presents many available positions. My use of feminist critiques of romance to facilitate this might seem inappropriate as *Romance* is not romance fiction but is instead *about* it. However, they are useful in opening up the terms of a debate to which Riley's novel is a contribution.

Feminist cultural critics have theorised popular culture in relation to gender, and have introduced analyses of texts aimed primarily at women — such as teenage magazines, day-time soap operas and romance fiction — onto cultural studies agendas. They have analysed how such texts construct and celebrate conventional, patriarchal femininity and attempt to position women in regressive ways. However, they reject the idea that these texts *simply* subsume readers into a process of identification with all things regressively feminine. Instead, by focusing on the practice of reading or viewing, feminist critics have shown how women's relationships to reading romance fiction are more complex than just affirming and condoning traditional, dependent femininity. They have theorised these readers as being sophisticated subjects with the power to read around texts to fulfil different functions, rather than just being passively constructed by the text. Also, the actual practices of reading these texts are examined as subversive acts through which women assert their dissatisfaction with patriarchy, and establish their rights to pleasure and leisure. This point is made by Janice Radway in her focus on the practice of reading rather than on a textual analysis of constructions of femininity in the genre.[18]

Does this text present Verona's reading as an assertion of her need for pleasure? As a black, working-class woman, Verona's access to pleasurable gratification is limited. The times she finds to read are carved for herself away from an unfulfilling job and domestic rituals.

> She found a quiet corner against one of the wide, full-length glass doors to the courtyard. Getting comfortable in the cushioned black chair, she arranged her four romance novels in a neat pile on the floor and stared pensively at the dripping ivy outside.[19]

Given this context, it is possible to interpret an assertion of time for pleasure and space to be alone as a subversive act. In the dominant culture, images of labour, rather than leisure, are represented around women like Verona but to then recast this as a radical act given her economic status, leaves open the question of why she needs to have a miserable existence. Verona is in the library because she has been unfairly dismissed from work and is afraid to defend herself against the charges. She finds it increasingly difficult to shelve her worries by reading as they intrude on her fantasy life. '*How am I ever gonna keep this from Des?* she wondered unhappily, making no attempt to start the book on her lap'.[20] Thus the act of reading is only limited in its potential for being a subversive act. *Romance* resists the conclusion that Verona has no critical skills and simply falls victim to the negative effects of romance fiction. On the other hand, neither is her reading simply seen as negative escapism. Rather, it acts as a way of signalling her problems.

Cora Kaplan has traced some of the historical roots of the debates around fiction and femininity.[21] She notes that Mary Wollstonecraft was concerned that fiction aimed specifically at women could be the path to, as Kaplan says, 'conventional, dependent, degenerate femininity — to the positioning of the female self in the degraded, dependent role as "object of desire".[22] She locates this attitude around the eighteenth century, when the effects of reading on people were a fundamental concern for the ruling class. She notes that the prevalent opinion was that people of 'lesser' subjectivities, such as women or colonised people, were more susceptible to being influenced through reading and so could be influenced into disrupting the social order. Kaplan suggests that such attitudes have continued to shape the idea that women are manipulated by romantic fiction, and suggests a less regressive reading of fantasy and fiction using Freudian psychoanalysis.

Like Kaplan, Alison Light has also rejected the idea that romance fiction can simply be read as 'a form of oppressive ideology, which works to keep women in their socially and sexually subordinate place'.[23] She says that this position is a moralistic one which treats women as victims. She notes:

> Feminists must baulk at any such conclusion which implies that the vast audience of romance readers (with the exception of a few up-front intellectuals) are either masochistic or inherently stupid. Both text and reader are more complicated than that.[24]

Light also notes that pleasure must be analysed within political and social relations rather than viewing it as an antidote to them. I think these positions are apparent in *Romance* as the circumstances causing Verona's retreat into the world of fiction are explored. In other words, one cannot simply assert Verona's act of reading as inherently subversive any more than one can simply trace it as a rejection of her blackness, an embracing of patriarchal myths and evidence of her gullibility. Verona's awareness of why she needs to retreat into these narratives exposes both positions as too simplistic.

Verona is aware that she is considered superficial and shallow for what she reads ('She closed the book, pushing it guiltily under her pillow'[25]), and is aware that the stories draw her into a world of white identification. However, Verona does not reject identification with black people; rather she engages in a conscious splitting of her subjectivity, with an acknowledgement of the function romance fiction has for her. *Romance* resists presenting Verona as a passive victim of romance's myths, or as a puppet of consumer culture, although it refuses subsequently to validate the activity as harmless or as empowering for her. Verona has a keen awareness of racism, sexism and state violence. It is she who tells Desiree not to let John, Desiree's husband, push her around, and herself stands up to his bullying. Similarly, she does not necessarily represent the unreconstructed figure in the text, even when compared to their friend Mara, who represents self-supporting, assertive, black womanhood. Mara and her friend Olu appear to be patronising Verona when they ask whether she has seen *Woza Albert*, the satirical play about apartheid in South Africa.[26] Verona realises that she avoids anything about South Africa because it makes her 'furious and depressed'. Hence her political awareness is not undermined by her taste in books; rather it is a question of her response to her anger. Verona's tactic of blocking out unpleasant facts of life draws attention to the fact that the political responses of black subjects are not uniform. By establishing that Verona does possess critical skills, the idea that she is a victim of false consciousness is rejected. As a result, the theme of romance fiction becomes a starting point for other issues such as women's dissatisfaction with marriage and importantly how women negotiate male violence.

Verona's rape is a crucial factor in her retreat into fiction. Tania Modleski also rejects the idea that romance fiction is read by women masochistically as a simple affirmation of dominant masculine ideology.[27] Modleski analyses the structure of mass-produced fictions in this genre, looking at how the male's brutality and initial rejection of the heroine in formulaic sagas is presented as his suppressed desire for her: 'Male brutality comes to be seen as a manifestation not of contempt, but of love'.[28] This interpretation, she feels, provides an outlet for women's resentments towards men. She notes that the extremes to which these novels resort to make men's hostility bearable show how deeply aggrieved women are by it.[29] In one of the few actual representations of a romance narrative, male violence is depicted as erotic: Verona is deeply engrossed as Alberto traps the heroine with his strength with an 'edge of violence' in his voice.[30] Here, a scene of violence can be recast as an act of seduction — a means of exorcising Verona's bad memories. However, the crucial point is that Verona uses a genre with white heroes and heroines because of her fear of young black men in particular, and because of the belief that her fat black body is not desirable; therefore 'race' and the romance require specific consideration.

Romance draws attention to how eroticism is frequently textually represented through the codes of cultural difference. In her fantasy life Verona takes on an identification with the white, female heroine. In her relationships she actively seeks dates with white men in order to fantasise these encounters into romance fiction scenarios. These images determine how she constructs her sexual relationships.

> Normally she would pretend Guy was one of the heroes in her novels and she was an innocent blonde-haired virgin. She would walk along feeling special, then she would catch a glimpse of their reflection in a shop window and depression would descend. It would be such a shock — the fat black woman looking squat and untidy, and the old leathery-skinned white man. But still she would continue the charade, hiding her disillusionment.[31]

This retreat from young, black men poses several questions. Does Verona associate the rape by Ronnie as being determined by his blackness and his youth? Or is it a case of her not wanting to be reminded of the incident by coming into contact with a similar body? Either way, this points to how 'race' and sex as discourses constantly invoke one another.

Cultural representations construct and reinforce sexual meaning in racial categories from a particular history of domination and subjugation. The sexuality of black bodies have historically been invested with particular meanings against which 'normal' sexuality can be measured.[32] Has the myth of the aggravated sexual potency of black men been internalised by Verona?[33] Would she have been fearful of all white men if a white man had raped her, or do the representations of white masculinity undermine the possibility of such a conclusion? If normative masculinity is constructed against the sexuality of the 'other' which is loaded with particular meaning, it is more difficult to extend the sexual aggression of one white man into a characteristic of a racial type, whereas the opposite is true for the sexual aggression of a black man.

What else happens when 'race' enters the matrix of fiction, femininity and the commodification of desire? In her fantasy life Verona positions herself within a discourse of beauty and desirability which necessitates her seeing her fat, black body as undesirable. The psychological impact of dominant cultural representations are interrogated as the text asks what damage is done as Verona shifts her subject position to realise the pleasures within the romance genre. Her fantasies show her masquerading as the ideal, feminine woman which her novels privilege, so conveying how her lack of sexual confidence and low self-esteem are related to the internalisation of this perception of herself as fundamentally undesirable to attractive men.

Verona's body is patrolled by a racist, patriarchal culture. She experiences feelings of invasion, distortion, displacement and being uncomfortable in her own body, which result from trying to marry a fantasy self-perception with what she sees in the mirror; desire and desirability become confused into a white configuration. The depiction of Verona's low self-esteem evokes how subjects experience the violences of racism both internally and externally. Stuart Hall notes:

It is one thing to position a subject or set of peoples as the Other of a dominant discourse. It is quite another thing to subject them to that "knowledge", not only as a matter of imposed will and domination, by the power of inner compulsion and subjective con-formation to the norm.[34]

Hall expresses how subjugated peoples can internalise dominant discourses, and judge themselves critically for failing to conform to them.[35] These power relations require an analysis of how meanings attached to a signifier, such as beauty, are experienced within individual psyches. One of the appeals of Black Power ideology was the challenge to beauty myths captured in the phrase 'black is beautiful' though black feminist critics questioned the notion that adopting African dress or 'natural' hair styles — which, particularly in the 1960s and 70s, was seen as an important indication of the rejection of white cultural imperialism — was the most significant contribution they had to make to political struggles.[36]

Racism, sexual violence and beauty myths are all culpable in turning Verona into an introverted and troubled person. Riley therefore sensitively addresses in *Romance* what she has tackled in previous novels: that is, how one of racism's severest manifestations is the turning in of racism against oneself.[37]

'Race' and femininity conspire to attach particular meanings to black and white womanhood; the absence of women like her in romance fiction perhaps subconsciously convinces Verona that she cannot expect to be treated as a 'real' woman because she does not conform to standards of desirable femininity. By posing the subtleties of the psychological violences which Verona has endured, Riley ensures that she cannot simply be dismissed as traitor to black consciousness.

The novel therefore also poses the question of whether there should be more images of black people in mass-produced consumer culture. Would Verona's emotional health improve by merely substituting a white romance heroine with a black one? African American critic Susan Willis considers black people's role as consumers, but not as producers, of dominant culture, and asks, 'can we conceive of mass culture as black culture? Or is mass culture by its very definition white culture with a few blacks in it?'[38] It is apparent that the presence of black 'super-models' such as Naomi Campbell, does not constitute a radical challenge to western beauty myths. Her emaciated body shape confirms the desirability of impossible thinness which tyrannises black and white women alike. It will be important in the future to see whether there is any correlation between the increase of thin, black models and the number of black girls affected by eating disorders.[39] Problems such as this challenge the idea that the inclusion of black women in mass-produced images is necessarily liberatory. Other issues of power require consideration when thinking about 'race' and representation, rather than simply including black subjects within dominant cultural images. Riley's novel also takes this position by presenting the complex operations of power in Verona's life which would make the existence of black romance heroines too simple a solution to her problems.

Verona's eventual rejection of romance does not result in her immediately embracing a 'black is beautiful' ethos, emphasising that the move from internalising white supremacist values to a rejection of them is neither easy, nor an unproblematic inversion of the terms of reference. When she is made pregnant and abused by a young and attractive white lover she has to reconsider her relationship to all men; therefore it is not a joyous revelation, but one born out of more sadness. At first it seems that Verona is going to fulfil the romance impulse and get her man. Steve is not like Guy but has an 'open, friendly face and a boyish grin that flashed out often'.[40] 'Now, with Steve, she wouldn't have to fantasise about the heroes in her novels'.[41] Verona believes he is a writer and persists in framing their relationship in romance terms. When she visits his flat and finds it in a mess she thinks:

It was just like in *Concertina Love*, she recalled, where Alain went into decline and April found him in squalor when his mother urged her to visit him. Verona felt happier thinking of it in that context. Poor Steve, no doubt he was so busy, so sunk in his work, he hadn't been able to find the time to clean up...and anyway it really was no job for a man.[42]

The persistence of these fantasies indicates there will be no happy resolution for her. After they have sex she stops at the library to read the 'story of *Harem Queen*' (the orientalist title again drawing attention to the intertwining of racist and sexist codes), still anxious that she doesn't have enough money for a bar of chocolate.[43]

Verona's sea change occurs through finally acknowledging that the promises of the romance narrative are illusory, and that 'the mistake she made was thinking they [bad men] only came in black skins'.[44] It is significant that, at the end, it is implied she is reading her last romance novel, with the children's book by a black author by her side as a signifier of the future. Verona's psychic journey is wrapped up in coming to terms with her own body. She puts behind her the recurring nightmare of her rape partly through confession to her sister, and through the realisation that avoiding black men will not help her. She asserts her independence from her sister which is signalled as necessary for her to mature. The gradual changes in response to her physicality are not literal, but in how her perception of her identity as a fat, black woman changes. At the end of the novel Desiree is shocked at how confident Verona sounds. 'Verona's voice nearly made her jump. Somehow she had expected that her sister would be full of melancholy, not sounding so strong and capable'.[45]

Overall, the position *Romance* reaches on Verona reading romance is similar to the conclusion Alison Light comes to: 'Romance reading then becomes less a political sin or moral betrayal than a kind of "literary anorexia" which functions as a protest against, as well as a restatement of, oppression'.[46] Verona's retreat into fiction and choice of lovers is a protest against her powerlessness and a means of healing herself. Sexual attack has brought about an internalisation of the pain and is manifested in forms of self harm. Being raped by someone known to her and her family, fuels her silence. Because she feels she cannot tell, her rejection of young, black men is a visible act of revenge on Ronnie, the man who raped her, and a way of channelling her anger. Through Steve she learns the futility of this method of survival the hard way. Her introversion is also a means of directing anger at Desiree for bringing Ronnie into their home, for not guessing what he did, and especially for not picking up the hints which Verona drops. Similarly, the romance theme allows Verona to be understood as both railing against, as well as being overcome by, a culture which has deemed her body undesirable and which has regulated her sexuality. She is both trapped, and in rebellion against being trapped. However, her strategies for coping are exposed as misplaced, as the novel considers how she may recover more successfully.

Through the contradictions and dilemmas which surface in *Romance*, Riley's characters emerge with a sharper critical consciousness. Although terrible things have happened to them, neither Verona nor Desiree can be seen as victims. Perhaps this is a good example of how black women can be represented 'positively', without recourse to brushing over complex issues of power. Riley does here what she always does: she tells stories of those seldom the focus of novels. *Romance* describes the body in relation to anxieties and dysfunctions in black women's lives, and figures themes of psychological and physical recovery, and the roles played by cultural identity and political consciousness. It considers how black women can become political agents, become emotionally fulfilled and deal with contradictions in their lives by learning to speak out. Consequently, it questions the nature of belonging, whether to a cultural or political community, or belonging within one's own body. Riley's narratives enable those who would otherwise be marginalised, not only from dominant white culture, but from the 'collective' memory of African-Caribbean women in Britain, to be part of that story. Rather than dwelling on whether or not Riley presents 'negative' or 'depressing' depictions, perhaps it would be more appropriate to understand her work as part of a body of writing which has told distinct, but related tales of being an African-Caribbean woman in Britain.

Notes

1. Joan Riley, *Romance*, London: The Women's Press, 1988. All references are to this edition.
2. Joan Riley, *The Unbelonging*, London: The Women's Press, 1985.
3. Jacqui Roach and Petal Felix, 'Black Looks', in Lorraine Gamman and Margaret Marshment (eds.), *The Female Gaze — Women as Viewers of Popular Culture*, London: The Women's Press, 1988, p.135.
4. See Patricia Duncker, *Sisters and Strangers — An Introduction to Contemporary Feminist Fiction*, Oxford UK and Cambridge USA: Blackwell, 1992, pp.247-49.
5. Riley, 1988, p.1.
6. Ibid., p.3.
7. Ibid.
8. Ibid.
9. Gabriele Griffin, '"Writing the Body": Reading Joan Riley, Grace Nichols and Ntozake Shange', in Gina Wisker (ed.), *Black Women's Writing*, Basingstoke and London: Macmillan Press, 1993, p.21.
10. Ibid.
11. Riley, 1988, p.4.
12. Ibid., p.17.
13. Ibid., p.34.
14. Ibid.
15. Ibid., pp.34-5.
16. Ibid., p.35.
17. Ibid., p.19.
18. Janice A. Radway, *Reading the Romance — Women, Patriarchy, and Popular Literature*, London and New York: Verso, 1987.
19. Riley, 1988, p.40.
20. Ibid.
21. Cora Kaplan, '*The Thorn Birds:* Fiction, Fantasy, Femininity', in *Sea Changes — Essays on Culture and Feminism* , London and New York: Verso, 1986, pp.117-46.

22. Ibid., p.121.
23. Alison Light, '"Returning to Manderley" — Romance Fiction, Female Sexuality and Class', in Terry Lovell (ed.), *British Feminist Thought — A Reader*, Oxford: Basil Blackwell, 1990, pp.325-44, p.326.
24. Ibid., p.326.
25. Riley, 1988, p.18.
26. Ibid., p.76.
27. Tania Modleski, *Loving with a Vengeance — Mass-Produced Fantasies for Women*, New York and London: Routledge, 1988.
28. Ibid., p.41.
29. Ibid., p.58.
30. Riley, pp.107-108.
31. Ibid., p.74.
32. For example, see Sander L. Gilman, 'Black Bodies, White Bodies: Toward an Iconography of Female Sexuality in Late Nineteenth-Century Art, Medicine and Literature', in James Donald and Ali Rattansi (eds.), *'Race', Culture and Difference*, London: Sage Publications in association with The Open University, 1992, pp.171-197.
33. For discussions on the representation of black masculinity and sexuality see Kobena Mercer and Isaac Julien, 'Race, Sexual Politics and Black Masculinity: A Dossier', in Rowena Chapman and Jonathan Rutherford (eds.), *Male Order — Unwrapping Masculinity*, London: Lawrence and Wishart, 1988, pp.97-164, particularly 'Territories of the Body', pp.131-141.
34. Stuart Hall, 'Cultural Identity and Diaspora', in Jonathan Rutherford (ed.), *Identity - Community, Culture, Difference*, London: Lawrence and Wishart, 1990, p.226.
35. See Frantz Fanon, *Black Skin, White Masks*, London and Sydney: Pluto Press, 1986, first published in 1952. Fanon's text remains a seminal work on the psychological effects of racism on black people.
36. See Lola Young's reading of the film *Burning an Illusion*, directed by Menelik Shabbazz, 1981, in Lola Young, *Fear of the Dark — 'Race', Gender and Sexuality in the Cinema*, London and New York: Routledge, 1996, pp.153-161.
37. Joan Riley in an interview with Marla Bishop, *Spare Rib*, 156, (July, 1985), 27.

38. Susan Willis, 'I Shop Therefore I Am: Is There a Place for Afro-American Culture in Commodity Culture', in Cheryl A. Wall (ed.), *Changing Our Own Words — Essays on Criticism, Theory, and Writing by Black Women*, London: Routledge, 1990, p.175.

39. The *Independent on Sunday*, 25 September, 1994 ran an article by Linda Grant on the different relationships that black and white women had with their bodies. It cited research carried out at the University of Arizona which, from a sample group of 250 teenagers, found that 90% of the white teenage girls expressed dissatisfaction with their own bodies, whereas the black teenage girls had a healthier attitude to their looks. The article considered how black women in Britain also have distinctly different attitudes to size and body shape. The black women's magazine, *Pride*, it noted, had consistently bigger models than those found in magazines such as *Elle*. The editor-in-chief of another magazine, *Visions in Black*, said she would not run a diet feature in her magazine, because although some black women did diet, her experience was many would rather defend their voluptuous figures. The article also talked about the Big and Beautiful contest for black women and noted that a 'similar contest, in the Caribbean, is a massive event, shown on television across the region and attracting major sponsorship'. Margaret Busby interviewed in the article said that with the visibility of more black women in the media one must take into account that 'the black faces you see in your newspapers are ones chosen by the white media'. If the white media choose black models who fit into white media conceptions of desirable shape and body size what will the implications for black women be? Grant ends her article by asking: 'In 10 years' time will Brixton Weight Watchers be full of black teenagers desperate to weigh seven stone?'

40. Riley, 1988, p.171.

41. Ibid., p.173.

42. Ibid., p.172.

43. Ibid., pp.176-77.

44. Ibid., p.225.

45. Ibid., p.222.

46. Light, "Returning to Manderley", p.342.

Imagining the 'Unimaginable'

Guadeloupean women writers and the representation of Black female desire

SAM HAIGH

Those writers whose names occur with the most frequency during discussions of women's writing of the 'French Antilles' are undoubtedly Maryse Condé and Simone Schwarz-Bart, both from Guadeloupe. The work of these writers, however, owes much to that of a slightly older generation of Guadeloupean women, a generation which includes writers such as Michèle Lacrosil and Jacqueline Manicom, writers whose work has certainly received some critical attention but which, out of print and out of favour, has of late begun to be forgotten. Here, I should like to remember these writers as important precursors — 'foremothers' even — while at the same time examining the relationship of their work to that of another, older literary foremother from Guadeloupe's 'sister island' of Martinique: Mayotte Capécia. Although Capécia's initial popularity as a writer was such that Lacrosil's editor suggested she capitalise on it by examining similar themes, she has now fallen into disrepute. Together, however, these three writers may be seen to have formed an important starting point for the ever-developing 'tradition' of black Antillean women writers.

Capécia wrote two novels *Je Suis Martiniquaise*[1] and *La Négresse blanche*,[2] and it is the former that I shall examine here. It tells the story — apparently autobiographical, but at least deeply personalised — of Mayotte, a young Martinican mulatto woman who, since discovering that her grandmother on her mother's side was white, has been driven by a single desire: to 'lighten the race' still further by marrying a white man. Shunning all black men who present themselves as potential partners, she eventually meets André, a white, French soldier stranded in Martinique during the second World War, and becomes his mistress. She admits to being in love, primarily, with André's blue eyes and his blond hair, and is delighted when she gives birth to a light-skinned son. Once the war is over, however, André returns to France, leaving her instructions to bring up their son in admiration of him.

From this, it is perhaps immediately obvious why Capécia's work is not terribly popular today, but its lack of popularity has much to do with a reading of *Je Suis Martiniquaise* which appears in Frantz Fanon's seminal text of 1952, *Black Skin White Masks*.[3] In his chapter 'The woman of colour and the white man', Fanon berates Capécia for having written what he sees as a thoroughly 'negrophobic' novel, and he accuses her of having betrayed both black men in particular and the black race in general. And this, despite the fact that the distinguished Martinican psychiatrist, writer and activist spends much of the rest of *Black Skin White Masks* analysing what has come to be known as the 'lactification complex': the collective, Antillean 'neurosis' which, according to Fanon, leads black, colonised subjects like Mayotte precisely to seek to 'become white'.

In great detail, Fanon explains what he sees as the very particular predicament of those peoples transplanted and colonised, specifically, by the French. As is well known, the French colonial enterprise was very explicitly presented not only as a 'civilising mission' but, more, as an attempt at the complete 'assimilation' of the colonised people and country. That is, at the wholesale importation and imposition of French culture in order, ostensibly at least, to remake the Caribbean colonies in the image of France, and to fashion their transplanted inhabitants in the image of the French.

Fanon describes how slowly, within this culture of assimilation, the Antillean people come inevitably to share the French worldview imposed upon it. Thus, for example, the black Antillean, like the white Frenchman, is negrophobic: 'in the [European] collective unconscious, black = ugliness, sin, darkness, immorality... If I order my life like a moral man, I simply am not a Negro'.[4] If the black Antillean feels 'the purity of [his/her] soul',[5] then s/he can convince him or herself that s/he is not black: s/he comes to regard him or herself not only as French, but as 'white'. Fanon goes on to describe, however, how this cultural identification, this sense of 'inner whiteness', is necessarily a very precarious one, since the French colonial enterprise was never actually to create French subjects in the colonies who would have the same status as those in the 'Metropole'. And it is this that the assimilated Antillean, according to Fanon, will eventually discover — when s/he goes to France (or when, as during the Second World War, 'France' comes to the Antilles) and encounters the white, French person's refusal to accept their black counterpart as equally 'French'.

Fanon describes his own such encounter as an assimilated Martinican in France, an encounter articulated, specifically, as one with the white gaze. He recalls being pointed out in the street by a white child — 'Look, a Negro, I'm frightened'[6] — and it is at this moment that he is forced to realise that, however culturally 'white' he feels, he will never, because of his black skin, be accepted as such. It is for this reason that Fanon speaks of the white gaze as something which is feared by the assimilated Antillean, for it destroys his/her sense of self, causing a split between a felt sense of 'inner whiteness' and visible, external blackness. However, he goes on to explain how, at the same time and apparently paradoxically, the white gaze is something which is also desired by the black Antillean, for it is the white other's recognition of the black Antillean's cultural whiteness which, alone, is capable of affirming his/her worth, of matching the way in which s/he is perceived by others with his/her self-perception. What the assimilated Antillean ideally seeks in the white other's gaze is desire: desire is the apogee of this self-affirming recognition by the other. As Fanon explains: 'I wish to be recognised not as black but as white... who but a white woman can do this for me? By loving me she proves that I am worthy of white love. I am loved like a white man. I am a white man'.[7]

It is this desire to be desired by the white other which may then lead on to the other, more extreme and more literal, attempt to 'become white', to bring external appearance into line with 'inner whiteness': that of miscegenation — the desire, like that of Mayotte, to escape one's blackness by marrying (in Fanon's terms) someone lighter than oneself and, ideally, by producing light-skinned children. Not only is the black Antillean thus recognised by the white other as worthy of white love, but s/he is able also to produce 'proof' of entrance into the white world.

In the light of his detailed and sympathetic account of the potentially damaging psychological consequences of the French colonial ideology of assimilation, Fanon's attitude towards Capécia's novel seems paradoxical indeed. And most especially given his attitude, in the parallel chapter 'The man of colour and the white woman', to a novel by René Maran in which the narrator Jean Veneuse, an educated and assimilated black Antillean, feels so distanced from black Antillean women that his only course of action is to attempt to marry a white woman, Andrée Marielle. Surprisingly, Fanon sees no evidence of 'betrayal' here, and treats Veneuse sympathetically, as a tragic figure.

The discrepancy, here, between Fanon's analysis of Mayotte and that of Jean Veneuse would seem mainly to reflect his inability, or unwillingness, to examine the huge difference that gender makes to the already complex, sexualised relationship between coloniser and colonised that he otherwise describes so eloquently. What becomes clear is that his analysis of the 'lactification complex' is highly gendered (perhaps because so highly personalised?): it is a model based upon Fanon's assumptions about the black, assimilated *man's* problems of self-identification, and attempts to solve them, and it does not transfer easily to the situation of the black, assimilated woman. In fact, despite occasional references to the possibility that the power relationship between a black man and a white woman may be different from that between a black woman and a white man, and despite a whole section devoted to what he calls the 'psychosexuality' of white women, Fanon admits quite readily, in answer to an imagined reader asking him what he has to say specifically about the 'woman of colour': 'I know nothing about her'.[8] The only piece of 'information' that he is able to offer is that, like the white woman, the black Antillean woman typically feels threatened by black men. And this, as he implies elsewhere in his study, is apparently because of the twin preoccupation of lactification: the fear of 'regression', of 'blackening' the race instead of lightening it.

What emerges here is Fanon's inability to dissociate black women from the most extreme, and literal, form that the lactification complex can take — miscegenation. Fanon has a clearly hierarchical notion of the different responses that may be provoked by lactification, and the desire literally to 'lighten the race', is at the bottom, valid only if regarded as a means 'supplementing' or confirming an already achieved degree of intellectual or cultural whiteness. While he has no difficulty imagining black men, like Jean Veneuse, who are capable of 'educating' themselves into whiteness first, he repeatedly finds it impossible to dissociate black women from the bodily, from the 'growing white from within' that pregnancy can be seen literally to represent for them.[9]

It is for reasons such as these that it becomes informative to examine the work of Antillean women writers such as Lacrosil and Manicom. In Lacrosil's 1961 novel *Cajou*[10] and Manicom's 1972 novel *Mon Examen de blanc*,[11] the 'gaps' in Fanon's analysis of the lactification complex and black female desire begin to be filled in, as the two writers also provide more rigorous analyses of the issues than did their foremother Capécia. Both Cajou, the narrator of Lacrosil's novel, and Madévie, the narrator of Manicom's, are assimilated, mulatto Guadeloupeans who, beginning where *Je Suis Martiniquaise* left off, have left their island for France. Here, like the assimilated Antilleans described by Fanon, they are made painfully aware of their misguided belief in the possibility of real assimilation, as they both embark upon relationships with white French men — blond-haired, blue-eyed Germain, nicknamed 'the Viking', in the case of Cajou, and the bourgeois fellow medical student Xavier in the case of Madévie. Both of these relationships mirror — often self-consciously — that of Mayotte and André in Capécia's novel. In actual fact, Madévie is shown to be more naïve even than Mayotte in her expectations of her relationship with Xavier. She genuinely believes that he will disregard her black skin in the light of her cultural 'whiteness' and having (in her terms) 'offered' him her virginity, she is shocked by his, and his family's, racism when she tells him that she is pregnant. Clearly echoing Capécia, she asks: 'Why wouldn't he marry her? She was prepared to become white to please him, and to give him little white children later on'.[12]

Eventually, she realises that neither he nor his family will ever accept her as a legitimate wife and she decides to leave and to take charge of the situation on her own — by aborting her four-month old foetus. It is this abortion which marks both Manicom's point of departure with Capécia, and her interrogation of Fanon, for it clearly signifies a refusal to submit to the apparently inexorable logic of the lactification complex — a refusal to submit to domination both by race and by gender. It is an attempt at resistance which, though rather self-destructive, sets a precedent for later, more positive moves towards self-liberation.

The relationship between Cajou and Germain is also marked by black female resistance. From the start, Cajou shows no interest in the alleged benefits of lactification. It is Germain who decides that the combined effects of a white man's desire and the production of his light-skinned child will cure her feelings of inferiority and self-loathing. Remembering her own struggles to come to terms with her difference from her pale-skinned mother, though, Cajou sees only what for her is the inevitable future pain of her mulatto child. Like Madévie, she chooses instead to refuse the logic of lactification and to rid herself of Germain's child — this time by throwing herself from a bridge into the river Seine.

This suicide, which Cajou herself sees in very positive terms, can be read not only as a refusal of lactification as domination by race but also, like Madévie's decision to abort her child, as a refusal to be dominated by gender — to have her fertility manipulated by the 'white master'. And as modes of resistance they both, of course, recall the legacy of slavery which is inevitably theirs. Within the strictly limiting situation of slavery, both suicide and abortion can be seen as amongst the only positive modes of resistance, just as within the limited situation in which Cajou and Madévie find themselves this may also be seen to be true. However self-destructive, it is an action which suggests that, in the light of the violence which has historically structured the relationship between black women and white men, the black Antillean woman may not desire the white man's whiteness in quite such an unproblematic manner as Fanon imagines.

This, too, is suggested by Cajou in other ways, for if Cajou is never portrayed as a desiring subject within the context of her relationship with Germain, black female desire is portrayed in Lacrosil's text as outside of the heterosexual domain. Cajou's final suicide can be read as a refusal not only of compulsory motherhood but, in another radical departure from Fanon's lactification script, also of compulsory heterosexuality. Just as Fanon's study of black-white relations is marked by a failure to address sexual difference, so it is marked by a failure to consider the possibility of same-sex interracial relationships, and by overt homophobia on the rare occasions that he alludes to the question of homosexuality at all. In fact, he confesses himself to be entirely unable to imagine what homosexuality 'means', saying: 'I have never been able, without revulsion, to hear a man say of another man: "he is so sensual!" I do not know what the sensuality of a man is. Imagine a woman saying of another woman: "She's so terribly desirable — she's darling!"'[13]

It is this 'unimaginable' desire which is fundamental to the narrative of *Cajou*: from the start, Cajou identifies with, and desires, women. Her 'first love' is Stéphanie, the white girl from next-door who provides her with an opportunity to discover what her own blackness represents when it is defined against the whiteness of others. She is obsessed with every part of Stéphanie's body, especially with her eyes and her hair, which is long, straight and European. She describes her very definitely sexual desire for Stéphanie in terms which are never echoed in her descriptions of her relationship with Germain, and which are recalled only in her later relationship with another woman, Marjolaine, her first friend in Paris and initially the lover of Germain. Like Manicom, Lacrosil succeeds in complicating Fanon's analysis of the lactification complex, imagining a form of desire unimaginable for him and suggesting once again that black female desire for whiteness cannot be reduced, as Fanon seems to imply, to the most basic desire for literal miscegenation. For Cajou, as for Jean Veneuse, what is important is gaining 'symbolic' (that is, cultural rather than biological) whiteness via *recognition* from the white other.

However, neither Stéphanie nor Marjolaine reciprocates Cajou's desire, and for Stéphanie in particular Cajou's adoration simply serves to consolidate her already-burgeoning sense of herself as white and superior. We are thus shown how same-sex relationships are by no means necessarily devoid of the play of power that structures heterosexual relationships, and especially within this particular interracial context. Whether heterosexual or homosexual, the lactification complex is based upon the desire simply to be desired, and it thus eradicates the possibility of *active* desire. It is only in Manicom's later text that alternative, less 'reactive', forms of black female desire begin to be imagined.

If Madévie's abortion can be seen to have represented an early, and limited, attempt at resistance, her life after her medical studies in Paris, working in a women's clinic in Guadeloupe, provides more positive examples of such resistance, as her former relationships with Xavier conditions her subsequent relationships with men. First, her relationship with Cyril, the white, French doctor with whom she works, is one which is characterised by the dual play of cultural and sexual power. He is constantly portrayed — and he portrays himself — as a representative of white French, culture and in this capacity he feels it necessary to offer Madévie and his other Guadeloupean staff gifts of 'culture' — books and records with which we know, from Madévie's narration of her relationship with Xavier, that she, at least, is perfectly familiar.

It is specifically his power as a white man which Madévie finds most disturbing, though she observes his overtly misogynistic treatment of his black, female patients. He treats their bodies with such violence and contempt that Madévie frequently becomes personally afraid of him, a fear which is almost always articulated as a fear of his 'ghostly' whiteness. The two, conjoined forms of power — cultural and sexual — which he exerts over her come to be represented by specific, and metonymic, parts of his body: his large, white shoulders which she imagines might suffocate her; his pink, sunburnt ears which recall the Creole term for French temporary residents of the Antilles, 'zoreilles'; and, above all, his gaze — a gaze which, like the black, assimilated Antillean described by Fanon, she constantly fears and desires upon her. Importantly though, and in contrast both with Fanon's apparently archetypal Antillean, and with her own former self as Xavier's lover, Madévie refuses to allow herself to become transfixed either by her fear or her desire. And this has everything to do with the level of self-awareness which she has achieved since, and because of, her relationship with him.

Since her return from Paris, Madévie has avoided examining her own reflection in mirrors, but after having recounted, and come to terms with, her relationship with Xavier, she suddenly experiences a wish to do so. As she stands before the mirror, she describes, in detail, the contours of her face — her skin, her hair, her lips. These are the signifiers of blackness which once filled her, like Cajou before her, with despair at the difference between her black reflection and her inner conviction of whiteness. Now, however, she recognises herself in her reflection and, having until now related her life story to Cyril entirely in the third person, she exclaims, as she looks: 'that's no longer really Madévie, it's me'.[14]

She is finally able to recognise herself, as Cajou never was, as a black, Antillean woman, and it's this fact which determines her relationship with Cyril. She no longer needs his gaze upon her; she no longer needs him to recognise her in order to feel assured of her self-worth. What she demands from him, if anything, is that he recognises her as black, as different from him, rather than as the same. But he is unable to do this — and for this reason he is represented throughout as fundamentally gazeless. He is always unable to see her properly, and she is always unable — or, perhaps she refuses — to discern his gaze: his eyes are hidden behind thick glasses which allow only what's described as 'an eyeless gaze'.[15] More than this, he is depicted as being afraid of her gaze upon him, for an active, black gaze threatens his own sense of himself as white and French — a sense of self dependent, like the colonial ideology of assimilation, on a conviction of cultural superiority.

Faced with Cyril's inability to recognise and to match her self-transformation, she turns away from their increasingly claustrophobic relationship and, instead, towards Gilbert, a black, Guadeloupean pro-independence activist. It is from him that she finally gains the external recognition of her blackness which is vital to her emerging sense of self. As she comments: 'he has such a beautiful gaze: long, narrow eyes — deep black, surrounded by pale blue. I'm sure that it's his gaze that gives me this feeling of well-being'.[16] Her relationship with Gilbert is unfortunately short-lived, for he is killed by the French police during a protest. It is also fundamentally flawed, for Madévie assumes an extremely subordinate position throughout: in many ways she simply moves from being fixed and objectified by the white male gaze to a position in which she is fixed and objectified by that of the black man. It is nonetheless, however, the most mutually satisfying relationship not only in Manicom's novel, but in all of the texts examined here. It is also, of course, the kind of same-race relationship which, while it is never explored as a realistic possibility (and certainly not in terms of the gendered power relations which may structure it) is implicitly held up as an ideal by Fanon, as he takes Capécia to task primarily for betraying black men for white.

Importantly, it is with this relationship — on which the novel ends — that the legacy of Capécia's novel also continues to be felt. Despite Mayotte's inability to form lasting partnerships with black men, *Je Suis Martiniquaise* does end on a slightly more positive, and less 'treacherous' note than Fanon is willing to admit. First, we see Mayotte's reconciliation with her father, a man much blacker than herself and her mulatto mother. Their relationship, though sometimes difficult, is the most enduring one of the entire novel — and she admits that she has with her father a level of understanding always absent from her relationship with André. Second, is the degree of self-awareness — admittedly extremely limited, to which even she accedes.

Although she continues to be proud of her white son, she is perfectly aware both that he by no means guarantees her access into the white world and that he actually separates her from the black community in which she now lives. She recognises the disapproval of her community — their accusations, pre-empting Fanon, that she has 'betrayed the race'. While it remains impossible for her to imagine having acted differently herself, she is conscious that attitudes generally are changing in post-war Martinique, as she notes the beginnings of a movement of what she calls 'emancipation'; of rebellion especially against the power of the local whites; and of black pride. What is striking, is that despite Mayotte's undeniable negrophobia, Capécia, in 1948, looks towards the future in terms of exactly the changing attitudes towards colour and self-liberation which, via the work of Lacrosil, we see articulated so much more clearly twenty four years later in Manicom's novel. And it is for this reason, in a way that Fanon's damning critique simply does not allow for, that she can be seen to have been an important precursor both to writers like Manicom, and Lacrosil, and then to subsequent generations of Antillean women who have gone on to look beyond the lactification complex, and to imagine the many and complex forms that female desire may take.

Notes

1.   Mayotte Capécia, *Je Suis Martiniquaise*, Paris: Corréa, 1948.
2.   Mayotte Capécia, *La Négresse blanche*, Paris: Corréa, 1950.
3.   Frantz Fanon, *Black Skin, White Masks*, trans., Charles Lam Markmann, London: Pluto Press, 1986.
4.   Ibid, p.155.

5. Ibid, p.156.

6. Ibid, p.112.

7. Ibid, p.63.

8. Ibid, p.179.

9. This association of man with 'mind' and woman with 'body' is extended also to the authors of the two texts examined by Fanon, for he repeatedly conflates Mayotte, the narrator of *Je Suis Martiniquaise*, with Capécia, its author, making an assumption of autobiography which he never makes with Maran's text, despite his acknowledged suspicion that it is highly autobiographical. Fanon seems prepared to imagine that Maran is capable, like himself, of reasoned analysis, of the 'objective' *representation* of the phenomenon of Antillean neurosis. He is apparently quite unable, however, to imagine that a woman such as Capécia is capable of anything more than naïvely recording a neurosis which she herself has experienced. Capécia, for Fanon, seems to *embody* the lactification complex in a way that Maran does not.

10. Michèle Lacrosil, *Cajou*, Paris: Gallimard, 1961.

11. Jacqueline Manicom, *Mon Examen de blanc*, Paris: Presses de la cité, 1972.

12. Ibid, p.41.

13. Fanon, *Black Skin, White Masks*, p.201.

14. Manicom, p.74.

15. Ibid, p.126.

16. Ibid, p.143.

Filial Resentment

and Maternal Desire

Reading poems by Georgina Herrera

CONRAD JAMES

Georgina Herrera (b.1936) is a black Cuban woman who has written several collections of poetry. Several of Herrera's poems recall aspects of women's history, explore questions of African cultural identity, or invoke seminal moments in Cuba's political history.[1] However the central concern in her work is the dynamics of maternity. Herrera's attitude towards motherhood is complex and sometimes trouble societal notions of obligatory love and respect between mother and child. In this essay I examine the construction of the experiences of motherhood and daughterhood which we find in her poetry. I provide a brief summary of some of the major feminist arguments on motherhood which have been advanced over the past two decades and consider Herrera's attitudes in light of some of the issues which are raised. I shall discuss poems from three collections *Gentes y cosas* (*People and Things*) (1974), *Granos de sol y luna* (*Grains of Sun and Moon*) (1978) and *Grande es el tiempo* (*Great is the Time*) (1989).

Evelyn Nakano Glenn's observation that in contemporary North American society 'mothering is contested terrain'[2] testifies to the success of feminist theory and practice over the past two and a half decades in foregrounding the need for the questioning and, in many instances, the radical reshaping of societal attitudes towards the practice of mothering. In the most general sense, feminist advocation for a change in the way motherhood is viewed has called for it to be seen not as a specifically female responsibility/destiny because of women's perceived natural, universal, and unchanging disposition towards it. Rather, feminist theory insists that motherhood should be seen as a relationship which takes place in and is mediated by particular social and political circumstances. Thus feminist theorising projects an understanding of motherhood as a social institution and not a biological imperative.

Motherhood and gender then, as Glenn reminds us, 'are clearly intertwined. Each is constitutive of the other'.[3] This point is also made by Elizabeth Spelman in *Inessential Woman* (1988), one of the many rebuttals of the universalist orientation of Nancy Chodorow's psychoanalytic interpretation of motherhood in *The Reproduction of Mothering* (1978). Summarising Chodorow's thesis concerning the relationship between the sexual division of labour and the different senses of self that boys and girls develop, Spelman states that 'we can't adequately describe gender differences without focusing on the different senses of self women and men have that are linked to their thinking or not thinking of themselves in ways that prepare them for mothering'.[4] More importantly, as Glenn also notes, because only women, and not men, can give birth, 'mothering more than any other aspect of gender has been subject to essentialist interpretation'.[5] One consequence of this fact is that 'regardless of whether women become mothers, motherhood is central to the way in which they are defined by others'.[6] It follows then that any project which is interested in understanding the different manifestations of the dynamic of gender in society must, at some point, consider the way mothering is constructed and de-constructed in particular social discourses.

Precisely because of the use of reproduction in different patriarchal systems as a means of justifying the gendering of motherhood, several early feminist works postulated reproduction as the cause of women's oppression. Shulamith

Firestone's controversial *The Dialectic of Sex* (1970) is paradigmatic of this position. According to Firestone, the biological inequality of the sexes is the basis of women's subordination. Essentially a feminist reworking of dialectical materialism advanced by Marx and Engels, the object of Firestone's work is the erasure of sexual distinctions in society; the creation of a world in which biological differences between men and women will cease to have cultural importance. She thus argues for a technological revolution which would eliminate women's need to experience childbirth and its associated traumas.[7] A similar thesis was advanced four years later by feminist sociologist Ann Oakley. Oakley does not, like Firestone, make technological revolution the object of her argument but by focusing on several widely held beliefs concerning motherhood she explodes what for her is the myth that all women need to be biological mothers. Similarly, the ideas that all women need their children and all children need their mothers are rejected as social myths which have come to be endorsed by 'pseudo-scientific backing'.[8]

This renunciation of biological motherhood was contested, however, by Adrienne Rich in *Of Woman Born* (1976). Whilst Rich recognised the oppressiveness inherent in the institution of motherhood, her work has been seminal in positing a distinction between the social institution and the experience of mothering. For Rich, female liberation does not need to be seen as antithetical to female biology. Biology has very radical potential, she argues, and it is important for women to view 'physicality as a resource'.[9] It is the patriarchal institutionalisation of biological mothering, Rich emphasises, that corrupts the positive potential of the mother/child relationship. The renunciation of biological motherhood, therefore, does not consider the possibilities that could arise if pregnancy and birth were to take place in a 'wholly different political and emotional context'.[10]

Calling into question the political contexts in which mothering takes place highlights the central contradiction between power and powerlessness in motherhood which is confronted by much feminist scholarship. Motherhood in most cultures is invoked as a symbol of power. Yet not only do the everyday tasks of mothering tend to be socially devalued,[11] but as an institution, mothering is 'named by the authoritative voice not of women but of patriarchal culture'.[12] Mothering is therefore essentially under male control. Because of the notions of sacredness often associated with motherhood, however, this political contradiction is invariably obscured and its perpetuation encouraged. As Evelyn Nakano Glenn puts it, 'because mothering is often romanticized as a labour of love, issues of power are often deemed irrelevant or made invisible'.[13] Thus, through ideology, patriarchy insists on its control over motherhood and over women.

Important issues of 'race' and class have also arisen from feminist attempts to challenge patriarchal ideologies on motherhood. Chief among these has been the failure of some theories to recognise the multiplicity of contexts in which mothering takes place. Works such as Nancy Chodorow's *The Reproduction of Mothering*, mentioned above, and Sara Ruddick's *Maternal Thinking* (1989) are thus attacked for generalising about mothering from narrow 'race' and class positions. Carole Boyce Davies contends, for example, that questions such as 'maternal thinking' and critiques of 'the perfect mother' advanced by Ruddick and Chodorow respectively 'become empty and limited understandings if they do not configure the issues of race and history'.[14] Patricia Hill Collins's discussion of this problem within feminist theorising on motherhood not only supports Boyce Davies's position but also identifies the elision of 'race' and class in feminist theories on mothering as a symptom of the overall 'decontextualization of western thought'.[15] Euro-American feminist work on mothering, Patricia Hill Collins emphasises, fails to focus on the importance of issues such as the need on the part of many mothers to work for their survival and that of their children. More importantly, the specific ways in which the dialectics of power and powerlessness involved in mothering affect non-white women escape the theoretical grasp of Anglo-American feminists.[16]

Like the perspectives discussed above, my reading of the poetry of Georgina Herrera is sensitive to patriarchal notions about mothering. However, a discussion of the place that motherhood seems to occupy in the social imaginary as well as the lived reality of revolutionary Cuba might be more useful in contextualising the perspectives we find in her work. The Family Code of 1975 served to institutionalise official policies on the family which were issued at different points between 1959 and 1975.[17] The egalitarian thrust of this document as far as the allocation of the duties of parental care are concerned are impressive. According to Lisandro Pérez it is an 'asexual' code, which contains no distinction between the sexes in matters of childrearing and caring. Gendered terms such as man, woman, wife or husband are thus substituted in the code by words such as spouse and partner.[18] Pérez highlights, however, one aspect of the Family Code which seems to point to the 'persistence of the traditional notion that women are more competent or suitable child-rearers'. This provision states that in the event of divorce, children reared with both parents should remain with their mothers unless in exceptional circumstances.[19]

Even if this apparently legal inconsistency is negligible the accompanying tenacity of cultural attitudes toward mothering is not. The import placed on motherhood in revolutionary Cuban society is undeniable. As Nissa Torrents suggests in her 1991 essay on women in male-authored Cuban texts, the emphasis placed on the celebration of Mother's Day in Cuba signifies an exaltation of the role of women in society. This role, she contends, despite the addition of new freedoms, 'remains the same as in old, patriarchal, pre-revolutionary times'.[20] Despite woman's entry into the labour market and her often indispensable function in insurrectionary political activities, in the Cuban societal ethos it is the role of mother that predominates as woman's most significant contribution to the revolutionary process. The refusal to jettison patriarchal linguistic limitations and talk of a new woman as well as a 'new man' is thus seen as a clear suggestion that it is primarily for her capacity of 'giving birth' fulfilling her 'biological condition', that the new regime ultimately hopes to incorporate woman.[21] Whilst this observation could be regarded as paying insufficient attention to the new images of woman in society fostered by the revolution, the persistence of the sexual division of labour within the household and the resultant 'double-shift' of mothers who work outside the house clearly corroborate Torrents's thesis.[22] Additionally, the new regime's endorsement of marriage could be seen as an endorsement of the nuclear monogamy inherited from Cuba's Spanish Catholic past.[23] As Smith and Padula (1996) observe, contrary to the expectations of enthusiastic feminist supporters of the revolution, the new socialist order was premised on deeply conservative views on the family.[24] The tendency to exalt the heroine's role as mother, both in popular culture and intellectual discourse, within the revolution (as in pre-revolutionary culture) also seems relevant here.[25]

Georgina Herrera

The discourse on motherhood in the work of Georgina Herrera complicates several major strands of feminist thought by demonstrating attitudes which could be read as both progressive and traditional. As far as the Cuban nation is concerned there are no tropes of idealisation and the mother figure is not used to represent nationalist politics. Her approach is self-reflective and explores some of the conflicts which inevitably arise in situations in which mothering takes place.

Herrera's representation of the experience of mothering corroborates the thesis of O'Barr, Pope, and Wyer (1990) concerning the interconnectedness of the experiences of motherhood and daughterhood in any given culture. 'So intertwined is the experience of being mothered to one's own experience of mothering', they suggest, 'that the meanings of either are indecipherable apart'.[26] Anguish and a sense of loss feature in most of Herrera's poetry and she herself has commented on the irony of the evolution of her poetic gift from a context marked by misery.[27] This emotional disquiet is often depicted as generating from or being exacerbated by an apathetic mother/daughter relationship. Motherhood is then inscribed as a therapeutic experience which redresses the psychological damage engendered by an emotionally distraught daughterhood.

Filial Resentment

Two consecutive poems from *Grande es el tiempo*, 'Mañana última' ('Final Morning') and 'El patio de mi casa' ('My Patio') are very poignant reconstructions of the emotional sterility of the poet's infancy.[28] Placed in a section of the collection entitled 'Lamentos' ('Laments') these two confessional poems highlight the daughter's early awareness of emotional pain. Here the subject's earliest consciousness of self is bound up with an almost primordial sense of loss, alienation, and entrapment:

'El patio de mi casa'

Nadie adornó su espacio con arecas...
Patio sin otro ruido
que el silencioso andarlo de mis pies descalzos.
Sitio para mi sola, donde la ternura
y su modo simple de crecer y darse
como la hierba fina,
me fue vedado.
Patio donde el sonido de la lluvia
dejó su oficio de agua
para ir cayendo, espesa y contenida,
más bien como lágrimas.
Ancho para una celda.

Georgina Herrera

(Nobody adorned its space with palms/...Patio without a sound/except the silent patter of my bare feet./A place for me only, where tenderness/and its simple manner of growing and giving/like tender grass/ was kept away from me./Patio where the sound of the rain/was no longer like water/ but fell thick and contained,/more like tears. /As wide as a cell).

The absence of floral adornment in the representation of the poet's childhood home is used to register the social dispossession which characterised her infancy and this is further emphasised through the early reference in the poem to her unshod feet. However, whatever effect economic marginalisation might have had wanes in the poet's consciousness in the face of the pain engendered by the extreme paucity of spiritual nurturing which the patio symbolises. Ideas of home are ironised in the poem which suggests a painful struggle to affirm a sense of place against a personal history of socio-economic and emotional deterritorialisation.

Tropes of silence and restraint are used in 'El patio de mi casa' to communicate the absence of happiness or familial communion in the subject's childhood and the patio becomes a metaphor for the emptiness which memory recreates. The sound of her feet is the patio's only source of animation and rain loses its regenerative potential in this context. Instead it becomes ominous phenomenon which exacerbates the child's condition of loneliness.

The poet's disavowal of her mother is achieved in 'El patio de mi casa' by writing her out of her childhood story completely but 'Mañana última' centres on the memory of the mother, although she is not named. The mother's death is used as the point of departure to reflect on the coldness and lack of communication which characterised the mother/daughter relationship. It is constructed as an inauspicious event, occurring 'sin adioses, sin reverencias' (without goodbyes/ without ceremonies). But it is also an extremely transcendental experience in the psychological trajectory of the subject. Not only is it her first experience of death but, despite an anguished attempt at subduing pain through rationalising, it also serves as the final foreclosure of any possibility of communion or solidarity between mother and daughter:

Y así empezó mi asunto con la muerte.
Seguro que hubo amor,
pero escaseaba el tiempo de mostrarlo
y hacer que lo entendiera.
Y a partir de ese día
todo fue ya inútil. Se hizo tarde
para sentarnos a hablar y conocernos
cuando yo fuese mayor y ella más vieja. (p.53)

(And so began my association with death/of course there was love/but not enough time to show it/and make it understood./And from that day/everything was useless. It was too late/for us to sit, talk and get to know each other/when I was more grown up and she older).

Hence the pain and sense of loss which are communicated in the poem are not so much a reflection of distress at the mother's death as a demonstration of regret at the lovelessness which her life epitomised. The portrait of the mother which emerges in 'Mañana última' also picks up on the motif of silence which features in 'El patio de mi casa'. She is constructed as a perpetually silent figure and her death, therefore, represents just another dimension of a characteristic inability to communicate. Thus in death she is: 'Callada como siempre' (Silent as always).

Herrera's poetic rejection of the mother is expressed in much more strident terms in 'Mami'.[29] *Gentes y cosas* is divided into three sections. The first section entitled 'Hijos' (Children) explores the poet's deep affection for her two children. The second, 'Vecinos' (Neighbours), presents a series of less emotionally involved portraits of different people who have at some point affected her life. It is in the third section, 'Otras gentes' (Other People), in which the focus shifts to bitter national and personal experiences that 'Mami' is placed. The emotional distance between mother and daughter which is lamented in 'El patio de mi casa' and 'Mañana última', then, is also the theme of 'Mami'.

The poem is a retroactive attempt to bridge the huge distance which existed between the two. It begins with an expression of this resolution: 'El día es propicio / para salvar distancias' (The time is suitable/to bridge gaps), and proceeds with an interrogative exploration of the lack of affection which characterised the relationship: '¿cómo pudo existir tan grande espacio / entre las dos? ¿cómo / vivimos tantos años, sin que nada fuese a ambas común?' (how could such a great void exist/between the two of us /how could we live together so many years without having anything in common). Far from leading to reconciliatory ends however, the subject's search simply rediscovers the bitterness of the past. It recalls the daughter's childhood experiences of psychological orphanhood:

Ahora
es que puedo entender.
Y te agradezco
el desamor, la angustia,
el desamparo. Y
la total ausencia de esa sustancia
elemental que me hace
vivir sin nadie, en medio
de mil manos, deseando
un mano que impida
mi perenne caída inevitable. (p.36)

(Now/I can understand./And I thank you for/the lack of affection, anguish/ neglect. And/the total absence of that elemental substance that makes me/live alone, among/a thousand hands, wanting/just one hand to stop/ my everlasting, inevitable fall.)

The title 'Mami' invokes a doubly significant irony; it underlines the subject's anguish at the lack of affection which dominated the speaker's past as well as the futility of attempts to redress this situation in the present. This ironic treatment of the mother/daughter relationship is taken to another dimension in 'Deseo' (Desire).[30] Adrienne Rich (following Lynn Sukenick) has termed the fear of becoming one's mother matrophobia.[31] Here, dispelling any semblance of this, the subject stages a passionate desire to defy the logic of history and become the mother of her mother: 'Si mami fuera mi hija, / ay, si yo fuera la mamá de mami' (If mami were my daughter,/oh, if I were mami's mother). The poem allows the subject to experience, at the level of fantasy, the exchange of affection between mother and daughter of which she feels cheated in reality. Thus in the fantasy both parties exchange loud kisses. But the poet's struggle to create a fantasy in which maternal endearment exists, is sabotaged by the intrusion of actuality and this is captured in a moving image in which the daughter attempts to lift the mother but finds that she is physically incapable of that demonstration of love. Physical incapacity is therefore used as a metaphor for the psychological difficulty involved in the project of reconciliation.

Despite its violent rejection of the failings of her mother, much of the poetry of Georgina Herrera constitutes a reflection on the way gender socialisation compounds the difficulty of mothering for women. 'Escena familiar' ('Family Scene') is a case in point.[32] Here the construction of the relationship between man and woman, father and mother, demonstrates a conditioning by the dominant 'casa/calle' (house/street) cultural attitude. The social context is one of dispossession. The paternal response to this social difficulty is to comment on it 'con los amigos, en la esquina / de algún café (with friends, on the corner/in some cafe)' leaving the task of mothering to the woman. Hence the experience of mothering comes to be defined by solitude: 'En casa quedan la mujer / y los chiquillos, alrededor / de la lámpara de luz brillante. / Ella se hace uso de su soledad' (At home the woman and children remain around the bright light of the lamp/She is used to loneliness). Maternal solitude is further complicated by fear. Mother and children are depicted as 'despavoridos' (petrified), and their existence is marred by the threat of unhappiness.

In a similar vein 'Muerte de Jesús' (Jesus's Death)[33] contextualises the maternal silence rejected in 'El patio de mi casa' and 'Mañana última' within the prescriptive traditions of patriarchal culture. The subtext of the poem is the slaying in the 1940s of the influential black Cuban trade union leader Jesús Menéndez Larrondo and the sense of national tragedy which it represents for the poet. But the boundaries between the private and the public are collapsed by the use of this event as the structural device to focus the conditioning of the parents' marital relationship by the 'casa/calle' ideology and the distressing emotional effects this has on the young female child. Oral communication between mother and father is limited and one-sided. The father enters the kitchen abruptly, delivers the news of the tragedy and of the imminent political reprisal and then leaves: 'Es que han matado a Jesús'... / 'La FNTA hará algo', dice mi padre y sale' (They have killed Jesus.../The FNTA will do something, my father says and leaves). No female speech features in this scenario since the mother accepts 'la costumbre antigua / de no hacer preguntas' (the old custom/of not asking questions).

But 'Muerte de Jesús' also demonstrates the attitude of filial resentment of the poems discussed previously. Unlike 'Escena familiar' in which mother and children experience fear together, in this poem the subject's distress derives from a feeling of isolation. Here we have yet another example of an ironic treatment of the mother/daughter relationship through the depiction of the child/subject as alienated even as both mother and father express solidarity with wider socio-political issues:

Por una hendija en el fogón, mis ocho años
van extrayendo la ceniza;
hierven aún las más recientes
pero
muy junto al corazón, una ceniza
más áspera me quema.

Georgina Herrera

(Through a crack in the stove, my eight years/draw ashes/the latest bits still burn/but/quite close to my heart/a harsher ash burns me)

Hence the substitution of the maternal voice with the demonstration of dismay does not inspire any empathy within the daughter. Rather her consternation compounds the daughter's feelings of abandonment:

moviendo de un lado a otro la cabeza
así, de un modo, como
si todos fuésemos ya huérfanos.

Georgina Herrera

(moving her head from one side to the next/as if we were all orphans).

Maternal Desire

While Herrera's treatment of the subject of mothering from a daughter's perspective goes against the grain of masculinist maternal idealisation, her poetry also challenges several notions advanced in western feminist theories on mothering. In particular, her poetic representation of the emotional and psychological aspects of her own experience as mother seriously troubles feminist scepticism of the existence of maternal love (Badinter, 1981) and of repudiation of the concept of a mother's need for her children (Oakley, 1974). Here not only do we find a construction of giving birth and child-rearing as processes of healing but there is also the presentation of mothering as an indispensable aspect of self-actualisation.

This idea is communicated forcefully in 'La solterona' (The Old Maid)[34] in which motherhood is posited as the quintessential context of completeness through the rejection of the childless woman. Here the callousness with which Herrera treats the 'solterona' reverses Rich's argument that 'the childless woman and the mother are a false polarity'.[35] Thus the poem reinforces the idea of distance between these two groups of women by constructing the life of the 'solterona' as one of negation:

No.
No has visto nunca amanecer,
que la mañana
es el poco de sol que hasta tus ojos
desde el abismo de otros ojos llega.

                                          Georgina Herrera

(No/ You have not seen dawn/morning is that little bit of sun that comes to your eyes from the depths of other eyes).

A similar attitude is expressed in 'La solterona — su muerte' (The Old Maid — Her Death)[36] in which the speaker's disapproval of the state of childlessness finds expression in violent deprecation of the body of the 'solterona'. Here as in

'La solterona' Herrera clearly transmits the orthodox masculinist perspective that woman's destiny is bound up with maternity. Tropes of dryness and tightness mock the lack of fecundity which defined the woman's life. Her cheeks are 'apretadas rosas' (tight roses) and her eyes are like 'hormigas secas' (dry ants). Additionally, the societal perception of distance between mother and childless woman is figured imagistically in the speaker's diminutivisation of the dead body of the 'solterona' whose form is described as an absurd little wisp.

The construction of childlessness as a state of lack in the poetry of Herrera contrasts with the portrayal of giving birth as a source of empowerment. This perspective is most clearly articulated in 'El parto' ('The Birth').[37] Through the juxtaposition of the legend of the stork with the reflection of the experience of giving birth the poem shatters patriarchally endorsed myths which obscure the realities of mothering:

He aquí que la cigüeña,
el patilargo pájaro de la mayor ventura,
desde hoy, acaba
sus funciones.
Mi realidad la deja sin empleo. (p.34)

(Well there you have it, the stork, / that long legged bird of great fortune / as of today terminates / its functions. / My reality leaves it unemployed).

The displacement of the story of the stork reveals a concern to confront the disregard of both the pleasure and the pain of childbirth which is often encoded in fairy tales. More importantly, however, it serves to inscribe the woman as agent:

acorralada
por el dolor más grande
y la más grande dicha por venir,
hago el milagro (my emphasis).

Georgina Herrera

(Cornered/by the greatest pain/and the greatest happiness for the future/*I work* the miracle).

Several poems from *Gentes y cosas* are passionate celebrations of the power which the speaker derives from the experience of mothering. In 'Los hijos' ('The Children'),[38] for example, this idea is communicated through the images of strength and immensity with which the children are invested: 'Ese árbol que son los hijos / casi se compara al cielo en su tamaño' (This tree which are my children/ almost compares to the sky in size). Similarly, 'Las dos mitades de mi sueño' ('The Two Halves of My Dream') constructs maternity as both therapy and protection from potential psychological disaster. Here the debilitating silence learned from the subject's experience of daughterhood is cancelled by a maternity through which she finds voice. She thus celebrates her two children:

Ambos me han hecho
una mujer hermosa.
Una mujer que tiene
la más inmensa historia
por contar.
Todo el dolor que venga
será pequeño, comparado
a tanto amor creciendo en sus tamaños.

Georgina Herrera

(Both of them have made me/a beautiful woman./A woman who has/ the greatest story/to tell./All the pain that may come/ will be small, compared/to all this love growing as they grow).

The image of the psychologically exiled mother who is rehabilitated by the young daughter reappears in 'Anaisa'.[39] The daughter is 'la mitad del canto indispensable / para quebrar esto de ser triste / casi por vocación' (Half of the indispensable song/to destroy this business of being sad/ almost as a vocation). In another poem, also entitled 'Anaisa',[40] in which the poet reflects on the daughter's birth and infancy the daughter's potential to make the mother happy is figured in religious imagery: 'Temblaba / de tanto gozo...ahora / representas mi diocesilla (I trembled/ from so much joy...now/ you are my little goddess). Here the daughter's birth is inscribed as the means through which the mother learns to cope with life's vicissitudes:

tu llorabas, recién
venida al mundo, para
que me aprendiera
definitivamente
a manejar la dicha y la agonía.

Georgina Herrera

(You cried, recently/arrived in the world/in order that I might learn/finally/how to handle joy and pain).

Many poems in *Granos de sol y luna* are explorations of the poet's feelings of love for her children. At times this is achieved by simply recording some of the ostensibly mundane aspects of maternal care. One example of this tendency is '¿De noche? Con los hijos' (At Night? With The Children) where the potential drudgery of child-rearing is presented as being compensated by its capacity to inspire love.

This idea is reinforced in poems such as 'Ella durmiendo' ('Her Sleeping') and 'Ella, otra vez durmiendo' ('Her Sleeping Again') where mundane activities take on transcendental significance. In the second poem the demonstration of maternal love is depicted as both an invaluable treasure and an indispensable source of sustenance. The first, however, is a more troubling reflection on the transience of happiness. The spectacle of the daughter sleeping peacefully is used as an occasion for the expression of maternal anxieties: 'A esta niña le llegará su hora, / la doblará el dolor más ambicioso' (This little girl's time will come/she will be bent by the greatest pain). Sleep thus becomes a metaphor for the insulation from grief which childhood can represent and the poem ends with the wish for the daughter's sorrows to be perpetually deferred: 'Por ahora, duerme apacible. Sea / lo más posiblemente largo / el sueño suyo' (For now, sleep

calmly/may your sleep last as long as possible). The poem
'Preguntas que sólo ella puede responder' is a suitable one
with which to close the discussion on Herrera's work:

Preguntas que sólo ella puede responder

Ojos de etíope, dime,
resuelve tú que puedes
este amasijo de ternura
en el que me debato.
¿Por qué te quiero hasta pisar los límites
del llanto?
¿Por qué la lastima,
si te estiras derecho hacia la felicidad?
Suave pedazo de lirio y mariposa,
hija
de estarme yo juntando, todas
las ganas de vivir, por vez primera...
¿Por qué no cruzo el mar
sino contigo, junto al pecho, como
un resguardo?

(Ethiopian Eyes, Tell me/resolve, you who can,/this bit
of tenderness/in which I flail./Why do I love you to the
limits of pain?/why the grief/ if you stretch out to joy?/
gentle fragment of lilly and butterfly/daughter/if I could
only bring together all of life's joys for the first time.../
why don't I cross the sea/without you close to my breast
as/my protection).

Here we find encapsulated several of the attitudes towards
mothering which feature throughout her poetry. The
complexity involved in motherhood which her work as a
whole conveys is presented in very succinct terms in this text
through the metaphor of emotional entanglement: 'este
amasijo de ternura'. The idea that maternal love is inextricably
bound up with pain is also underlined.

Another important element of Herrera's perspective on
motherhood is signalled in the title of the poem. Through its
interrogative formulation the maternal persona is revealed as

having a variety of psychological needs which the daughter has the capacity to resolve. Mother, then, is not the source of infinite knowledge. Here Herrera's perspective on motherhood differs markedly from some attitudes found in Cuban poetry written by black men in which the mother is a heroic figure adept in creating opportunity out of adversity. Here the 'superstrong black mother' (Hill Collins, 1994) is replaced by a maternal figure who is perplexed and fearful.[41] By debunking such notions of maternal insight and omnipotence in 'Preguntas...' then, Herrera approaches the demystification of mothering which is indispensable in ridding it of essentialism.

Finally, the link which the poem establishes with Africa is extremely important. Here questions of motherhood are linked to ideas of 'race', history, and nationality. What is significant is that it is the daughter and not a revered deity who is used as the vehicle for the subject to re-establish her connections with the past. Ultimately mothering is inscribed as an agentic experience which can serve as the vantage point from which to grapple with questions of identity.

Reading poems by Herrera concurs with the suggestion that 'the geography of mothering is a complex and shifting terrain'.[42] While she presents complex woman-centred approaches to motherhood her work seems to contradict much of feminist theorising on mothering. Not only does her poetry disregard female solidarity through its candid rejection of the childless woman but it also inscribes maternity as the ultimate means of self-fulfilment. Quite apart from serving as the key to women's oppression motherhood is represented as a liberating experience.

Notes

1. See Catherine Davies, 'Writing the African Subject: Two Women Poets of Cuba', *Woman, a Cultural Review*, 4, 1 (1993), 32-48.
2. Evelyn Nakano Glenn, *Mothering, Ideology, Experience & Agency*, London: Routledge, 1994, p.2.
3. Ibid., p.3.
4. Elizabeth Spelman, *Inessential Woman: Problems of Exclusion in Feminist Thought*, London: Women's Press, 1988, p.82.
5. Glenn, p.3.

6. Ann Pheonix et al, *Motherhood: Meanings, Practices and Ideologies*, London: Sage Publications, 1995, p.13.
7. See Shulamith Firestone, *The Dialectic of Sex*, New York: Bantam Books, 1970, p.242.
8. Ann Oakley, *Woman's Work: The Housewife Past and Present* , New York: Pantheon Books, 1974, p.186.
9. Adrienne Rich, *Of Woman Born*, New York: W.W. Norton, 1976, pp.31-32.
10. Ibid., p.174.
11. Pheonix, p,13.
12. Jean O'Barr et al., *The Ties That Bind: Essays on Mothering and Patriarchy*, Chicago: Chicago University Press, 1990, p.1.
13. Glenn, p.16.
14. Carole Boyce Davies, *Black Women, Writing and Identity*, London: Routledge, 1994, p.137.
15. Patricia Hill Collins, *Black Feminist Thought*, London: Routledge, 1990, p.45.
16. Ibid., p.53.
17. Lisandro Pérez, 'The Family in Cuba' in Man Singh Das and Desser (eds.), *The Family in Latin America*, New Delhi: Viking, 1980, p.244.
18. Ibid., p.246.
19. Ibid.
20. Nissa Torrents, 'Women Characters and Male Writers: A Cuban Approach' in L.P. Condé and S.M. Hart (eds.), *Feminist Readings in Spanish and Latin American Literature*, New York: Edwin Mellen Press, 1991, p.177.
21. Ibid., pp.176-177.
22. For a spirited discussion of some of the images of the Cuban woman presented in two popular national magazines, *Mujeres* and *Muchachas*, in the 1980s see Verity Smith (1995) 'What Are Little Girls Made Of Under Socialism?: Cuba's *Mujeres* and *Muchachas* in the period 1980-1991', *Studies in Latin American Popular Culture*, 14, 1-15.
23. Under 'operation family' the Cuban government promoted a massive institutionalisation of previous consensual unions. Quoting from a 1968 weekly review in Cuba, Lisandro Pérez indicates that in just four years after the revolution there were about 106,063 such formalisations. See Pérez, p.243.

24. Lois Smith and Alfred Padula, *Sex and Revolution: Women in Socialist Cuba*, Oxford: Oxford University Press, 1996, p.145.

25. For a detailed discussion of one example of this tendency see Jean Stubbs 'In Search of an Unchaperoned Discourse on Mariana Grajales Coello: Social and Political Motherhood of Cuba' in Bridget Brereton and Verene Shepherd (eds.) *Engendering History: Caribbean Women in Historical Perspective*, London: James Currey, 1995, pp. 233-257. A notable exception to this pattern is the 'testimonio', *Tania la guerrillera inolvidable* (1970). Tania who dies at the age of thirty never becomes a mother and what the story stresses is her revolutionary and political commitment. See Verity Smith, 'Tania la guerrillera as testimonio' (1993).

26. O'Barr et al., p.1.

27. See Margaret Randall, *Breaking the Silences*, Vancouver: Pulp Press, 1982, p.112.

28. See p.53 and p.55 respectively.

29. Georgina Herrera, *Gentes y cosas*, 1974, p.36.

30. Georgina Herrera, *Granos de sol y luna*, 1978, p.39.

31. Rich, p.235.

32. Georgina Herrera, *Grande es el tiempo*, 1989, p,56.

33. Ibid., p.52.

34. Herrera, 1978, p.24.

35. Rich, p.250.

36. Herrera, 1974, p.29.

37. Herrera 1978, p.34.

38. Herrera, 1974, p.9.

39. Ibid., p.13, Anaisa is the real name of Herrera's daughter who was killed in a motor vehicle accident in 1991.

40. Ibid., pp.10-11.

41. Here I am thinking specifically of Eloy Machado. The image of the mother searching for answers from the child in 'Preguntas que solo ella puede responder' is the polarised opposite of the figure of Jacinta in a poem such as 'Tu lo sabias' (*Jacinta ceiba frondosa*, 1991, p.9), for example. Here the mother is invested with the prophetic insight which allows her to foresee the toppling of neo-colonialism in Cuba and the establishment of a new social and political order.

42. O'Barr et al., p.1.

'Politically Correct' Marginalisation and Early Narratives of the West Indies by White Women

EVELYN O'CALLAGHAN

The place of Jean Rhys in the West Indian literary tradition has long been subject to controversy. The exchange between Peter Hulme and [Edward] Kamau Brathwaite in the pages of *Wasafiri* has reopened the debate, and once again, Rhys's contested placing linked to her race has surfaced. True, there are other issues mentioned, such as the fact that she left her native Dominica in her late teens and only returned for a visit; but Jamaica Kincaid also emigrated from Antigua at seventeen, intending never to return, much as V.S. Naipaul did from his native Trinidad. Then there is Caryl Phillips who arrived in England at the 'portable age of one', only returning to St Kitts for intermittent residential periods in his late twenties. And yet their work has been readily admitted to courses on West Indian literature in the region and abroad. True, not all of Rhys's fiction is set in nor deals explicitly with the region; but this is also true of the writing of Phillips, Naipaul, Kincaid and many other authors long resident outside the West Indies. Domicile and subject matter appear to vary widely as determining factors in the categorisation of a writer/work as 'West Indian'. Race, however, seems to have been against Rhys.

235

This debate has once again inserted the discourse of race into the notion of regional identity. In what follows, I attempt to suggest some approaches to other (earlier) prose narratives of the West Indies by white women and, more generally, to ask questions about the nature of what has come to be known as 'Caribbean women's writing'.

My thesis is that the anomalous position of such early narratives in the history of West Indian literature has, as in the case of Rhys, less to do with regional identity, but rather reflects certain political assumptions on the part of critics. Predominantly, it seems that the race of author and/or character is the determining factor for what qualifies as a 'woman writer's text' in the West Indies. I examine various critical statements to challenge such a position. Additionally, though with a somewhat different focus from Brathwaite, I discuss the appropriation or rejection of such texts by certain post-colonial and feminist positions, again with the aim of interrogating marginalisation based on currently sanctioned notions of 'political correctness'.

West Indian Women's Writing: Says Who?
I am presently researching prose narratives by women of the nineteenth and early twentieth centuries which deal with representations of the anglophone Caribbean. I have found a fascinatingly varied body of writing. Not all of it is particularly readable, but on the whole the project has yielded some valuable insights into how the region was perceived in 'long time story'. However, to even begin to summarise this perplexingly uncategorisable corpus is impossible in the present context. Therefore, what I try to do in what follows is to identify some possible critical approaches to the material. Could it, for example, come under the heading of West Indian women's writing? And what exactly does this term mean? To all who care about 'Caribbean women's writing' the questions raised in this paper may encourage us to think a little more about the nature of this label.

Moira Ferguson, in her comprehensive study *Subject to Others* (1992)[1] which deals with women's anti-slavery writing to 1834, finds that 'no African-Caribbean slave women are known to have written before the publication of Mary Prince's narrative in 1831'.[2] To the best of my knowledge, no other prose works by non-white West Indian women — besides Prince's *History* and (free coloured) Mary Seacole's autobiographical *Wonderful Adventures* (1857) — saw, or has survived in print before Alice Durie's *One Jamaica Gal* in 1939.

This is not to say that there was no West Indian women's writing during the nineteenth and early twentieth centuries. Far from it, Brenda Berrian's 1989 *Bibliography of Women Writers from the Caribbean*[3] gives Mary Prince's narrative first place as the earliest female-authored text from the anglophone region, followed by Seacole's; subsequently she cites Pamela Smith's collection of folklore (1899), Mary Lockett's novel *Christopher* (1902), a poem by Clarine Stephenson (in the 1909 edition of the *Jamaican Times*) as well as her novel *Undine* (1911). My own research discovers other, earlier texts[4] and I have no doubt my findings represent only the tip of the iceberg.

Nonetheless, it has become commonplace to speak of writing by West Indian women as a mid to late twentieth century phenomenon. Erika Smilowitz, for example, asserts that after Aphra Behn's pioneering *Oroonoko* (1688), 'the West Indies have ... been a remarkably barren region as far as women writers are concerned'.[5] She acknowledges Lady (Maria) Nugent's *Journal* (1839) in passing and several abolitionist novels written about the region by English women in the eighteenth century, but 'as far as published women of stature ... there were merely a handful from Mrs Behn straight through several centuries to the very recent past'. Aphra Behn was, like Maria Nugent, an Englishwoman, but unlike Lady Nugent, there is still speculation as to whether she actually visited the region, so it is unclear why her work is implicitly considered to relate in some way to West Indian literature by women while that of Lady Nugent gets only a mention. Whether or not the selection of the 'handful' has to do with literary quality is unclear. What I want to concentrate on here is the supposed 'barrenness' of the female literary scene in the nineteenth and early twentieth century period of Caribbean literary history. For what Smilowitz suggests is that the body of writing by women about the West Indies since *Oroonoko* just does not count.

Carole Boyce Davies and Elaine Savory Fido, editors of *Out of the Kumbla: Caribbean Women and Literature* (1990), begin their introduction with the statement: '[t]he concept of voicelessness necessarily informs any discussion of Caribbean women and literature'.[6] By voicelessness they mean:

> ...the historical absence of the woman writer's text; the absence of a specifically female position on major issues such as slavery, colonialism, decolonisation, women's rights and more direct social and cultural issues. By voicelessness we also mean silence: the inability to express a position in the language of the 'master' as well as the textual construction of the woman as silent. Voicelessness also denotes articulation that goes unheard ... Understanding 'voicelessness', immediately puts into perspective the sparseness of the female literary terrain.[7]

Like Smilowitz, the assumption here is that the 'female literary terrain' is, if not barren, sparsely populated. And yet Davies and Fido continue, '[t]here has been a long history of women writing in the Caribbean', although it is only recently that 'these invisible writers are being seen'.[8] For example, they cite Elizabeth Wilson's assertion that 'prose works by women from the francophone Caribbean appeared before the end of the nineteenth century, perhaps even earlier'.[9] Importantly, they clarify that these were produced by 'women of color'. Further, they acknowledge Marjorie Engber's bibliography (1970) as containing references to 'many unknown women writers'[10] but nothing more is said about these 'unknowns'. So it would appear that far from being a barren literary terrain, there is a body of West Indian (and more widely, Caribbean) narratives by women dating from at least the nineteenth century. The question is why they have been ignored, rejected, forgotten, rendered voiceless?

It seems necessary at this point to 'unpack' some of the assumptions underlying the generally supposed 'absence of the woman writer's text' in the region until recently. First, there is an unquestioned notion of what constitutes this 'woman writer's text'. This notion appears to presuppose a concept of representation as transparent: 'the woman writer's text' represents 'a specifically female position' on life as lived; what was written is what was lived/felt/thought at the time by 'women' (unspecified). Texts, it is generally considered at present, are constructions. So too, I would maintain, is the so-called absence of the 'woman writer's text'.

Therefore, Elaine Showalter (1978)[11] and more recently, Virginia Blain et al (1990) have demonstrated that female-authored texts are not so much *missing* from the particular national archive, as ignored or deemed unworthy of notice. Showalter points out the double critical standard which has operated with reference to women's writing, so that individual achievements were subsumed under a relatively unfavourable group stereotype: woman first, writer second (if at all).[12] Blain et al, in their introduction to *The Feminist Companion to Literature in English*, detail the difficulties of accessing women's writing in English, and critical response, until a generation ago, rarely unmarred by automatic condescension. The content of 'quality' of the narratives is almost irrelevant. The texts themselves are simply ammunition (or, as the case may be, dross) in what is essentially an argument about the ideological or historical interpretation of a *literature*. But as demonstrated by the studies of Showalter and Blain et al, the wish to define narratives that express a 'specifically female position' is informed by a feminist ideology, and this in turn will involve the 'discovery' and re-claiming of texts quite different to those which a nationalist project would identify.

While I would subjectively judge some of these early narratives as of 'poor quality', yet it may be profitable for now to suspend the issue of literary value and focus more on the other reasons for their rejection. Who are the arbiters of value at a particular time? What are their criteria and what ethnocentric or gendered discourses inform these? Are women's novels devalued because of their 'female' concerns (the home) and features (sentimental)? Are women's texts marked as inferior *because* they are the products of 'lady novelists'? Are their writings excluded because of the low status of the literary vehicle they choose (the journal, for example or the travel narrative)? Are early narratives devalued because of their assumed political (retrogressive) stances, or because they are badly written by our standards? Are they valorised because of their apparently coded progressive stance, even if they are of dubious literary merit by our standards? 'Standards' of course is the issue: and there is no 'standard' fixed in stone, for the anomalous body of work I focus on here.

It is now generally acknowledged that in eighteenth and nineteenth century Britain, women writers were incredibly productive and that women readers formed a stable market for their publications. But despite the popularity of their texts they have been deemed of limited quality and importance — with a few exceptions — so that until recently, the existence of hundreds of writers and thousands of texts was forgotten. The relation between 'popular' and 'quality' writing is problematic in all literary production: there is no fixed inverse ratio. Yet again, the texts themselves are simply grist to the various mills of literary/ideological authority.

Another issue that needs to be examined is what exactly qualifies as a 'woman writer's text' in the West Indies. Currently, race would appear to be the determining factor: that is, the West Indian woman writer's text is one written by/about black women. Selwyn Cudjoe's historical overview in the introduction to *Caribbean Women Writers: Essays from the First International Conference* (1990)[13], seems to take it as given that Caribbean women writers, with few exceptions, are non-white if not black. One may ask which black women? For the majority of women (black or white) in the region do not write fiction or poetry or drama; many still lack more than basic literacy skills. Yet, as noted by Denise DeCaires Narain and Evelyn O'Callaghan,[14] there has been a tendency recently for anthologies and critical studies of Caribbean women's writing to feature cover illustrations of working-class black women. Does this suggest that the writer, or the writer's subject matter is specifically defined by such a representation? And if so, why is this the case — a marketing strategy perhaps, one which yet again packages the 'exotic' Caribbean for a paying audience with preconceived expectation?

If this is indeed the situation vis à vis the West Indian woman writer's text, a certain carry-over from nineteenth century racialist language appears to be operating.

Unquestionably, race is a key issue in the region, perhaps still *the* most important. Nonetheless, this should not be utilised to reinforce the binary oppositions at work in the claim that only women of one race can be 'authentically' West Indian. Cudjoe's overview moves from the writing of (black) Mary Prince and (free coloured) Mary Seacole, in the anglophone Caribbean, through a void when it seems nothing was written by women of this region until well into the twentieth century: in general, Cudjoe opines, 'there appears to be a significant gap in the recorded novelistic writings of Caribbean women after the later half of the nineteenth and the early part of the twentieth centuries'.[15] As noted above, this gap is one of perception, given that many women were writing in the region; but for reasons of race or otherwise, they remain invisible. The literary territory, he too suggests, was 'barren' as far as women were concerned.

I feel it is necessary to refuse any simplistic equation of 'West Indian' with 'non-white'. Certainly, these early women writers, by virtue of their race and the elite status this generally conferred, represent 'outsiders' perspectives on the majority of the region's inhabitants, and the voices of non-whites are therefore silenced in their accounts. As noted in Hulme's survey, Kenneth Ramchand one of the first critics to write comprehensively on the West Indian novel initially included texts by white West Indians in the literary canon, seeing their texts as 'socially relevant' in the articulation of the 'terrified consciousness' of elites in the decolonising process. Given the 'demanding context of Black nationalism', he saw this was an unpopular stance: in the 1950s and 1960s, West Indian critics were naturally concerned with redressing the balance of centuries of colonial exploitation and racism, and with the promotion of the voice of the oppressed.

Ramchand seems to have come around to the latter view, as he subsequently argues that West Indian literature is a twentieth century phenomenon and, as for the earlier body of narratives, when it

...was not the production of planters and planter-types, government officials, visitors, missionaries and other birds of passage writing from alien perspectives, it was the writing of a small group or class either pursuing its own narrow interests or committed to the idea of Europe as home and centre.[16]

Perhaps Ramchand is not disqualifying these narratives because of the race of their authors, but because of their implicitly colonial vision, a point made by post-colonial critics and one to which I will return.

However, for another important theorist of Caribbean literature, Edward Kamau Brathwaite, race *is* (as we have seen) a crucial factor in the debate. 'There are of course, 'white people' in the West Indies', he admits, 'but these are regarded either as too far apart to count or too inextricably mixed into the whole problem to be considered as separate'.[17] Now, given his prolific analytical output in the last three decades, it is dangerous to take any of Brathwaite's critical statements as definitive. Nonetheless, one can safely say that he has been fairly consistent in positing 'the folk' or 'the broadly ex-African base' as the matrix of Caribbean culture. Logically, then, white writers (those who have been 'inextricably mixed' are presumably no longer a separate entity?) represent only the 'outsider's voice' and can make no contribution to a West Indian 'norm and model':

White Creoles in the English and French West Indies have separated themselves by too wide a gulf, and have contributed too little culturally, as a *group*, to give credence to the notion that they can, given the present structure, meaningfully identify or be identified with the spiritual world on this side of the Sargasso Sea.

One can debate what changes have taken place in 'the present structure' to account for the recent literary production of 'white' West Indian writers like Robert Antoni, Michelle Cliff, Lawrence Scott and Jane King-Hipolyte, or indeed to ask whether such writers constitute 'a *group*', but the focus on race as a criterion for inclusion in West Indian literature would now seem to be in need of revision. With reference to the *earlier* writers, however, Brathwaite's argument as I understand it is that the historical and ideological nature of colonialism raised insurmountable barriers between white West Indians (writers included) and the racial and cultural mainstream, so that the texts of the former could not constitute a truthful 'recognition of the realities of the situation. Again, is there not an assumption here of representation as transparent?

I would wish to refuse this position and to argue against prescriptive classifications of 'West Indian' as well as to refuse, for the moment, a racially-based concept of 'relevance'. It seems more productive to adopt Brathwaite's spirit of inclusiveness, as discussed in his theory of creolisation as *creative* as well as imitative acculturation. It is Brathwaite, after all, who opposes the view of Caribbean culture as a static plural entity in favour of a vision of productive friction. In art, he feels the goal is a 'meaningful federation of cultures'. '[T]here will be no 'one West Indian voice' in West Indian literature', he concludes 'because there is no '*one West Indian voice*' (italics mine).[18] White West Indian writers, then, may or may not demonstrate textually that their interests do not coincide with the interests of black West Indians. Again, this is largely a matter of reading. It implies that a white person writing about the West Indies can only write about 'white' experience of the place — whatever that might be, exactly — and that experience is perceived by the reader to be irrelevant to black culture at the specific historical moment. This may be an accurate assessment, but is quite different from claiming that it is irrelevant to *West Indian* culture. In the end, the West Indian experience includes that of whites and any definition of the region's writing needs to take this into account.[19]

A related issue that needs to be considered here is the assumption in much critical work that the publication process is invisible. The presumption is that once the woman writer's text makes it into print, we can access 'a specifically female position'. But if we consider the case of Mary Prince, for example, the invisible amanuensis is shown to have a great deal of power over the narrative. Mary Prince's *History* presents itself as an autobiographical 'slave narrative'; but her account, it is noted, has been through two sets of mediation by the time it appears in print. Prince's narrative is *dictated*, her editor Thomas Pringle tells us, to 'a lady who happened to be at the time residing in my family as a visitor' and is further 'pruned' (italics mine) by himself, 'to exclude redundancies and gross grammatical errors, so as to render it clearly intelligible'.[20]

While *all* texts undergo editorial shaping, the very nature of the slave narrative as a genre with its own internal rules as to structure and content suggests a significant ordering and selection process, and renders the term autobiography — that is, self-authored — somewhat problematic in the case of Mary Prince's *History*. Certainly, Moira Ferguson speculates as to the involvement of Pringle and his amanuensis in the articulation of Prince's life, and notes the 'contending agendas of such a multi-tiered narrative'.[21]

Given the above, who exactly is the West Indian woman writer here? What exactly is 'her' text? Which 'specifically female position' can be identified? Perhaps the disagreeably unanswerable nature of such questions illuminates the odd treatment of the texts in question. Indeed, does the difficulty of 'pinning down' such texts into comfortable categories contribute to the invisibility, the 'voicelessness', of many of the early narratives, as to the apparently questionable 'place' of *Wide Sargasso Sea* in the West Indian literary tradition?

In an attempt to transcend such problems of categorisation, I have tried to move beyond conventional labels. What particularly interests me is the common motifs that emerge in these early depictions of *the West Indies*, and on querying *why* these might have been important to writers and readers then, as well as now. Again, the intention is not to point out what is or is not 'true' about the region, what 'they' said about 'us', but rather to investigate *what* images the discourse circulated and to suggest possible reasons *why* these proliferated in the specific texts. After about 1865, the writing offers a somewhat more recognisable picture of the West Indies as we currently conceive it through historical sources; prior to this, the images tend to belong to the terrain of the romanced in many texts. But even in the early twentieth century, it is clear that white Creole or expatriate writers were generally unable to transcend certain stereotypical representations of the territory. Nonetheless, these are a *part of* the body of race and gender, for example — that it implicitly or explicitly raises. Rather, I am seeking to identify the presuppositions and assumptions that inform the literature, to ask why it was unable in most cases to transcend colonial/racist parameters, and to suggest some alternative readings.

In dealing with the type of slippery texts that I have encountered, it is important to avoid rigid critical positions. If the texts complicate easy classification, it is counterproductive to employ theoretical approaches which limit themselves to categorical boundaries and tend to homogenisation in the interest of ideological or formal constraints. As the texts themselves often resist neat labels, as evidenced by the multiple claims on (or repudiation of) Rhys's work, so too should readings. Nevertheless, I envisage my project as contributing to the post-colonial/feminist project of 'recuperating lost and silenced voices' and interrogating the role of these voices in the construction of the West Indies from a woman-authored perspective.

As noted earlier, for certain political reasons, early West Indian novels by women also consigned to oblivion by the arbiters of the West Indian literary canon — with a few exceptions — have been considered unrewarding subjects for post-colonial and, sometimes, feminist enquiry. Simply because they have been ignored or forgotten is, of course, no reason to claim them as worthy of merit; just as asserting the value of any writing — for example, by marginal groups — simply because it deals with oppression, seems to me to be condescending, if not insulting. Nonetheless, like Peter Hulme, I feel that accreditation — particularly in matters of 'literary value' and worth — is always partly informed by political (gender, race, class, cultural separatism) discourses in which the reader is situated, and which we as readers and critics need to interrogate and acknowledge from time to time.[22]

Sidonie Smith concludes her essay on 'The Other Woman and Racial Politics' with the following comment on a specific and, in this context relevant aspect of contemporary feminist theory:

The concern for the 'other woman' that now weaves throughout feminist theory in the West derives from a profound rethinking that problematises with postmodernism generally the Western notion of a sovereign 'self', but also a rethinking that insists that historical specificities are the 'grounds' outside the text that position us complexly and relationally in consciousness, behavioural practices, and politics. The shift derives also from a rethinking that rejects any simplistic or romanticised notion of 'marginality', recognising instead that position of marginalities and centralities are nomadic, that each of us, multiply positioned in discursive fields, inhabits margins and centres.[23]

The rejection of essentialising generalisations; of fixed and transparent notions of the 'self'; the importance of historicising; the refusal to valorise marginality as, for example, a celebration of victimhood; the need to recognise shifting — and thus often relative — power positions: all these 'feminist' concerns seem to me to be crucial to the post-colonial project. It is with these considerations in mind that I read the texts in question.

Theoretical Politics: 'Politically Correct' Marginalisation?
I have thus far sketched some of the theoretical inputs which have informed my approach to the material under study, a kind of amalgam of aspects of post-colonial and feminist theories. Nonetheless, in the light of a certain 'hardening' of attitudes regarding critical eclecticism,[24] it is necessary to note that this body of early texts by Creole or expatriate white women would seem to be a most unfavourable site for such an investigative program. Post-colonial critics like Homi Bhabha and Edward Said have been criticised for their concentration on colonialist documents as subjects of enquiry, to the detriment of counter-discursive 'native' productions; a criticism that is reminiscent of Brathwaite's and Spivak's position on *Wide Sargasso Sea*. As Brydon and Tiffin[25] put it, '[d]econstructing imperial representations of the colonised is useful to a point, but if it replaces listening to the voices of the colonised themselves ... it may, however innocently, act repressively'.[24] Surely Brathwaite is closer to the 'post-colonialists' here than he might think! Given that my focus is also on the deconstruction

of representations of the gendered *coloniser*, no doubt the reservations are even graver.

Certainly Gareth Griffiths seems to dismiss such 'first texts produced in a post-colonial society' as the proper subject of theoretical investigation, given that they represent 'the viewpoint of the colonising center' since their writers ('gentrified settlers, administrators ... travellers, sightseers') appear 'to have been born hand in hand with the Imperial enterprise'. Ashcroft, Griffiths and Tiffin[26] reinforce this stance:

> The first texts produced in the colonies in the new language are frequently produced by 'representatives' of the imperial power ... and, even more frequently, their memsahibs ... their claim to objectivity simply serves to hide the imperial discourse within which they are created.[27]

And indeed, many of the early narratives I will be discussing *are* implicated in the colonising project. For example, as Moira Ferguson has pointed out, patently negrophobic colonialist 'histories' like that of Bryan Edwards (1793), were utilised as research material in the construction of early fictions[28] — for example, Harriet Martineau's 'Demerara' (1832) — which purported to represent the West Indies (Martineau had never visited the region). Thus the fictions recirculate negative myths and continue to perpetrate racist representations of 'the native'.

Ferguson's thesis, in *Subject to Others*, is that much early abolitionist writing by British women (1670-1834), despite its worthy intentions, nonetheless wrote Africans and West Indians as a totalised, undifferentiated mass, projecting onto this stereotyped group their own female sense of social invalidation: a kind of gendered 'Orientalism', so to speak. Nonetheless, as Brydon and Tiffin remind us there is no 'uncontaminated alternative space outside imperialist discourse from which the subaltern may speak'[29] and, given that the textual construction of the colonised is inseparably bound up with that of the coloniser, I would still suggest that it is useful to approach these early narratives from several post-colonial perspectives. Outsider's texts they may be, in several cases, but as Brydon and Tiffin also acknowledge, '[t]he outsider's perspective may prove a particularly valuable one, provided that it is recognised as such'.[30]

If the face and class (and sometimes national) markers of many of these early authors is equated with 'elite' and 'colonial', and their texts thereby problematic as subjects of post-colonial analysis, similar objections can be raised as far as a feminist approach is concerned. As discussed above, Cudjoe examines the work of selected West Indian women writers from Mary Prince to Una Marson and attempts to fit them into a 'radical' tradition, as articulations of feminism (as well as of nationalism and often, black racial pride).[31] He does not include the narratives by white women. Presumably, such accounts, being the production of a predominantly elite group of women and firmly in the conservative mode as far as feminist politics are concerned, would not fit the paradigm. In the same volume, Rhoda Reddock (1990) examines the early Women's Movement in the anglophone Caribbean (1900-1950) and notes that among 'middle-strata' women (the group within which most writers discussed here would be placed) and women of 'the colonial elite',

...there was general acceptance of the colonial housewife ideology, which identified the dependent housewife and male breadwinner as the key actors of the bourgeois family ... however [they] accepted the right of women to earn an income even though they felt this should be done in activities suitable to women's sex and station in life.[32]

The point is that the majority of women writers in the nineteenth and early twentieth century West Indies, who — like Rhys — would have come from a middle class or elite background, educated and 'cultured', would have been socialised into values which are, by *present* feminist standards, 'conservative'. As Reddock explains, such a group might have 'radical' politics insofar as many women were nationalists, but their sexual politics were very much of their time.[33] They internalised 'modern' (that is, 'Western') values of family, economy and society and considered (Eurocentric) education as the key to enlightenment, with the concomitant rejection of African derived 'backward' practices (like the matrifocal family and female economic autonomy) in favour of 'the Euro-Christian Western nuclear family' as the ideal, a unit in which Erna Brodber (1982) describes the women as an entirely supportive figure, 'the angel in the House'.[34] In short, the writers of many of the early narratives were not writing from what we now term a feminist perspective. Does this render them unworthy of analysis? Why the insistence on reading their texts solely from politically correct, but historically premature, pespectives?[35]

What I have tried to illustrate is the futility, as I see it, of the kind of simplistic equations that might be phrased as follows: these early texts are coloniser's voices which have silenced those of the colonised, and are thus unworthy of study; these early narratives are implicated in some way in the colonising project, and are thus unworthy of attention; these early writings are not feminist enough, and thus should not be analysed; these early works are not nationalistic enough, and are thus undeserving of literary exegesis. Implicit in such — admittedly oversimplified — formulae, is a kind of *reverse* Manichean allegory. For JanMohamed (1985), 'colonialist literature' is defined, following Franz Fanon's account of the Manichean structure of the coloniser/colonised relationship, as the writing produced by the European coloniser, a monolithic discourse structured around this central concept of the 'Manichean allegory'.[36] In a sense, the kind of formulae I have rehearsed above act as inversions which nonetheless follow the same 'Manichean allegory' identified by JanMohamed as fundamental to 'colonialist literature'. Refusing attention to the construction of this 'monolithic' colonising subject, or to disparities of power within 'the European colonisers' as a group (which consisted, after all, of men and women from all kinds of classes), those who disparage the study of 'colonialist literature' are themselves following a Manichean line with the terms reversed, so that the voice of the white colonial is unquestionably to be silenced and that of the black native to be unquestioningly privileged.

It is unsurprising that texts *per se* can yield varied, even totally opposite readings according to the reader's positionality and the political ideology that always informs critical interpretation. While I have eschewed a monologic approach and acknowledged the theoretical strands which seem useful to my interpretation of particular texts, I recognise that while the early narratives can profitably be investigated by contemporary literary theories, they do not easily yield either 'feminist' or 'post-colonial' reading and as a result are easy targets for branding with the pejorative terms 'conservative' and 'reactionary'. As with several other labels mentioned above (including 'West Indian'), I want to keep 'conservative' and 'radical' in play for the most part, and attempt readings that avoid dogmatic polemic while retaining sensitivity to the historical and social contexts of the texts. If this strategy anticipates critical, if not hostile reception, it is a corollary of what I believe to be the need for a re-examination of some of our presuppositions as scholars and readers and admirers of women's writing about the West Indies.

Notes

1. *Subject to Others: British Women Writers and Colonial Slavery, 1670-1834*, New York and London: Routledge, 1992, p.26.
2. Mary Prince, *History of Mary Prince, a West Indian Slave, Related by Herself*, in Henry Louis Gates Jr. (ed.), *The Classic Slave Narratives*, New York: New American Library, 1987, first published 1831.
3. Brenda Berrian, *Bibliography of Women Writers from the Caribbean*, Washington: Three Continents Press, 1989.
4. See for example, Charlotte Elizabeth [Mrs C. Tonna], *The System: A Tale of the West Indies* (1823); Mrs Carmichael's *Domestic Manners* (1833); Mary Ann Hutchins, *The Youthful Female Missionary* (1839); and other texts included in the select bibliography.
5. ' 'Weary of Life and All My Heart's Dull Pain': The Poetry of Una Marson', in Erica Smilowitz and Roberta Knowles, (eds.), *Critical Issues in West Indian Literature*, Parkersburg, IA: Caribbean Books, 1984.
6. Carole Boyce Davis and Elaine Savory Fido, (eds.), *Out of the Kumbla: Caribbean Women and Literature*, Trenton, New Jersey: Africa World Press, 1990.
7. Ibid., p.1.

8. Ibid., p.2.

9. Myriam Warner-Vieyra, *Juletane*, London: Heinemann, 1987, Introduction, p.v.

10. See Marjorie Engber, *Caribbean Fiction and Poetry*, New York, Center for Inter-American Relations, 1970, p.2. Engberger has compiled a list of 'fiction and poetry by Caribbean authors published in the United States and Great Britain since 1900' (p.5). In fact, the list is very partial and contains inaccuracies (Paule Marshall is said to hail from Jamaica) that cast some doubt on the usefulness of the work as a bibliography. Of the entries for the anglophone Caribbean, under the headings 'short stories' and 'novels', there were few by women writers all of whom are quite well known, excepting perhaps Mary Lockett, whose novel *Christopher* (1902) in fact contains virtually no Caribbean material. After Lockett, Engber's list includes the work of Ada Quayle and Esther Chapman (both of Jamaica) from the 1950s. Generally speaking, then, Engber's text is a disappointing resource as far as discovering 'many unknown women writers' of prose narratives.

11. Elaine Showalter, *A Literature of their Own: British Women Novelists from Bronte to Lessing*, London: Virago, 1978; Virginia Blain et al., *The Feminist Companion to Literature in English*, London: B.T. Batsford, 1990.

12. Virginia Blain et al., *The Feminist Companion to Literature in English*, London: B.T. Batsford, 1990.

13. *Caribbean Women Writers: Essays from the First International Conference*, Wellesley, Mass: Calaloux, 1990.

14. 'Anglophone Women Writers', in Anna Rutherford et al eds. *Into the Nineties: Post-Colonial Women's Writing*, Mundlestrup: Dangeroo Press, 1994, p.625.

15. Cudjoe, p.15.

16. Kenneth Ramchand, 'West Indian Literary History: Literariness, Orality and Periodization', *Callaloo* 11, 1, 95.

17. Edward Kamau Brathwaite, 'Roots: A Commentary on West Indian Writers', *Bim* 10, 37 (July-December) 1963, 16.

18. 'Caribbean Critics', *Critical Quarterly* 11, 3 (Autumn) 1969, 270.

19. The situation of the white African woman writer is relevant here: see Brenda Cooper (1994) 'Literated Repressions: Escaped Thoughts of a White South African Critic', *Wasafiri* 19 (Summer) 40-50. Attempting to break the cycle of futility in which writers and critics are questioned (and, in turn question others) about where they

derive the authority to speak, Cooper posits — from the work of Edward Said and Gayatri Spivak — 'the recognition of the possibilities inherent in intellectual work of developing beyond the determining forces of one's background and of making a progressive intervention' (p.47). While her essay is to a large extent concerned with making 'the necessary point that not only blacks can critique blacks, Jews understand Nazism or Elizabethans understand Shakespeare' (p.48), her discussion is relevant here if we substitute 'write about' for 'critique' in the quotation. It would seem that this is tacitly taken for granted in Susheila Nasta, *Motherlands*, London: Women's Press, 1991, which includes supposedly white writers like Jean Rhys and Marjorie Macgoye under the subhead 'Black Women's Writing from Africa, the Caribbean and South Asia'.

20. Prince, p.185.
21. Ferguson, 1992, pp.282-3.
22. See Peter Hulme in *Wasafiri* 20, Autumn 1994, 5-11.
23. See Sidonie Smith, 'The Other Woman and the Racial Politics of Gender: Isak Dinesen and Beryl Markham in Kenya', in Sidonie Smith and Julia Watson eds. *De/Colonizing the Subject: The Politics of Gender in Women's Autobiography*, Minneapolis: Univ. of Minnesota Press, 1992, pp.431.
24. See for example, Mike Sanders's review of Aijaz Ahmad', *Theory: Classes, Nations, Literatures* (1992) in *Wasafiri* 21 (Spring) 82-84. Sanders reads Ahmad's book as a challenge to the fundamental assumptions of 'contemporary literary radicalism', and 'an eschewal of the currently fashionable theoretical eclecticism' in favour of a 'clear and consistent theoretical commitment', in this case to 'a form of Marxism'. Perhaps Brathwaite's defensiveness, regarding 'Prosperean' critical schools such as post-colonial and feminist theories might be part of the same trend.
25. Diana Brydon and Helen Tiffin, *Decolonising Fictions*, Mundlestrup: Dangaroo Press, 1993, p.26.
26. Gareth Griffiths, 'Imitation, Abrogation and Appropriation: The Production of the Post-Colonial Text', *Kunapipi* 9, 1, 1987, 13.
27. Bill Ashcroft, Gareth Griffiths and Helen Tiffin, *The Empire Writes Back: Theory and Practice in Post-Colonial Literatures*, London and New York: Routledge, 1989, p.5.
28. Ferguson, 1992, p.227.
29. Brydon and Tiffin, p.26.

30. Ibid., p.21.
31. Cudjoe, pp.11-25.
32. Rhoda Reddock, 'Feminism, Nationalism and the Early Women's Movement in the English-Speaking Caribbean', in Selwyn Cudjoe (ed.) *Caribbean Women Writers*, 1990 pp.61-81.
33. Ibid., p.63.
34. Erna Brodber, *Perceptions of Caribbean Women: Towards A Documentation of Stereotypes*, Cave Hill, Barbados: ISER, 1982.
35. An analogous reading that perhaps illustrates the desire to find contemporary 'correct' values in an apparently reactionary body of fiction from an earlier period, is Claudia Tate's *Domestic Allegories of Political Desire: The Black Heroine's Text at the Turn of the Century* (1993). As I understand it, Tate seeks to justify a reading of 'domestic novels' by African-American women in the late nineteenth/early twentieth century as allegories of racial and sexual liberation by demonstrating that 'domestic' plots — apparently politically conservative tales of light-skinned heroines, involved in somewhat maudlin love affairs — in fact fit into a tradition of black female protest and self-expression. This protest, of course, is anything but obvious; indeed, traditionally such stories have been pejoratively compared with more socially conscious and 'responsible' fictions by black women of the period. However, Tate argues, because slaves were denied the right to marry, the institution of marriage for African-Americans in the nineteenth century became a symbol of material freedom, and the emphasis on marriage in these texts was an indication of black women's refusal of the myth of retrogression (i.e. that blacks, post-slavery, inevitably reverted to barbarism) and a statement of their material advancement.

For a black woman writer in the late nineteenth century to 'normalise' images of a successful black family, was — in context — a radical move. Tate's subtext is the necessity of attention to cultural and historical contexts of narrative in the allocation of literary value, and is a consideration not to be taken lightly. However, my brief and sketchy synopsis of her strategy serves merely to reinforce the difficulty of forcing feminist — or 'radical' — readings of early texts by women.

36. 'The Economy of Manichean Allegory: The Function of Racial Difference in Colonialist Literature', *Critical Inquiry* 12 (Autumn) 59-87.

'Dark and Unfathomable Beyond Control': Women Writing the Deviant Male

PAULA E. MORGAN

How are Caribbean women writers using the hegemonic mantle of the storyteller to treat cultural paradigms of masculinity? What accounts for the making of the criminal as a young man who possesses no notion of private ownership unless it is of his right of enjoyment of that which he has stolen; no respect for life, perhaps not even his own?[1] This paper, part of a larger work on the language and literature of violence, focuses on the portrayal of the deviant male in the hands of female writers.[2] Predictably, this character appropriates a portion of the fictional stage, even as he appropriates the collective dreaming and waking reality, creating vulnerability and wide spread intimidation in the psyche of women fearful for themselves and their families.

I argue that any attempt to understand and / or to alleviate violence must take regard of interlocking concepts of gender and power. Moreover, it must also grapple with the complexity of constructing gendered identities within a Caribbean framework. As Christine Barrow explains:

Barbadian men and those of the wider Caribbean internalise and demonstrate their masculinities within a gender system which has its origins in more than one cultural heritage (European, African, Indian, etc.) and has developed into a complex mosaic of gender ideologies and values. The patriarchy of slavery, colonialism and the post-colonial state dictates the behaviour and symbols of 'proper' masculinity, but is challenged by subcultural, subordinate male constructs. The result is not an unchanging, uniform masculinity to which all conform but one of variety, ambiguity, contradiction and change.[3]

Jean Rhys's 'Our Gardener' (the last creative work published in her lifetime) is a grim poem in which a child witnesses the brutal murder of her parents by the gardener. It begins:

> I thought Ken was a nice man
> Ken was a pal
> His other name was Taylor
> My name was Sal

And the poem culminates:

> People came running
> Ken didn't look round
> He laughed as he was striking
> Mum on the ground

> Went on laughing
> And this is what he said
> 'White flesh, white flesh'
> Talking to my Mother, dead.[4]

The horror of the scene and the complex web of racialised interactions on which it is built are masked by the childlike perspective and the simplicity of the ballad quatrain. The writer also exploits the traditional ballad's convention of non-judgmental understatement. Subtle markers of race and colour relations abound. True to appropriate form for master servant relations, the child calls the adult gardener by his first name. Moreover they are discursively linked by the abab end rhyme:

'I thought Ken was a pal / ...my name was Sal.' Complicit with the infantalisation of slaves/servants as happy children, Sal sees high entertainment value in her pal Ken, so much so that when he advances, cutlass in hand, she thinks 'it new game Isn't he grand'. The potential motivation for the crime is alluded to in Ken's only words, which thud in heavy iambic rhythm, to echo the lethal chops, 'White flesh, white flesh'.

Rhys (1894-1979), the offspring of a white Creole mother and Welsh doctor, was familiar with incipient violence within the black/white colonial and post colonial encounter and with the folly of the happy nigger stereotype which was crucial to the coloniser's rationalisation of enslavement. The dangerously naïve infant's perspective in 'Our Gardener', parallels that of Mr. Mason who underestimates the ex-slaves' potential for violence, in a sequence which leads to the conflagration of the Great House in a post emancipation scenario of *Wide Sargasso Sea*.[5] The physical and social landscape of enforced submission to enslavement/servitude has long been (mis)represented in the narration of conquest, as the idyllic paradisaical garden, which contextualises the hierarchy of white masculinity and racialised dominance within the Western imaginary.[6] It is in the tropical garden that the white male demonstrates his inherent superiority as the natural basis of dominance, showcases the pure flower of white womanhood and reduces the black to invisibility and servitude.

But Rhys's gardener, who represents the enslaved or the servant class divinely ordained for toil in the garden, emerges from the shadows. Even as the ascendant male, armed with the camera seeks to capture his crowning glory — the white woman picking flowers in the midst of the garden — the true labourer, Ken, who is represented 'pottering out of sight', moves from peripheral invisibility to centre stage to execute the heinous act. The criminal act extends beyond challenging the ascendancy of white flesh over black. Greater venom is reserved for the woman who has been rarified as the symbolic repository of ethnic superiority, desirability, visibility and inviolability. The poem speaks fundamentally of loss which goes beyond the loss of life. It is also the loss of the landowning class's illusory garden, loss of the reductive unidimensional identity construct and ownership of 'OUR' gardener.

The poem demonstrates that the epistemic violence inherent in master class/race and servant class/race relations has the potential to generate retaliatory acts of violence. Indeed the *Wide Sargasso Sea* scenario implies that it is sheer power, not fabricated bonds of love and loyalty, or puerile constructs of happy, childlike Negroes, which keeps such violent eruption at bay. Where there is a weakening of the power base, the oppressed underclass is likely to erupt, albeit in self-destructive, criminal or even insane acts of revenge. The underlying, warped complex of class and ethnic relations in the Caribbean manifest themselves in the present in repeated incidents of violence, crimes committed by impoverished employees against prosperous upper and middle class employers of all ethnicities. Even today, the focal point of white/coloured upper/middle class animosity and distrust is likely to be the male rather than the female servant. Most chilling of all, is that the latent violence seems more prone to eruption where there is some measure of social interaction-cordiality and even acts of kindness exchanged between the potential criminal and the potential victim.

This formula is repeated with only minor variations in Michelle Cliff's *No Telephone to Heaven* (1987).[7] Cliff sketches a grim portrait of post-independent Jamaican society with its dismal economic prospects, sharply stratified classes, extremes of wealth and poverty, insensitive, intolerant and invariably light-skinned upper-middle class. This scenario is aggravated by a decadent, wasteful frivolity within the upper echelons and a mindless and incredibly brutal violence within the lower strata. Cliff writes of Jamaican society in crisis well on its way to becoming what Harriot defines as 'crimogenic', that is, one in which criminality is 'embedded', 'internalised moral inhibitions against criminal acts are increasingly neutralised' and there is 'pervasive criminality and disregard for law across all social classes'.[8] Acts of violence against the person are portrayed here as a subset of a pervasive culture of social injustice, poverty, inequity and hopelessness. L. Gunst, in *Born Fi' Dead*, chronicles the politically motivated instigation and patronage of gang warfare as a consequence of which young male 'sufferers' of the urban slums are socialised into a violent alternative masculinity, exploited by politicians for gang warfare, and then turned over to the police for persecution (as opposed to prosecution) and sometimes blatant assassination, when they have outlived their usefulness.[9] In her construct of the violent subculture of Jamaica, Gunst emphasises the correlation between institutional state violence and the making of the criminal:

> For almost fifty years the people of downtown Kingston have lived with intensifying violence – institutionalised warfare with the police, political banditry, and the quieter brutality of being bulldozed or torched out of their tenements so that one politician or another could build a housing project for his supporters. This has been going on, in one wave after another, since Jamaica went into the first birth pangs of nationhood in 1938.[10]

One consequence of the growing maelstrom of violence and social unrest in the 1970s was mass migration of white and coloured Jamaicans to North America. Cliff zeroes in on a single representative of the countless violent crimes against the wealthy, coloured middle class during this period. She plays the tensions of the scene with sensitivity and strategy. She positions the account of the brutal murder of the wealthy family, after the chronicle of the decadent wasteful lives led by the children of the rich. She sketches the scene twice; first as it unfolds to the pampered, self-indulgent son who returns from all-night carousing to find his family slaughtered. Paul initially recounts the defenses which secure the wealthy within their domestic fortresses, only to find they have been breached. The implied reader sympathetically shares Paul's horror at his discovery of his family's brutal killing, but the character immediately attracts censure when he treats the maid's death as an inconvenience because of her invisibility — she possesses no last name, no address, no family to his knowing — hence her remains are an inconvenient liability. Significantly, we can place in Paul's mouth the words of the naïve infant of Rhys's narrative—'I thought Chris was a nice man / I thought he was a pal'. Blissfully blind to the trauma and hostile intent of his childhood playmate turned yard boy, Paul neatly facilitates his own death.

Adding to the polyvocality of the novel and expressing the text of the criminal, Cliff retells the distasteful scene a second time, just as convincingly, through the crazed eyes of Christopher, but not before sketching in his harsh oppressive, loveless, background and revealing the skewed reasoning which leads to the murders. Indeed for the acts which Paul label as bestial, Cliff in the second recounting of the scene, supplies a skewed, insane, highly subjective reason, but nevertheless a reason for the making of the beast.

Christopher could well be a descendent of Rhys's Ken Taylor, who emerges when the social crisis has ripened to create the dungle, an urban slum constructed on a garbage heap. The factors which feed into his making are absentee parenting (an invisible father and a mother who deserts him through becoming a prostitute with a truncated lifespan); an aging poverty-striken grandmother whose best efforts are inadequate, as well as hunger, poverty, eventual homelessness, lack of human love and connection and despair. The seething rage comes to surface in relation to a lack of rootedness, an unaccommodation so deep that he is unable to perceive it in relation to himself. The drunken, irrational houseboy invades the master's bedroom at night seeking a burial plot for his grandmother who has been dead for some thirteen years. He is persuaded that her duppy cannot rest because she was given a pauper's burial. The pursuit of a resting place in the land is related to ancient burial rituals and ancestor veneration which in African cosmology is pivotal to the individual and communal well being. Christopher's example again demonstrates the propensity to inflict the greatest damage where there has been kindness. Because of what he reads as loyalty to her employers as opposed to him, he reserves the worst of his already extreme brutality for the maid who has befriended him. Note that Cliff evokes markers of commonality — master and servant are united by common nation language — Jamaican Creole. By his murderous act, he releases the spirit of the family to join his grandmother as wandering duppies.

Whereas Rhys and Cliff portray violent acts as an overflow of deeply rooted rage and/or insanity, it is to Olive Senior and Barbara Lalla that we must turn for sketches of the professional criminal.[11] Harriot describing changing trends in Jamaican society explains: 'The general direction of violent criminality has been towards greater rationality and its instrumentality as means to commonly valued ends (wealth, power, status, respect). Since the mid-1980s, murder has been largely associated with income generating activity in the underground economy'.[12] In recognition of the professional who has now become integral to the Jamaican social landscape, Senior introduces The Dispatcher, Jack Spratt:

People who say
overpopulation is the greatest
curse of the nation should
give medal to Jack Spratt
for what we over-produce
Jack Spratt will reduce
with efficiency and dispatch[13]

Naming is instructive. The lovable nursery rhyme character validates the right to choose opposing alternatives. Senior's sinister Jack Spratt exemplifies an alternative, anti-heroic view of manhood. His is the culturally enshrined, fairy tale transformation of the pauper into the prince. He is the poor, ignorant, country boy who starts with no resources, comes to town and makes good. He affirms the assumption that hard work, efficiency and diligence create success. In a society in which the pursuit of power is an extremely desirable heroic objective, he becomes a repository of personal power and representative of institutional power, a public servant, contractor, potential medal earner. He is set on a clearly demarcated and well-travelled fast track and shows every indication of arriving at the upper echelons of the criminal world with his characteristic dispatch. Moreover, as the central authority figure, the supreme signifier of his world, he has apparently attained an ultimate human quest objective, the power over life and death. Miller argues that men marginalised from the material means of sustaining masculinity take recourse to 'the personalistic idiom of power within narrow territorial boundaries and the use of violence to establish authority and respect within this area':[14]

Jack Spratt
have the might and the right
to decide who sleeping
in tonight and who outside
in Hope River Bottom
or in cold Sandy Gully.[15]

The musicality generated by the internal rhyme 'might' and 'right' and the initial rhyme 'in' and 'in', ironically affirms the sense of the appropriateness of the order created by Jack Spratt and his machinations.

The strength of the poem is the extent to which Senior introduces the ironic sense of normalcy into the deviant criminal world. The exploits of Jack Spratt are related with a flat ironic detachment as if it were a communally recognised and accepted success story. The poem zeroes in on the professionalism which is increasingly characterising the criminal scene in Jamaica, and its impact on the young males who are its primary practitioners. How does killing become natural and even commendable? The dispassionate tone of the poem parallels the dispassionate mask which the young perpertrators learn to wear until violence becomes their second nature. In *Born Fi' Dead*, a young posse member turned star witness explains from a New York prison:

I felt like I killed before. I think maybe Hollywood had a part in the rude boy thing, with the movies they put out, like certain Westerns ...
     When I *shot at people*, I felt like I did it before. It wasn't like I was trembling and asking, What is this I'm doing? It was like I was into it all along. And I think that's just from social settings, from growing up around all that violence, the way Jamaica was with the politics. The way it was when I was a youth comin' up.[16]

This testimony speaks reams. Young men habituated to violence in the socio-cultural environments from youth, are further inured by televised images which add style and glamour to the ugly and gory. Peer pressure and group affirmation contribute to the process. The values of the subculture which valorise killing as a marker of masculinity encourage them to multiply murders and thereby add notches to their guns. Moreover, the political instigation and patronage that represent affirmation by the compromised hegemonic hierarchy, further lower inhibitors and help to make murder normative. Note the verbal evasion despite the assertion: Delroy [the gang leader] 'shoots people' but I shoot '*at people*' (my emphasis).

There is a minute step from this scenario to the process of normalising and ascribing social usefulness to criminality. Crime becomes embedded with other networks of social relations:

But in these communities, violence even when manipulated in an offensive mode may be considered legitimate. The 'morally legitimating principle is communally bounded utilitarianism, the moral boundaries of which co-terminate with the social community boundaries of the moral subject. To exist beyond this communally established boundary is to fall beyond the pale of morally accountable action. To exist beyond this boundary as an enemy (political, social) is to qualify as a legitimate target'.[17]

Senior's tongue-in-cheek allusion to the social effectiveness of the professional criminal points to the potential for the subculture to come to see in murder and mayhem, the means to a socially productive ends. Moreover the poem stands as an indictment against tension between valorised cultural norms for manhood which automatically deny access to subgroups, which, in turn, create other more accessible markers. Finally, it also passes judgment on the extremely materialistic measure of hegemonic manhood based on the size of one's member, one's car and bank balance, the number and attributes of one's women, and the extent of personal and institutional power one is able to wield.

'Country of the One Eye God' questions the contribution of home and upbringing in the making of the criminal.[18] The domestic setting is the proud rural community with its values of hard work, decency and stringent morality. Here Jack Spratt, reduced to the diminutive Jacko, has fallen into adverse circumstances and returns to his Grannie seeking money to escape from the police. As far as Jacko is concerned, his outcome is natural and logical given his upbringing. It is written of Jack Spratt:

his grannie
did beat him
with supplejack cant done
boy so tough
never cry
grannie say
is bad seed

The child is nurtured on a steady diet of 'licks' to beat out the bad blood and rejection based on the hope, deferred year after year, of his parents (who have migrated to the promised foreign land) sending for him. The outcome is a man who recognises no constraint of morality or religion, love or duty, decency or social order. His criminal actions of robbing and conceivably killing his grandmother for the burial money which she jealously guards on her person, are framed in his mind as reciprocity for the abuse which he received in the name of an upbringing. The effectiveness of dispensing corporal punishment in the home, in the absence of affirmations of love and clear moral and ethical direction comes into question. For Jacko, the constant beatings merely manifested his outsider status.

Yet Ma B's beatings of all her children to eliminate 'bad ways' were proffered out of concern and ignorance of more humane child-raising strategies. True to life, Senior intentionally problematises the situation — had child abuse been sufficient cause, Ma B would have raised a generation of criminals, not only one. Hence, she searches further afield for a cause: 'She had coldly cast her mind back to everything she knew about every single member of the family to discern if there was something hidden in her tribe that betokened this ending and she could find nothing that warranted such a hard and final cruelty'. Moreover, she searches the range of circumstances successfully confronted by her forefathers and her descendent: 'deaths, starvation, hurricane, earthquake, cholera, typhoid, malaria, tuberculosis, fire, diphtheria and travel to dangerous and distant places in search of work'.[19] Here too, she draws a blank for at no time in the past has this series of adversities produced a hardened criminal.

If Ma B and Jacko sat down to dialogue, the criminal would have posited nurture, that is excessive punishment, rejection, poverty and adverse circumstances. And the primary nurturer would have posited nature: 'bad seed' and predestination; it is written that the youth raise up 'the ways of their destruction'.[20] Each of these may be a contributing factor, but neither of these is sufficient enough to nullify the individual's power of choice.

A focal point in the story and the poem is the formulation of life's objectives and particularly the personal and culturally shared correlations between representation and desire. For Jacko and unfortunately for a substantial cross-section of our population, 'foreign' represents the culmination of wealth and well being. It represents the home and comforts that he has never had, and the parents for whom he has longed in vain. Even with his impressive credentials as a professional 'thief, a murderer, a hired gunman, a rapist, a jailbird, a jailbreak, and at nineteen a man with a price on his head' he is poised to shed his grandmother's blood to facilitate his much longed for homecoming:

'What? Yu plan to go foreign?
'What else? Don't I have mother, don't I have father in foreign?'[21]

To what extent can we 'trace' Jacko? This hardened criminal values his own life and retains the power to dream. He is portrayed as coldly, methodically, fighting for life which translates for him, into the illusory dream space of 'foreign'. In the exchange, Jacko reverses the traditional social structure which privileges respect for the authority of age and the respect for the mother figure based on allegiance and gratefulness for her sacrificial acts on behalf of kin.

Of greater significance for this argument is the power confrontation between alternative masculinities and a weakening matriarchy – both of which are responses to marginalisation within the hegemonic system. I will not enter into the dialogue here the disem(power)ment of the reluctant matriarch except to mention that empowerment (for both figures) would best be understood by mapping their position on a matrix of power markers instead of on empowerment, disempowerment binary. Ma Bell is financially impoverished by any external standards, but she is rich in the currencies which have imparted transcendence to the African-Caribbean families in simpler times –contentment, love, loyalty, self-sacrifice, faith, resourcefulness, patience, endurance, and so on. The passing matriarchal order invested hope and future in children and sought precious little of this world's goods, with hope of gain oriented towards the next life. Her modest, hoarded cache is intended to see her on her way. The final triumph over a life of poverty and meanness is the resplendent coffin in which she will lie in state to receive tribute to the wealth, beauty and order which she never acquired previously.

Conversely, Jacko, representative of a new generation and an emerging counter-hegemonic masculinity, defies and defiles the traditional values of respect for seniority, authority and for the mother figure (both of which are rooted in the ancestral tradition), heightened by gratitude for her sacrifices on behalf of kin. He embraces a ruthless pragmatic materialism whose god is self-centredness and material gain. And from this stance he challenges the traditional female-centred power base. Despite his fear and anxiety, as a wanted man running for his life, he retains the stance of a masterful, threatening, authority figure holding over his grandmother, the power of life and death. She who treats her excitable nephew as a child because he had never acquired her calm, is constrained to bow to the evil life force in him: ' In the pale light, Ma Bell wondered how such a little boy could suddenly grow so huge as to fill all the spaces in the room. She felt shrivelled and light, compressed into the interstices of space by his nearness'.[22] It is from this position that he presents his new order supported by his own logic and rationale. The issue of personal immorality is subverted for him by the essential injustice of the world.

The criminal is essentially justified in his own eyes. His (im)moral vision supersedes that of the Almighty who Jacko labels reductively as a 'one eyed god', who has aligned himself with the unjust social power structure: 'Him no business with ragtail and bobtail like unno. God up a top a laugh keh keh keh at the likes of you'.[23] Ironically, like his grandmother he is a man of faith. Since all power and meaning resides in the material world, he in turn vests his belief in an essentially unjust God of the materially prosperous, which leaves him free to create his own alternative existential reality as sovereign over a new order in which man turns beast — a dog eat dog world in which he can affirm his ascendancy as top dog.

The irony is that whereas the birth parents have rejected him, the state is hunting him and his posse has disappeared. The only place of belonging he will ever possess is in the unconditional love of the grandmother who, despite her innate knowledge of his reprobate nature, rejoices, when fleeing from the police, he answers the call of blood and returns to her sheltering. He systematically desecrates the only home that he will ever have, a place in the heart and loyalty of this mother woman. The weakened matriarchal order is executed by the counter hegemonic new masculinity, and the region is yet to experience the ripening of the outcome.

Whereas Senior locates her criminal character within the underworld subculture and the family, Lalla's canvas includes the entire broad sweep of Jamaican society and its people past and present. *Arch of Fire* is an ambitious and complex historical novel whose plot draws members of each ethnic group and historical experience into a vast interlocking network.[24] Lalla's text does much. It valorises family and tradition. It celebrates Jamaican landscape, customs and language. It grapples with its utter social breakdown and gross gratuitous violence which swamped this nation and, for many of the privileged, destroyed even the possibility of life as they knew it. It is pierced through with a nostalgia for a fine, cultured, prosperous and decent lifestyle. It explores the possibility for the reconstructed plantation as a physical and psychic space for the displaced in the urban society. Each major character encounters a personal debilitating tragedy and casts about for some avenue of transcendence.

Much of the evil in the novel crystallises around Lalla's clear-eyed gangland boss. Austin Louis is a shadowy character developed in flashes throughout the episodic text. He is at the core of the mystery which develops at the culmination of the narrative. Moreover, the unveiling of the character to the reader coincides with a process of self-revelation in which Louis's inner man is being unveiled to the self through a process of reconstructive memory, symbolised by the opening of doorways into the dark and unfathomable caverns of his mind.

The fabric of criminal character is woven and revealed through these flashes of memory — the stinking squalor of his shanty, hours tied to a bed post while his mother worked, the said mother crafting a voodoo doll for revenge on her employer, the faithful servant who stabs the vengeful one, the child wallowing in pools of his mother's congealed blood and emerging born again so to speak but not into the fraternity of human beings: 'The hag mounted his mind and whipped it to remember forever. Sharper and clearer. The steel pierced into his soul as his own humanity seeped with his mother's blood'.[25]

Lalla's sketches parallel worlds which resist all attempts to keep them apart — bright beauty, order, abundance, fragility and love / darkness, disorder, poverty, starvation, crime. Initially, the stark class differentiation dictates that they remain separate except for the workers who come and go. Eventually, Austin Louis the criminal on whom the plot resolution eventually hinges becomes the point of convergence. And Lalla's novel seems, to my reading, to strain at this point of convergence, when amiable, well meaning, old people exhume the corpse of their son and nephew seeking the identity of the criminal.

Underlying and in contestation within Lalla's novel are the pat class, race and gender certainties which are associated with upper strata Jamaican society. Indeed a significant dimension of the text is the palpable longing of upper middle class, fair-skinned Jamaican for the possession of his/her lush post-colonial Kingdom. Instead, as the novel progresses, the aging ones are marooned in an urban cul de sac appropriately named Oxford Close. While mass hysteria rises, neighbours migrate, properties are deserted, and a mass of unwashed humanity encroaches.

This notwithstanding, the text steers clear of predictable polarities sketching instead a tight web of connections and cause and effect relationships. It points to shared social and historical responsibility of all social groups for the outcomes. Whereas the criminal Austin must constantly deal with the trap doors that swing open unbidden in his mind to readmit memories of latrines and stench, abuse, blood, pain, fear and utter despair, Grace Goldman, secure in her family's love, must needs dredge the memory for discordant images that are not there. And the text itself becomes an assertion that the images, debilitating and empowering, are the collective inheritance of the Caribbean people. No social group can live an airtight existence. All must share culpability and credit for the common inheritance.

Lalla is careful to rebut the upper class discourse of racism. The clearest demonstration is in the portrayal of the Rats Man Lion. Not only is he an honourable man; he is also of honourable lineage. He and his father are both credited with redeeming the lives of vulnerable young boys and restoring them to their families. They bear favourable comparison with Senior's 'Brother Justice' who stands guard presumably to save a boy from sodomy — potential criminal assault which is alluded to in Senior's *Summer Lightning*. They also resemble Hodge's nurturing men and draw attention to hitherto submerged cultural paradigms of African-Caribbean masculinity which have been subject to sweeping generalisations and negative stereotyping.[26]

As the desecration of the matriarchal order, community, love and belonging is at the core of Senior's short story, the affirmation of family as the last vanguard against the hurtling social chaos is at the core of Lalla's. Moreover, the text features a visual motif, a sprawling family tree which links all of the major characters, and all of the ethnic groups into one family despite the hostilities of history and existing challenges. This vision which resembles that of Brodber in *Jane and Louisa* provides a glimpse of utopic possibility in a narrative dedicated to documenting encroaching social chaos.[27]

In the final analysis, the forces which generate the criminals, and what they in turn generate destroy their hope of belonging to family, even to the community of men. The redemptive figure in Austin Louis's life is Les who held a different door open — the door of inclusion into a generous and loving family. If a portion of Louis was slaughtered when his mother was murdered, he personally assassinates any possibility for rebirth, when he arranges the murder of the man who loved him completely and demonstrated to him the possibility of a better life.

Together, the fictions point to a range of causes which create the criminal mind. Gender overlaps with race, colour, age and class, to create multiple jeopardy for a cross section of young male. Many young criminals are spawned in starvation, abuse, loneliness, deprivation, stench and physical and moral filth. The situation is intensified in the case of absentee parenting whether in the form of the absent father or the absent mother. Migration aggravates the situation by adding to absenteeism, an unattainably 'imaginary homeland', a dream space which the child assumes will impart fullness of self.

Add to these the inaccessibility of markers of masculinity valorised in hegemonic society (wealth, status and secure advantageous employment) and criminal subcultures which valorise alternative masculinities are prone to emerge to provide alternative pathways. The negative impact of criminal subcultures is heightened in which children are habituated to these values from youth. Professional criminals who may emerge from such a procedure create their own legitimising meaning systems and assume dispassionate masks which allow them to murder with impunity. State officials and politicians who exploit gang violence heighten the anomie and blur the boundaries between the dominant culture and the subculture. Criminal networks and subcultures become embedded when they interact with a range of social networks and come to be legitimised, as inherent to the social well being.

Finally, how do the women writers of privileged class deal with the representation of the dark and monstrous other? This nightmarish figure holds a place of significance in the literary imagination recalling Kenneth Ramchand's evocation of the white Creole's 'terrified consciousness'. Their ambivalent positions as beneficiary of the institutional violence of slavery, the legacies of which are working for the privileged class of all ethnicities today, have created a paradoxical stance. The ongoing dependence on a 'black' servant class to ensure the privileged middle class lifestyle, which is open to upwardly mobile social groups of all shades and ethnicities, creates the ongoing necessity of and the fear of connection. The criminals may appear dark and unfathomable beyond control, but the writers probe the possibility and even tacitly acknowledge complicity as secret sharers in the systems of privileges, which continue to shape the 'monstrous other'. Moreover, the ideological imperative of creating a gendered, anti-establishment reconstruction of history demands exposure of the root and source of the violence.

The authors demonstrate a deep sensitivity to the connection between the existing mayhem and the inherent criminality behind historical forces at work. The modern Caribbean nation states were crafted in immense violence against the human person. The institutionalised violence of slavery and indentureship, racism and cultural denigration, perpetrated in the interest of mammon, has not been widely acknowledged as a crime against humanity. No absolution has been sought. No restitution has been made. Despite the substantial gains in terms of self government, development, and the establishment of prosperous, creative and humane Caribbean societies, institutional and personal violence escalate since the seeds were nestled within the grounding of our societies and well nurtured thereafter.

The writings explored here portray the grim criminal sensibility with honesty, artistic integrity and with a measure of sympathetic identification. As the writers display the overwhelmingly bleak socio-cultural scenario, they also affirm thematically and through cleverly deployed narrative strategies, a measure of identification with and perhaps even a hint of 'literary' atonement for the process. They simultaneously engage with and undermine denigrating stereotypes to create a case for understanding; they inscribe complicity with inequitable power relations and expose their consequence; they document resultant familial chaos and affirm the healing balm of enriching family love and community.

Notes

1. See Anthony Harriot, 'The Changing Social Organization of Crime and Criminals in Jamaica', in *Caribbean Sociology: An Introductory Reader*, Christine Barrow and Rhoda, (eds.), Kingston: Ian Randle Publisher, 1992. Writing on the changing social organisation of crime and criminals in Jamaica, Harriot indicates that the majority of victims are young (65%), urban based (70%) male (89%,) unemployed or self employed (59%).

2. See, for example, my paper 'Under Women's Eyes: Literary Constructs of Afro-Caribbean Masculinity', presented at the Symposium on 'The Construction of Caribbean Masculinity: Towards a Research Agenda', The University of the West Indies, St. Augustine, January 1996.

3. Christine Barrow, 'Caribbean Masculinities and Conjugal Relations: Idealogies and Contradictions', in *Gender and the Family in the Caribbean*, Wilma Bailey (ed.), Mona, Institute of Social and Economic Research, 1998, p.49.

4. Jean Rhys, 'Our Gardener', in *The Penguin Book of Caribbean Verse in English*, Paula Burnett, (ed.), Harmondsworth: Penguin, 1986.

5. Jean Rhys, *Wide Sargossa Sea*, London: Penguin Books, 1968.

6. This motif recurs in Senior's *Gardening in the Tropics* as well as in Walcott's *Pantomine* in which Jackson forcibly constrains Trewe to admit that Crusoe's occupation was not a delightful meander through a tropical paradise to be romantised in flowery language, 'O silent sea, O wondrous sunset' (148). Rather, it involved violent, self serving appropriation of the resources of the New World to meet his needs. See Mary Louise Pratt, *Imperial Eyes: Travel Writing and Transculturation*, London: Routledge, 1992.

7. Michelle Cliff, *No Telephone to Heaven*, London: Methuen, 1988.

8. Harriot, pp.512-27.

9. L. Gunst, *Born Fi Dead: A Journey into Jamaican Posse Underworlds*, London: Henry Holt, 1995.

10. Ibid., p.65.

11. Some elements of this discussion of Olive Senior's work are included in, 'Under Women's Eyes: Literary Constructs of Afro-Caribbean Masculinity', presented at the Symposium on 'The Construction of Caribbean Masculinity: Towards a Research Agenda', January 1998.

12. Harriot, p.519.

13. Olive Senior, 'The Dispatcher', in *Voiceprint*, Stewart Brown, Mervyn Morris and Gordon Rohlehr, (eds.), London: Longman, 1989. But compare Senior's figure with that in the Nursery rhyme:

> Jack Spratt could eat no fat
> His wife could eat no lean
> And so betwixt them both you see
> They licked the platter clean.

14. Errol Miller, 'Gender and the Family: Some Theoretical Considerations', in *Gender and the Family in the Caribbean*, 1990, p.26.

15. Senior, in *Voiceprint*.

16. Gunst, p.9.

17. Harriot, p.521.

18. Olive Senior, *Summer Lightning*, Essex: Longman, 1986.

19. Ibid., p.16.

20. Ibid., p.19.

21. Ibid., p.21.

22. Ibid., p.23.

23. Ibid., p.24.

24. Barbara Lalla, *Arch of Fire*, Kingston: Kingston Publishers, 1989.

25. Ibid., p.184.

26. Paula E. Morgan, 'Merle Hodge, Interview with Paula Morgan: Merle Hodge, Author and Activist', *Supporting Women and Development (WDS) Group News*, 3:2 (February, 1996), 12-18.

27. See also, Erna Brodber, *Jane and Louisa Will Soon Come Home*, London: New Beacon Books, 1980.

'Long Memoried' Meanings: Underpinnings of African-Caribbean Women's Writing

JOAN ANIM-ADDO

From dih pout
of mih mouth
from dih
treacherous
calm of mih
smile
you can tell
i is a long memoried woman
Grace Nichols

I take as my starting point Grace Nichols's preface, above, which lends the title to her 1983 Commonwealth Poetry award-winning collection, *i is a long memoried woman*.[1] The epigraph, which turns inescapably on a visual metaphor, begs the question: whose gaze is being privileged, that of the 'long memoried' woman or the implied reader, the 'you' of the text? Nichols's poem, grappling with issues of visibility and voice, audience and reading, resistance and testimony, allows rich beginnings for an exploration of some 'long memoried' underpinnings of African-Caribbean women's writing.

Texts by Merle Collins, Beryl Gilroy and M. Nourbese Philip similarly embed meanings crystallised in Nichols's text; similarly evoke remembrance. June D. Bobb writes:

The act of re(member)ing addresses the African's violent separation from the original body. It also addresses the New World need for reconnection to the original body and the creation of an identity out of the ruins of the past.[2]

The 'act of re(member)ing' is germane to this discussion. Similarly, the particular qualities with which Grace Nichols's text imbues the gendered act of remembering figured within the poem are also significant. Specifically, the text brings the woman's body into play as an embodiment of defiance since it is, after all, towards both 'pout and smile' that the reader is directed. Secondly, the ideological stance of the text signifies, like that of the woman's body it represents, an act of resistance. Thirdly, the text functions as an act of testimony which is affirmative, if possibly aggressive, and fourthly, the text reveals its meanings through a 'double consciousness'.[3] Nichols's instance of 'double consciousness' may be read as such, not only because of its African-Caribbean woman's voicing but also because of the way in which it invokes memory while implying a 'treacherous' retributive response consequential upon the wrong perpetrated. It is a text simultaneously reconstructing memory while rewriting history.

Only the mouth in pout and smile is highlighted but so much more is implied particularly the physical / psychological stance, offering a familiar enough 'everyday' figuration of the Caribbean female.

Nichols establishes direct contact between reader and narrator through the strategic juxtapositioning of the second and first person pronouns 'you' (line 7) and 'i' (line 8) of the text. This contributes powerfully to the second person / first person confrontation which the poet stages and which the text, through its staccato opening lines, immediately enforces upon the consciousness of the reader. I refer to the reading of the face, figured in 'pout', 'mouth' and 'smile', that is at once public, since it can be read by anyone; and intimate, by virtue not only of the 'treacherous' knowledge which the reader is made to share, albeit minimally, but also by the fact of the facial reading itself. That the reader's focus is directed first upon the 'pout' (line 1) followed by the 'smile' (line 5) implies interaction with a living subject. The acts of pouting and smiling, necessarily sequential gestures, underscore the living status of the subject which the first person creole variant of the present indicative tense, 'i is' reinforces.

The theory of the gaze, articulated variously by Caribbean Frantz Fanon[4] and North American Beth Newman[5] — among others — are of interest here. At the theoretical core of this discussion, however, I am concerned to foreground textual interpreters whose access to 'informing literary traditions' and 'real-world contexts' as described by American critic, Annette Kolodny[6], includes those in which the texts are rooted. In line with Kolodny's position on this, Valerie Lee's persuasively argued essay, 'Testifying Theory: Womanist Intellectual Thought' calls for the foregrounding of black women theorists still significantly absent as readers of texts by black women.[7] Valerie Lee asks two key questions. The first interrogates what happens to black women's literature when it is 'subjected exclusively to critical approaches' albeit 'useful and illuminating', which do not foreground or give primacy to 'black women's experiences and intellectual traditions?'[8] The second asks what happens to (black) students when they are denied access to black women's theorising? While Lee's essay reflects upon the African-American situation, the questions similarly draw attention to African-Caribbean literature as I have commented upon it elsewhere.[9]

Lee's concerns in some measure underline my own interest in questions about the theoretical framing of African-Caribbean women's literarture.[10] In part, this paper continues the development of that thinking. The first question, therefore, is whether African-Caribbean women theorise and if so how that theorising is made explicit. One might be forgiven for asking this question given the paucity of references to African-Caribbean women's theorising in the larger body of critical writing. At the same time, the paradox of critical silence into which many texts fall, is problematic relative to the proliferation of African-Caribbean women's writing in the final decades of the twentieth century. I am interested to address the role played by 'long memoried' African-Caribbean women's writing in making theorising explicit and to interrogate how memory has shaped that writing. Taking the lead from Nichols's text, womanist-feminist enquiry is offered which examines theorising through the texts which simultaneously reconstruct memory while rewriting history.

Returning the gaze

The theory of the gaze engages with a range of issues including whether the 'gaze' is necessarily male,[11] the centrality of visibility for women in relation to the gaze[12] and how the meaningfulness of the visual metaphor of the 'gaze', might itself be assessed.[13] That such preoccupations reflect culture-specific concerns may be illustrated by Fanon's seminal account of 'the gaze' or, having 'to meet the white man's eyes', which reflects upon a sensitivity equally alert to the male adult's response, as to the child's articulation of this in the statement, 'Mama, see the Negro! I'm frightened'.[14] Nichols's text, published thirty six years after Fanon's, succeeds in subverting a good many notions of the gaze by insisting upon first directing the gaze upon the female body, that is, visibility for the female subject and an objectifying of the gazer ('you') which parallels the objectifying of the one viewed ('i').

Nichols's narrator's demand for visibility may be paralleled with the long-memoried demand for black women critics which Valerie Lee makes. Lee's citation of Barbara Christian's analysis of the power dynamics contributing to the absence of black women theorists might also apply to the present day context of invisibility for African-Caribbean women theorists:

My concern, then, is a passionate one, for the literature of a people who are not in power has always been in danger of extinction or co-optation, not because we do not theorise, but because what we can even imagine, far less who we can reach, is constantly limited by societal pressure.[15]

While the steady publication of new titles since the nineteen eighties attests to there being little current danger of the 'extinction' of Caribbean women's literature, a concern about 'co-optation' resounds in Lizabeth Paravisini-Gebert's critique of present day realities. Paravisini-Gebert argues for example that, 'Black women — given their gender and race — have become the subject of almost feverish study; Caribbean women, by virtue of their race, gender and postcolonial condition, have become the other's other, a valuable commodity'.[16] By this analysis, Paravisini-Gebert signals an unwelcome visibility which goes hand in hand with an absence of theoretical power. Carole Boyce Davies's caution that, 'at the same time one must not concede all the theoretical positions of power to men and white women' is consequently the more poignant for Paravisini-Gebert's analysis.[17]

Of course, Nichols's poem returns the gaze textually. Such a textual context of interest to literary debate similarly concerns USA feminist, Beth Newman, whose perspective on the gaze leads to the questioning of the validity of the visual metaphor in the light of novels being 'verbal structures rather than visual ones'.[18] These 'verbal structures' have, nonetheless, been important vehicles allowing movement from a status of invisibility to one of visibility; from powerlessness to author-ity for African-Caribbean women writers. A result of this is evidence of theorising, if not through direct 'theoretical positions of power' then through the texts which are published.

M. Nourbese Philip writes of texts which hold 'to the centre of remembrance'.[19] These may be said to be *actively* long memoried and, like Merle Collins's *Angel* (1987) and Beryl Gilroy's *Boy Sandwich* (1989) imaginatively engage with acts witnessed.[20] Gilroy's *Boy Sandwich*, for example, treats the racism of post-fifties Britain; while central to Collins's *Angel* is the political upheaval of post-independence Grenada. Both texts function, in terms of memory trace, as historical-testimonial texts so that *Boy Sandwich*'s addressing of the racism of post-fifties Britain is not as the narrative of victims but as the backdrop to a significant period in the lives of three generations of an African-Caribbean family resident in London. Writing autobiographically of the period, Gilroy notes:

The world of the young Commonwealth immigrant of the early fifties was full of political talk. People slept, dreamt and lived politics.... We were all going to put this world to rights in five or six moves.[21]

Gilroy's 'five or six moves' captures with irony the idealism and confidence of the 'young Commonwealth immigrant', or more specifically, the student emigré interested to effect change. *Boy Sandwich* tells a different and altogether harsher story. Instead of the thrill of political involvement and debate, the Graingers, economic migrants, who find loss and the constant threat of erasure of the self within their new home setting, London, describe their experience as 'days of woe and weepin'.[22] The text theorises further upon the experience of post-war immigrant existence in London, 'even today they seem to understand only suffering. It is like the mortar that holds the bricks of their lives together'.[23] What is more, such 'suffering' which holds their lives together applies not only to the migrants. The situation is equally problematic for the young adults of the Grainger's grandchildren's generation. The particular flavour of the racism of the fifties is subsequently summed up in Grandpa Grainger's observation: 'It bad to be a foreigner and worse to be coloured'.[24]

At a textual level, the author's theorising is evident in her summation of suffering through endemic racism, which becomes a fundamental part of the African-Caribbean migrant experience: 'It is like the mortar'. Yet the need to socialise a new generation to a sense of belonging, despite the racism, becomes paramount and young Tyrone, notwithstanding the experience of his grandparents and parents, asserts, 'I belong regardless of those who say I don't'.[25] An effect of this is that the text which introduces the Graingers, at the point at which they are objects of hatred in the racists' gaze, also returns the gaze and, like Nichols's text takes delight in the focusing and directing of the returned gaze.

Privileging Voice
The statement 'i is a long memoried woman' privileges voice. Further, it privileges the vernacular voice of the Caribbean, an

ideological stance which remains as problematic within the Caribbean as outside of the region. M. Nourbese Philip writes in 'Who's Listening?' an essay in the collection, *Frontiers* (1992):

Language has been and remains — as the South African example shows — a significant and essential part of the colonisation process; the choice between Caribbean demotic and standard English becomes, therefore, more than a choice of audience.[26]

For some African-Caribbean women writers, the 'choice' to which Philip refers, itself signifies the African-Caribbean experience. Indeed Philip's discussion of the demotic leads pointedly to issues of power and control. Nichols's narrator claims both in her distinct evocation of the colonised experience. She affirms herself as woman, African-Caribbean and colonial in the deceptively simple but loaded 'I is' statement. Merle Collins in interview refers to the 'voices of my early socialisation' as a dominant influence upon her writing.[27] In her case, this particular 'long memoried' nexus is a crucial one. To be 'long memoried' is, in the first instance, to be active in the recording or publishing of signs from 'before and now'[28] of significance to the self or community. For African-Caribbean women writers like Collins, language is a crucial sign of such community. This is not to suggest that the complex Caribbean language situation and that of individual writers resident in any number of diasporic locations is solved by a binary choice between either standard English or a Caribbean variant. For writers of an earlier generation in the anglophone context, few options existed. Mimetic reproduction of standard English was highly valued. Gilroy recalls:

Since Independence, you could or you could not speak English. I wrote about this in *Sunlight On Sweet Water*. We were told, Don't say papaya, say paw-paw and my aunt would tell us what to say; teach us how to be mimetic.[28]

But the demand for mimetic reproduction of the colonial language came to straining point precisely at the historical moment when many African-Caribbean women became seriously engaged with the process of reconstructing and recreating the self. It is at that point in the nineteen eighties that Nourbese Philip's cry, 'A foreign anguish is english' is palpably understood.[29] At a textual level, resistance to the 'bile of a colonial language' becomes articulated as both text and sub-text for many African-Caribbean women writers who, like Philip are only too well aware of seeing 'no way around the language, only through it'.[30]

The language of Merle Collins's writing is interesting in its 'long memoried' stance towards that which Philip describes as 'the bile of a colonial language'. As in Philip's writing, language for Collins readily becomes sub-text. In *Angel*, Collins's first novel, the following extract illustrates how language operates as both text and subtext.

'Hear how de boy talking bad, non!'...
'So youself you talkin better den?' someone asked.
'He not talkin bad. He's speaking a different language, that's all. It's no better or no worse than English.'
'Is not that Cambridge want though!'
'True! So we learn English, but it isn't better than our own language'.[31]

The extract depicts a Caribbean classroom accurately reflecting some of the language forces at work. Not only is 'talking bad', that is, the popular creole medium, under attack, but a level of irony also applies. This is because the discussion, initially about the American 'invasion' of the island had interrupted the teaching of the established literary canon. The teacher had abandoned Shakespeare's *Macbeth*, no less, in order to facilitate her students response to the 'invasion' of Grenada. Yet 'colonial' investment in Standard English (SE) is acknowledged in the student's statement: 'Is not that Cambridge want though!' That is to say, the language of status and power is widely known to be *not* the Caribbean variant, not the popular language of the people, but the language of text books and an elite local minority. The devalued view of the mother tongue is, not surprisingly, widely internalised by the educated, those aspiring to educated status, and educators, hence the reference to 'talkin bad'. Trinidadian author and critic, Merle Hodge takes issue with the blanket valuing of the higher status SE to the exclusion of Creole as follows:

> Educators at the highest level become too hysterical to argue rationally when they are presented with the very simple proposition that Caribbean people can be *armed with both standard English and their own mother tongue, Creole...*[32] (italics mine).

It is, to use Hodge's terms, the linguistic armoury comprising 'both Standard English and their own mother tongue, Creole', which the fiction of Caribbean women particularly in the eighties and nineties submit to literary crafting.

Testimony

To be 'long memoried' is also to be prepared to testify as Nichols's narrator does. Testimony, Valerie Lee suggests, plays a crucial part in womanist writing.[33] From further direct testimony, Philip notes:

> But as a writer nurtured on *the bile of a colonial language*, whose only intent was imperialistic, I see no way around the language only through it, challenging the mystification and half truths at its core[34] (italics mine).

Collins's *Angel,* like Gilroy's *Boy Sandwich* similarly testifies, though their settings differ, to 'days of woe and weepin'. Collins states that the novel, '*Angel* is more consciously concerned with the historical, about the colonial and neo-colonial existence'.[35] Furthermore, asked about the way in which she addresses political and socio-economic issues in the text, she asserts, 'politics is life'.[36] In contrast to *Boy Sandwich*, the narrative of *Angel* theorises at the intersections of race, gender and class. Like Gilroy, Collins's rootedness in African-Caribbean realities at the centre of which is the extended family, leads to an exploration of 'generational shifts'.[37] Three generations of black women are brought into focus; the youngest, Angel, becomes the first to benefit fully from post-war educational opportunities for girls. Angel's mother, Doodsie, proud of her achieving daughter, regularly exhorts her to take advantage of the opportunities for which she has striven. She warns, 'Ah have nutting to leave for you when ah dead all ah have is in you head so make de best of it'.[38]

The narrative, structured partly through highlighting the mothertongue, achieves the effect of theorising rooted in everyday practice literally writ large within the text. Proverbs, riddles, pithy popular Creole sayings, in bold type face, signal and substantiate the philosophy and 'everyday' theorising of the community upon which the novel is focused. Of some fifty plus examples, the following offer an indication of the range and replication of both language and philosophy: 'one han' caan clap';[39] 'don't sit on nobody eyelash so dat when they wink, you fall'[40] and 'sa ki f'ew?' (what to do?)[41] Collins has referred to the indigenous style of philosophising, indicated above, as speaking 'in headlines'.[42] She explains:

> When I say we speak in headlines, I am referring to the way of encapsulating a whole philosophy of life into a short proverb. For example, Doodsie might say to Angel, 'Look child, don't live on nobody's eyelash so that when they wink you fall.' Immediately, Angel understands that this is relevant to a conversation that they may have had some ten minutes ago or is the substance of a conversation which will follow. This is what I mean when I say we speak in headlines. The proverbs. The philosophy of life.[43]

The headlines, proverbs and pithy sayings, testimony to a theorising community, function as signifiers of remembrance as well as contemporary theorising in literary texts across the region, regardless of language barriers. Francophone author, Simone Schwarz-Bart's *Bridge of Beyond*, for example, is a novel richly textured with such examples of folk wisdom.[44] Why such widespread emphasis on folk wisdom? Bobb's analysis points firmly to the value of the word itself within

Caribbean communities. She notes that 'the experience of Caribbean people has been built on suppression and silence, but a silence under which the 'word' was carefully preserved'.[45] It is such silence, broken in relation to black women, at the level of publication of African-Caribbean women's literary texts, which now remains to be broken through an insistence upon the valuing of practice described by African-American, Patricia Hill Collins as 'Black women's intellectual tradition'.[46] The nature of such a tradition extends from the 'everyday' Caribbean-rooted theorising, often the preserve of matriarchs and other wise, ancestral women, to be found in the literary texts; to the theoretical texts written from a knowledge base valued by prestigious western institutions of learning. The significance of the 'everyday' heightened within the literary text remains yet to be valued in critical practice.

Resistance and Memory
The role played by memory in Caribbean women's literature has, until recently, been little theorised. Myriam Chancy, in *Framing Silence* (1997),[47] contributes to this important area of debate in relation to Haitian women writers so as to highlight the way in which memory functions as a 'crucial element of the politics of representation in the Haitian woman's novel'.[48]

Signalling caution, part of Chancy's project lies in indicating how the process of change from dependence on an oral culture to the establishing of a scribal culture through colonisation 'resulted in a tragic falsification of memory'.[49] The extent to which the Haitian situation might resemble that of the anglophone Caribbean is subject to conjecture at this moment in the literary history of the region. Yet what is beginning to emerge in respect of the anglophone African-Caribbean novel is the scope of memory in first-wave longer fictional texts.

Chancy's analysis points to memory as a 'signifier of identity'. In Gilroy's novels, identity founded upon a 'long memoried' knowledge of the self is of particular importance. Furthermore, it is within such ontological rootedness that Gilroy's characters, like Nichols's narrator referred to above, find the necessary resources for effective resistance against the trangressor's hurt. *Boy Sandwich*, set both in London and on 'the island', like several of Gilroy's works, presents elderly black characters. Though spanning three generations, the novel maintains a central focus upon London born and 'culturally adapted' Tyrone. Identity and notions of home are among the themes explored in the text. What sustains Clara and Simon Grainger in their difficult old age in London is their memory of who they are. It is during this period that they are deprived of even the material benefits of metropolitan existence and are forced, rather, to experience the indignity of eviction from the house they have struggled to afford. Their family album, described as 'the most treasured of his possessions — this album of pages overburdened with photographs' becomes crucial to sustaining the memory of identity.[50] Thus a more everyday function of memory as a cohesive force within family or community is also treated in Gilroy's work. For this reason in *Boy Sandwich*, Gilroy employs the Grainger's family album as an important focus for the sharing of family stories binding the generations together. Gilroy writes: 'the album is an amalgam of remembered tales, some amorphous, others observational and yet others romanticised'.[51]

While this man-made construct for preserving memory serves a clear function in the Grainger's household as aide-memoire, its significance is only surpassed by the bag of island soil which Clara Grainger clutches through all her troubles. For Gilroy, the role of identity in the creation of character is paramount and highlights 'the fear of being forgotten and of avoiding chaos and anxiety as well as the confusions of social and psychological space'.[52] Memory, then, serves a plurality of functions among which as in Nichols's text is the positive role of resistance.

A feature of particular significance to each of Gilroy's texts, memory is also firmly related to the body. For example, Gilroy pays attention to the body as recipient or 'store house' of memory. She refers, too, to 'body text' which, she suggests survives in the memory. She refers to the body as mortuary where dead memories and past hurts remain unresolved. In comparison, it is the active, living memory which positively contributes to the resistance required to survive in hostile conditions.

The context of immigration as experienced by the Graingers represents such a hostile environment. Yet the impact of acute change upon memory is a minor part of the adjustment that is implied in the use of the term 'immigrant' or 'immigration'. A good many of Gilroy's characters are immigrants for whom acute change has left its emotional scars. Such 'change' brought about by the process of immigration plays a key part in the new literature of the diaspora. Gilroy writes that 'change by immigration is a crucial and comprehensive step. It calls for dramatic and external orientation'.[53] If such 'orientation' is evident in the characterisation by Gilroy and other writers, how might this be understood?

The recuperative meanings of memory and diaspora are beginning to be revealed in a range of recently published texts. It is, for example, at the beginning of *Boy Sandwich* that Claire and Simon Grainger assess the extent of their enforced re-orientation and the toll it has taken upon their lives. Furthermore, recent memories are displacing older ones as new generations represented by characters such as Adijah and Tyrone in *Boy Sandwich* discover the complexities of their diasporic identity. In many respects, the texts I have foregrounded are those which, like Philip's, 'undermine the culture of silence in the ordeal of testimony'.[54] 'The grief sealed in memory' continues to be transformed as publication. What remains is the reading of it.

Notes

1. Grace Nichols, *I Is a Long Memoried Woman*, London: Karnak House, 1990.
2. June D. Bobb, *Beating A Restless Drum: The Poetics of Kamau Brathwaite and Derek Walcott*, New Jersey: Africa World Press, 1998, p.38.
3. W.E.B. DuBois, *The Souls of Black Folk* (first pubd.1903), New York: Dover Publications, 1994, p.2. See also, Paul Gilroy, *Small Acts: Thoughts on the Politics of Black Cultures*, London: Serpents Tail, 1993, pp.160-61.
4. Frantz Fanon, *Black Skin, White Masks*, London: Pluto Press, 1986, p.110.

Joan Anim-Addo

5. Beth Newman, "'The Situation of the Looker-On": Gender, Narration and Gaze in Wuthering Heights', in robyn r.warhol & diane price herndl, *Feminisms*, Hampshire: Macmillan, 1997, pp.449-66.
6. Annette Kolodny, 'Dancing Through the Minefields: Some Observations', in warhol & herndl, (eds.), p.180.
7. Valerie Lee, 'Testifying Theory: Womanist Intellectual Thought' in *Women: A Cultural Review*, 6, 2, (Autumn 1995) 200-206.
8. Ibid., 201.
9. I refer to unpublished conference papers.
10. The conference, 'Framing The Word' and the critical collection of the same title which followed began to address such issues in relation to Caribbean women's writing.
11. E. Ann Kaplan cited in warhol and herndl, (eds.), p.449.
12. Luce Irigary, "Another "Cause" Castration" from *Speculum of the Other Woman*, in warhol and herndl, (eds.), p.428.
13. Newman, ibid.
14. Fanon, 1986, p.110.
15. Barbara Christian cited in Lee, p.200.
16. Lizabeth Paravisini-Gebert, in Adele Newsom and Linda Strong-Leek, (eds.) *Winds of Change*, New York: Peter Lang, 1998, p.161.
17. Carole Boyce Davies cited in Lee, p.200.
18. Newman, ibid.
19. M. Nourbese Philip, *She Tries Her Tongue, Her Silence Softly Breaks*, London: Women's Press, 1993.
20. Merle Collins, *Angel*, London: Women's Press, 1987; Beryl Gilroy, *Boy Sandwich*, London: Heinemann, 1989.
21. Beryl Gilroy, *Black Teacher*, London: Cassell, 1976, p. 103.
22. Gilroy, 1989, p.21.
23. Ibid.
24. Ibid., p.22.
25. Ibid., p.30.
26. M. Nourbese Philip, 'Who's Listening?' Artists, Audiences & Language', in *Frontiers: Essays and Writings On Racism and Culture*, Ontario: Mercury Press,1992, p.37.
27. 'Merle Collins Interview with Joan Anim-Addo', *Mango Season*, 5, (April 1996) 5.

286

28. Beryl Gilroy Interview with Joan Anim-Addo, *Mango Season*, 3, (August 1995) 4-5.
29. Philip, 1993, p.30.
30. Ibid, p.32.
31. Collins, 1987, p.236.
32. Merle Hodge, 'Challenges of the Struggle for Sovereignty: Changing the World Versus Writing Stories', in Selwyn Cudjoe, (ed.), *Caribbean Women Writers*, Massachusetts: Calaloux, 1990, p.204.
33. Lee, ibid.
34. M. Nourbese Philip, 1992, p.77.
35. Brenda Berrian, "We Speak Because We Dream'. Conversations with Merle Collins", in Carole Boyce Davies, (ed.), *Moving Beyond Boundaries*, Volume 2, London: Pluto Press, 1995, p38.
36. Ibid., p 39.
37. See Houston Baker, *Blues, Ideology and African-American Literature*, for an African-American discussion of the concept.
38. Collins, 1987, p.90.
39. Ibid., p.34.
40. Ibid., p.52.
41. Ibid., p.22.
42. Berrian, p.39.
43. Ibid.
44. Simone Schwarz-Bart, *Bridge of Beyond*, trans. Barbara Bray, London: Heinemann, 1982.
45. Bobb, 1998, p.40.
46. Cited in Lee. See Patricia Hill Collins, *Black Feminist Thought: Knowledge, Consciousness and the Politics of Empowerment*, Boston: Unwin Hyman, 1990, p.15.
47. Myriam J.A. Chancy, *Framing Silence*, New Jersey: Rutgers University Press, 1997.
48. Ibid., p.74.
49. Ibid.
50. Gilroy, 1987, p.5.
51. Beryl Gilroy, *Leaves in the Wind*, London: Mango Publishing, 1998, p.74.
52. Ibid., p.73.
53. Ibid., p.104.
54. Philip, 1993, p.70.

EPILOGUE

Interview with the Shantytown

ALBA AMBERT

After many years, a woman returns to the Puerto Rico shantytown where she was born.

SHANTYTOWN:
Hey, long time no see.

WOMAN:
Not long enough.

SHANTYTOWN:
Staying?

WOMAN:
Just passing through.

SHANTYTOWN:
So, what can I get you *mamita*? Some ganja, an AK, nose candy, nice primos, some Fu Manchu chocolate, a good edge. Jagged or smooth. You name it. Any shit you want, I got it.

WOMAN:
Nothing more from you, thanks.

SHANTYTOWN:
What's the score then?

WOMAN:
(Looks around and hums) *The shantytown, the bitter shantytown has nailed me to a cross.*

SHANTYTOWN:
You keep humming that Carlos Gardel song. Man, what a downer.

WOMAN:
You should know.

SHANTYTOWN:
Whatcha talking about?

WOMAN:
Don't you torture and kill people? Rob them of all hope. (Humming) *The shantytown, the bitter shantytown has nailed me to a cross.*

SHANTYTOWN:
Who are you, anyways?

WOMAN:
You don't remember my name? I didn't think so. But it really doesn't matter. Call me *arrabalera*, shantytown dweller. I wasn't born from the sea. Though I could have been. This is an island after all. Surrounded on all sides by the sea and I had to be born in this fetid mud. I was born nameless. Right here. In you.

SHANTYTOWN:
Yeah, I could tell right away that you was one of mine. But I don't remember exactly. I seen so many. When was it?

WOMAN:
When a bolt of lighting cleaved my mother in two and I swam to the shores of her thighs.

SHANTYTOWN:
So, that's what this is all about! I remember now. Your mami was a gorgeous piece of ass, you know. I couldn't get why your papá dumped her. That other bitch he ran off with wasn't half as good. But hey, it ain't my fault if someone pushed her into the swamp. And she was pregnant, right? Was that you in her belly?

WOMAN:
What do you think?

SHANTYTOWN:

You shouldda died like all those other babies.

WOMAN:

Nothing moves you, does it?

SHANTYTOWN:

I'm just saying. Your father split, your mother died, so it's a miracle you survived. But hey, you can't blame me for nothing. Look at you. You left and now you're looking sooo good, *mamita*.

WOMAN:

I left, but you didn't. You stayed. Hounded me like a stalker. Everywhere I went, there you were, my punishment, my curse. Squeezing tightly around my heart. I'll always be an *arrabalera*. Don't you get it? I'm sewn to your cross.

SHANTYTOWN:

Cut out that cross business already! You ain't dying or nothin'.

WOMAN:

That's where you're wrong. All my life I've been dying because I don't know how to live. What did I learn from you that could help me survive out there?

SHANTYTOWN:

Where?

WOMAN:

Out there where babies aren't dying, where men don't get shot and women's faces aren't slashed open.

SHANTYTOWN:

Oh, you mean where white folk live. That ain't no place for one of mine. You shouldda known better and stayed here. I couldda gave you a lot more than that boring crap.

WOMAN:

Such as?

SHANTYTOWN:

Livin' *mi vida loca*, baby! Stuff to take your mind off things, you know what I mean? Make you doze under the sun all day and earn some quick pesos by just opening your pretty thighs. Get some heavy action at the corner hangout.

WOMAN

Like the bar where my godfather was riddled with bullets?

SHANTYTOWN:

Did you see when they smoked him?

WOMAN:

From here, I've seen all there is to see.

SHANTYTOWN:

Bet you don't get that kind of action out there. You gotta come back. Stay here where you belong.

WOMAN:

Don't you understand that I don't belong here, just as I don't belong there? Do you see what I mean? It's like living in a lightless hole where nothing survives. Only a chill deep in my bones. It's fear that circles around me, I know that. A fear of being stranded in the middle of nowhere. And every night I look out at the dense darkness and press my knees against the sky so the fear won't enter me.

The woman looks out at the cardboard and wooden shacks built on high stilts in the marsh. A breeze lifts the stench of the sewage that collects in the marsh and she turns around, putting her hand over her nose. The shantytown is quiet and still under the blazing sun.

WOMAN:

At night I lie in bed studying the ceiling and fall into a restless dream. Then I'm shrouded by mist. A shadow that's so thick it crusts over my eyelids. I don't dream any more, but drown in darkness every night. A darkness that's so suffocating, so dense, it sucks me into itself avidly, desperately. In the depths of this dreamless sleep, I feel terror. The terror of knowing without images. In the absolute darkness of sleep, I soak in the humiliating stench of rotten moss.

SHANTYTOWN:

Listen, *mamita*, you're too sad. I can get you something for that. Make you feel real good.

WOMAN:

For how long?

SHANTYTOWN:

As long as you want. *Por vida*, for life, if that's what you want.

WOMAN:

I told you I don't belong here.

SHANTYTOWN:

You just told me you don't belong there.

WOMAN:

No, I don't belong there either. I live on the border. On the edge of the tongue, the edge of the mind, the edge of consciousness. Flapping like a rag over the border and back, never knowing quite where that border ends or begins. What's a border, anyway?

SHANTYTOWN:

You lost me.

WOMAN:

You don't know what it means to live on the edge, to subsist on knives and blades and shards of glass, do you? What it means to step ever so carefully, all the time afraid of stumbling over your own tongue. The edge isn't a shore or a frontier. The edge is a knife, a blade. The edge is the humiliation of a turned back, the sting of a slur, the rage of impotence. The edge is an end with no beginning. The edge is living the jabber of a foreign language.

SHANTYTOWN:

So, what you're saying is that you live on some kind of edge that's sort of between here and there.

WOMAN:

I guess that's the answer. I inhabit the edge, a place of perpetual banishment. Always looking back to the impossible return.

Selected Bibliography

Allison, A.W. et al., (eds.), *The Norton Anthology of Poetry*, New York, 1983.

Anim-Addo, Joan (ed.), *Framing the Word : Gender and Genre in Caribbean Women's Writing*, London: Whiting and Birch, 1996.

_____ 'Merle Collins Interview with Joan Anim-Addo', *Mango Season*, 5, April, 1996.

_____ 'Beryl Gilroy Interview with Joan Anim-Addo', *Mango Season*, 3, August, 1995.

Ashcroft, B., Griffiths, G. and Tiffin, H., *The Empire Writes Back: Theory and Practice in Post-Colonial Literatures*, London and New York: Routledge, 1989.

Badinter, Elisabeth, *The Myth of Motherhood*, London: Souvenir Press, 1981.

Baugh, Edward, 'Goodison on the Road to Heartease', *Journal of West Indian Literature*, 1(1), 1986.

Benjamin, W, in Arendt, H. (ed.), *Illuminations*, trans. Zohn, H. London: Fontana, 1973.

Bernabé, J.P. Chamoiseau and R. Confiant, *Eloge de la Créolité*, Paris: Gallimard, 1990. English translation, 'In Praise of Creoleness', *Callaloo*, 13, 1990, 886-909.

Berrian, B. (1989) *Bibliography of Women Writers from the Caribbean*, Washington: Three Continents Press, 1989.

_____ ' "We Speak Because We Dream'. Conversations with Merle Collins", in Boyce Davies, C. (ed.), *Moving Beyond Boundaries*, Volume 2, London: Pluto Press, 1995.

Birbalsingh, F. (ed.), *Frontiers of Caribbean Literature in English*, London: Macmillan, 1996.

Bishop, M., 'Interview with Joan Riley', *Spare Rib*, 156, (July), 1985.

Blain, V. et al., *The Feminist Companion to Literature in English*, London: B.T. Batsford, 1990.

Bobb, J.D., *Beating A Restless Drum: The Poetics of Kamau Brathwaite & Derek Walcott*, New Jersey: Africa World Press, 1998.

Bolland, O.N., 'Creolization and Creole Societies: A Cultural Nationalist View of Caribbean Social History', in *Intellectuals in the Twentieth-Century Caribbean*, Volume 1, *Spectre of the New Class: the Commonwealth Caribbean*, Hennessy, H. (ed.), London: The Macmillan Press, 1992.

Brand Dionne, *San Souci and other Stories*, Ontario: William Wallace, 1989

_____ *In Another Place, Not Here*, London: The Women's Press, 1997.

Brathwaite, E.K., 'Roots: A Commentary on West Indian Writers', *Bim* 10, 37 (July-December), 1963.

_____ 'Timehri', *Savacou*, 2, (1970), 35-44.

_____ *The Arrivants: A New World Tragedy*, London: OUP, 1975; Oxford: Oxford University Press, 1967.

_____ *The Development of Creole Society in Jamaica 1770-1820*, Oxford: Oxford University Press, 1978.

_____ *A History of the Voice*, London: New Beacon, 1984.

_____ 'Caliban's Guarden', *Wasafiri*, 16, 1992.

Brodber, Erna, *Jane and Louisa Will Soon Come Home*, London: New Beacon, 1980.

_____ *Perceptions of Caribbean Women: Towards A Documentation of Stereotypes*, Cave Hill, Barbados: ISER, 1982.

_____ *Myal*, London: New Beacon Books, 1988.

_____ 'Fiction in the Scientific Procedure', in Cudjoe, S. (ed.) *Caribbean Women Writers: Essays from the First International Conference*, Wellesley: Calaloux, 1990.

Brown, S., Morris, M. and Rohlehr, G. (eds.), *Voiceprint*, London: Longman Caribbean Limited, 1989,

Brydon, D. and Tiffin, H., *Decolonising Fictions*, Mundlestrup: Dangaroo Press, 1983.

Campbell, E., 'Afterword' to Allfrey, P.S., *The Orchid House*, London: Virago, 1990.

Capécia, M., *Je Suis Martiniquaise*, Paris: Corréa, 1948.

_____ *La Négresse blanche*, Paris: Corréa, 1950.

Carmichael', Mrs, *Domestic Manners*, 1833.

Carrington, Roslyn, *A Thirst for Rain*, New York: Kensington Books, 1999.

Césaire, I., *Mémoires d'Isles*, Paris: Editions Caribéennes, 1985.

Chamberlin, J. Edward, *Come Back To Me My Language: Poetry and the West Indies*, Toronto: McClelland and Stewart, 1993.

Chancy, M.J.A., *Searching for Safe Spaces: Afro-Caribbean Women Writers in Exile*, Temple University Press: Philadelphia, 1997.

_____ *Framing Silence*, New Jersey: Rutgers University Press, 1997.

Chodorow, Nancy, *The Reproduction of Mothering*, Berkeley: University of California Press, 1978.

Clifford, James, 'Diasporas', *Cultural Anthropology*, 9(3), 302-338, 1994.

Collins, Merle, *Angel*, London: Women's Press, 1987.

Collins, Patricia Hill, *Black Feminist Thought: Knowledge, Consciousness and the Politics of Empowerment*, Boston: Unwin Hyman, 1990.

Condé, Maryse, *Les Derniers Rois mages*, Paris: Mercure de France, 1992.

_____ *Heremakhonon*, Paris: Union Générale d'Editions; English translation (1982) *Heremakhonon*, Washington: Three Continents Press, 1976.

_____ *Moi, Tituba, Sorcière noire de Salem*, Paris: Mercure de France, 1986. English translation, *I. Tituba, Black Witch of Salem*, Charlottesville: University Press of Virginia, 1992.

_____ *Ségou: Les murailles de terre*, Paris, Laffont, 1984.

_____ *Ségou: La terre en miettes*, Paris, Laffont, 1985.

_____ *Rihata*, Paris, Laffont, 1981. English translation, *A Season in Rihata*, London: Heinemann, 1998.

_____ *Traversée de la mangrove*, Paris: Mercure de France, 1995. English translation, *Crossing the Mangrove*, New York: Anchor Books, 1995.

_____ *La Vie scélérate*, Paris: Seghers, 1987. English translation, *The Tree of Life*. New York: Ballantine Books, 1992.

Condé, Mary and Lonsdale, Thorunn (eds.), *Caribbean Women Writers: Fiction in English*, Hampshire and London: Macmillan.

Cooper, C., 'Afro-Jamaican folk elements in Brodber's *Jane and Louisa Will Soon Come Home*', in Boyce-Davies, C. and Fido Savory, E. (eds.), *Out of the Kumbla*, Trenton, NJ: Africa World Press, 1990.

_____ *Noises in the Blood*, London: Macmillan, 1993.

Cudjoe, S., *Caribbean Women Writers: Essays from the First International Conference*, Wellesley, Massachusetts: Calaloux, 1990.

Cumber Dance, D. 'Go Eena Kumbla: A Comparison of Erna Brodber's *Jane and Louisa Will Soon Come Home* and Toni Cade Bambara's *The Salt Eaters*', in Cudjoe, S. (ed.) *Caribbean Women Writers.*

Danticat, E., *Breath, Eyes, Memory*, London: Abacus, 1995.

Davies, C.B., *Black Women, Writing and Identity: Migrations of the Subject*, London: Routledge, 1994.

Davies, C.B. and Savory-Fido, E., *Out of the Kumbla*, Trenton, New Jersey: Africa World Press, 1990.

Davies, Catherine, 'Writing the African Subject: Two Women Poets of Cuba', in *Women, A Cultural Review*, 4(1), 1993, 32-48.

Dilger, G., 'Jamaica Kincaid Talks to Gerhard Dilger', in *Wasafiri*, 16, (Autumn), 1992.

Donnell, A., 'Contradictory (W)omens? Gender Consciousness in the Poetry of Una Marson', *Kunapipi*, XVII(3), 1995, 43-58.

_____ 'Writing for Resistance: Nationalism and narratives of Liberation', in Joan Anim-Addo (ed.), *Framing the Word: Gender and Genre in Caribbean Women's Writing*, London: Whiting and Birch, 1996, 12-27.

Donnell, A, and Lawson Welsh, S. (eds.), *The Routledge Reader in Caribbean Literature*, London: Routledge, 1996.

Dracius-Pinalie, S., *L'Autre qui danse*, Paris: Seghers, 1989.

DuBois, W.E.B., *The Souls of Black Folk*, New York: Dover Publications, 1994 (first pubd.1903).

Duncker, P., *Sisters and Strangers — An Introduction to Contemporary Feminist Fiction*, Oxford, UK and Cambridge USA: Blackwell, 1992.

Durie, Alice, *One Jamaica Gal*, Kingston: Jamaica Times, 1939.

Eco, U., *Travels in Unreality*, London: Picador, 1980.

Elizabeth, C., [Mrs C. Tonna], *The System: A Tale of the West Indies*, 1823.

Engber, M., *Caribbean Fiction and Poetry*, New York, Center for Inter-American Relations, 1970.

Fanon, F., *Black Skin, White Masks*, trans., Charles Lam Markmann, London: Pluto Press, 1986.

Ferguson, M., *First Feminists: British Women Writers, 1578-1799*, Bloomington: Indiana University Press, 1985.

_____ *Subject to Others: British Women Writers and Colonial Slavery, 1670-1834*, New York and London: Routledge, 1992.

Firestone, Shulamith, *The Dialectic of Sex*, New York: Bantam Books, 1970.

Freud, S. *Totems and Taboos*, New York: Routledge.

Fulani, I., *Seasons of Dust*, New York: Harlem River Press, 1997.

Garner, E., *Duet in Discord*, London: Arthur Barker Ltd, 1936.

_____ *A Flying Fish Whispered*, London: Arthur Barker Ltd, 1938.

_____ *Winter Is in July*, London: Jonathan Cape, 1948.

Gilman, S.L., 'Black Bodies, White Bodies: Toward an Iconography of Female Sexuality in Late Nineteenth-Century Art, Medicine and Literature', in Donald, J. and Rattansi, A. (eds.), *'Race', Culture and Difference*, London: Sage Publications in association with The Open University, 1992.

Gilroy, B., *Black Teacher*, London: Cassell, 1976.

_____ *Boy Sandwich*, London: Heinemann, 1989.

_____ *Leaves in the Wind*, London: Mango Publishing, 1998.

Gilroy, Paul, *Small Acts: Thoughts on the Politics of Black Cultures*, London: Serpent's Tail, 1993.

_____*The Black Atlantic: Modernity and Double Consciousness*, London: Verso, 1993.

Glenn, Evelyn Nakano et al., *Mothering: Ideology, Experience, and Agency*, London: Routledge, 1994.

Glissant, E., *Caribbean Discourse: Selected Essays*, M. Dash, trans, Charlottesville: University Press of Virginia, 1989.

_____ *Poetics of Relation*, (*Poétique de la relation*, Gallimard, 1990), trans. Betsy Wing, Michigan: University of Michigan Press, 1997.

Goodison, Lorna, *I Am Becoming My Mother*, London: New Beacon Books, 1986.

_____ *Heartease*, London: New Beacon Books, 1988.

_____ *Selected Poems*, Michigan: University of Michigan Press, 1992.

_____ *To Us All Flowers Are Roses*, Urbana: University of Illinois Press, 1995.

Greene, Gayle and Coppelia, Kahn, (eds.), *Making a Difference: Feminist Literary Criticism*, London: Routledge, 1991.

Griffin, G., '"Writing the Body": Reading Joan Riley, Grace Nichols and Ntozake Shange', in Wisker, G. (ed.), *Black Women's Writing*, Basingstoke and London: Macmillan Press, 1993.

_____ 'Imitation, Abrogation and Appropriation: The Production of the Post-Colonial Text', *Kunapipi* 9, 1, 1987.

Gunst, L., *Born Fi' Dead: A Journey into Jamaican Posse Underworlds*, New York: Henry Holt and Company, 1995.

Hall, S., 'Cultural Identity and Diaspora', in Rutherford, J. (ed.), *Identity - Community, Culture, Difference*, London: Lawrence and Wishart, 1990.

Hannay, M.P., ' 'Your vertuous and learned Aunt': The Countesse of Pembroke as Mentor to Mary Wroth' in Miller, N.J. and Waller, G. (eds.), *Reading Mary Wroth: Representing Alternatives in Early Modern England*, Knoxville: University of Tennessee Press, 1991.

Harriot, Anthony, 'The Changing Social Organization of Crime and Criminals in Jamaica, in Christine Barrow and Rhoda Reddock (eds.), *Caribbean Sociology An Introductory Reader*, Jamaica: Ian Randle Publishers, 1992, 512-527.

Herrera, Georgina, *Gentes y cosas*, La Habana: Cuadernos Unión, 1974.

_____ *Granos de sol y luna*, La Habana: Ediciones Unión, 1978.

_____ *Grande es el tiempo*, La Habana: Ediciones Unión, 1989.

Hodge, Merle, *Crick Crack Monkey*. London: Andre Deutsch, 1970.

_____ 'Challenges of the Struggle for Sovereignty: Changing the World Versus Writing Stories', in Cudjoe, S. (ed.), *Caribbean Women Writers*, Massachusetts: Calaloux, 1990.

Hutchins, M.A., *The Youthful Female Missionary*, 1839.

Juneja, R., *Caribbean Transactions: West Indian Culture in Literature*, London and Basingstoke: Macmillan, 1996.

Kaplan, C., '*The Thorn Birds:* Fiction, Fantasy, Femininity', in *Sea Changes — Essays on Culture and Feminism*, London and New York: Verso, 1986.

Katrak, K., 'Decolonizing Culture: Toward a Theory for Postcolonial Women's Texts', in *Modern Fiction Studies*, 35(1) (Spring), 1989.

Kelly-Gadol, J., 'Did Women have a Renaissance?' in Bridenthal, R. and Koonz, C. (eds.), *Becoming Visible*, Boston: Houghton Mifflin, 1977.

Kincaid, J., *Annie John*, London: Picador, 1985.

_____ *A Small Place*, New York, Farrar; London, Virago, 1988.

_____ *Lucy*, London: Plume, 1991.

_____*The Autobiography of My Mother*, London: Vintage, 1996.

_____ 'My Brother', in *Transition*, 72, (Winter), 1996.

Kirshenblatt-Gimblett, Barbara, 'Spaces of Dispersal', *Cultural Anthropology*, 9(3), 1994, 339-44.

Kolodny, A. 'Dancing Through the Minefields: Some Observations', in warhol, r.r. and herndl, d.p., *Feminisms*, Hampshire: Macmillan.

Lacrosil, M., *Sapotille et le serin d'argile*, Paris: Gallimard, 1960.

_____ *Cajou*, Paris: Gallimard, 1961.

_____ *Demain Jab-Herma*, Paris: Gallimard, 1967.

Lalla, Barbara, *Arch of Fire*, Kingston: Kingston Publishers Ltd, 1989.

_____ *Defining Jamaican Fiction*, Tuscaloosa: University of Alabama Press, 1996.

Lamb, M.E., 'The Cooke Sisters: Attitudes Towards Learned Women in the Renaissance' in Hannay, M. (ed.) *Silent but for the Word: Tudor Women as Patrons, Translators, and Writers of Religious Works*, Kent, Ohio: The Kent State University Press, 1985.

_____ 'Introduction', in *Gender and Authorship in the Sidney Circle*, Madison: University of Wisconsin Press, 1990.

Lee, V., 'Testifying Theory: Womanist Intellectual Thought', in *Women: A Cultural Review*, 6, 2, Autumn, 1995.

Light, A., '"Returning to Manderley" — Romance Fiction, Female Sexuality and Class', in Lovell, T. (ed.), *British Feminist Thought — A Reader*, Oxford: Basil Blackwell, 1990.

Lockett, M., *Christopher, A Novel*, New York: Abbey Press, 1902.

Machado, Eloy, *Jacinta ceiba frondosa*, La Habana: Letras Cubanas, 1991.

Manicom, J., *Mon Examen de blanc*, Paris: Presses de la cité, 1972.

Martineau, Harriet, 'Demerara: A Tale', in Harriet Martineau *Illustrations of Political Economy*, Volume 2, London: Charles Fox, 1832.

Mercer, K. and Julien, I., 'Race, Sexual Politics and Black Masculinity: A Dossier', in Chapman, R. and Rutherford, J. (eds.), *Male Order — Unwrapping Masculinity*, London: Lawrence and Wishart, 1988.

Miller, N.J. and Waller, G., 'Introduction: Reading as Revision' in Miller, N.J. and Waller, G. (eds.), *Reading Mary Wroth: Representing Alternatives in Early Modern England*, Knoxville: The University of Tennessee Press, 1991.

Modleski, T., *Loving with a Vengeance — Mass-Produced Fantasies for Women*, New York and London: Routledge, 1988.

Mohanty, C.T., *Cartographies of Struggle: Third World Women and the Politics of Feminism,* Indiana: Indiana University Press, 1991.

Momsen, Janet H. (ed.), *Women and Change in the Caribbean,* London: James Currey, 1993.

Mordecai, Pamela, 'Wooing with Words, Some Comments on the Poetry of Lorna Goodison', *Jamaica Journal,* 45, 1981.

Morgan, Paula E., Under Women's Eyes: Literary Constructs of Afro-Caribbean Masculinity, in Proceedings of the Symposium on the Construction of Caribbean Masculinity: Towards a Research Agenda Centre for Gender and Development Studies, UWI, St Augustine.

_____ 'Interview with Paula Morgan. Merle Hodge Author and Activist', *Supporting Women and Development (WDS) Group News,* 3, 2, February, 1996, 12-18.

Morrison, T., *The Bluest Eye,* St Albans: Panther, 1970.

Napier, E., *Youth is a Blunder,* London: Jonathan Cape, 1948.

Nasta, S., *Motherlands,* London: Women's Press, 1991.

Nettleford, R., 'This Is Ours', in the *Globe and Mail,* 9 July, 1988.

Newman, B., 'The Situation of the Looker-On': Gender, Narration and Gaze in Wuthering Heights', in warhol, r.r. and herndl, d.p. *Feminisms,* Hampshire: Macmillan, 1997.

Nichols, G., *I Is a Long Memoried Woman,* London: Karnak House, 1983.

Nora, P. 'Between Memory and History: Les Lieux de Memoir' in Genevieve Fabre and Robert O'Meally, (eds.), *History and Memory in African-American Culture,* New York: OUP, 19.

Nugent, Maria, *Lady Nugent's Journal of Her Residence in Jamaica from 1801 to 1805,* London: Printed for private circulation, 1839. Revised and ed. Philip Wright, Kingston: Institute of Jamaica (1966).

Oakley, Ann, *Woman's Work: The Housewife Past and Present,* New York: Pantheon Books, 1974.

O'Barr, Jean et al., *The Ties that Bind: Essays on Mothering and Patriarchy,* Chicago: Chicago University Press, 1990.

O'Callaghan, E., 'Literature and Transitional Politics in Dominica', *World Literature Written in English,* 24(2), 1984, 349-59.

_____ *Woman Version: Theoretical Approaches to West Indian Fiction by Women,* London: Macmillan, 1993.

Ormerod, B., *An Introduction to the French Caribbean Novel,* London: Heinemann, 1985.

_____ 'French West Indian Writing since 1970', in Burton, R. and Reno, F. (eds.) *French and West Indian*, London: Macmillan, 1995, pp.167-87.

Paravisini-Gebert, L., in Newsom, A. and Strong-Leek, L. (eds.) *Winds of Change*, New York: Peter Lang, 1998.

Patteson, Richard, 'The Fiction of Olive Senior: Traditional Society and the Wider World', *Ariel*, 24(1), 1993, 13-33.

Pérez, Lisandro, 'The Family in Cuba' in Das, M.S. and Jesser, C. (eds.), *The Family in Latin America*, New Delhi: Vikas, 1980, pp.235-69.

Philip, Nourbese M., *Frontiers: Essays and Writings On Racism and Culture*, Ontario: Mercury Press, 1992.

_____ *She Tries Her Tongue Her Silence Softly Breaks*, London: Women's Press, 1993.

_____ *A Genealogy of Resistance*, Ontario: Mercury Press, 1997.

Phoenix, Ann et al., *Motherhood: Meanings, Practices and Ideologies*, London: Sage Publications, 1995.

Pineau, G., *La Grande Drive des Esprits*, Paris, Le Serpent à plumes, 1993. English translaion Dash, J.M. to appear soon, working title, *The Great Drifting of the Spirits*.

_____ *L'Espérance Macadam*, Paris: Stock, 1995.

Pollard, V., *Considering Woman*, London: The Women's Press, 1989.

_____ 'Mothertongue Voices in the Writing of Olive Senior and Lorna Goodison', in Nasta, S. (ed.) *Motherlands: Black Women's Writing from Africa, the Caribbean and South Asia*, London: Women's Press, 1991.

Poynting, J., 'Literature and Cultural Pluralism: East Indians in the Caribbean', unpublished Ph.D thesis, School of English, University of Leeds, 1985.

Prince, Mary, *History of Mary Prince, a West Indian Slave Related by Herself*, Tho. Pringle, London, 1831. Westly, F. and Davies, A.H. (eds.), Collected in Henry Louis Gates Jr. (ed.), *The Classic Slave Narratives*, New York: New American Library, 1987.

Radway, J.A., *Reading the Romance — Women, Patriarchy, and Popular Literature*, London and New York: Verso, 1987.

Ramchand, Kenneth, *The West Indian Novel and Its Background*, London: Heinemann, 1970.

_____ 'West Indian Literary History: Literariness, Orality and Periodization', *Callaloo* 11, 1.

Randall, Margaret, *Breaking The Silences*, Vancouver: Pulp Press, 1982.

Reddock, R., 'Feminism, Nationalism and the Early Women's Movement in the English-Speaking Caribbean', in Cudjoe, S. (ed.) *Caribbean Women Writers*, 1990.

Rhys, Jean, *Wide Sargasso Sea*, London: Penguin Books, 1968.

Rich, Adrienne, *Of Woman Born: Motherhood as Experience and Institution*, New York: W. W. Norton, 1976.

Riley, J., *The Unbelonging*, London: The Women's Press, 1985.

_____ *Romance*, London: The Women's Press, 1988.

Roach, J. and Felix, P., 'Black Looks', in Gamman, L. and Marshment, M.(eds.), *The Female Gaze — Women as Viewers of Popular Culture*, London: The Women's Press, 1988.

Roberts, J.A. (ed.), *The Poems of Lady Mary Wroth*, Baton Rouge: Louisiana State University Press, 1993.

Rowell, Charles, 'An Interview with Olive Senior', *Callaloo*, 11(3), 1998, 480-90.

Ruddick, Sara, *Maternal Thinking: Towards a Politics of Peace*, Boston, Mass.: Beacon, 1989.

Sampath, N.M., 'An Evaluation of the 'Creolization' of East Indian Adolescent Masculinity', in *Trinidad Ethnicity*, Yelvington, K. (ed.), Knoxville, Tennessee: University of Tennessee Press, 1993.

Sanders, M., 'Review of Aijaz Ahmad's', *Theory: Classes, Nations, Literatures'*, in *Wasafiri* 21 (Spring), 1992.

Scarry, E., *The Body in Pain: The Making and Unmaking of the World*, Oxford: OUP, 1980.

Schwarz-Bart, S., *Pluie et vent sur Télumé Miracle*, Paris: Seuil, 1972. English translation (1974), *The Bridge of Beyond*. New York: Atheneum.

_____ *Ti Jean L'horizon*, Paris: Seuil, 1979, English translation (1981) *Between Two Worlds*, New York: Harper & Row.

_____ *Bridge of Beyond*, trans. B. Bray, London: Heinemann, 1982.

_____ *Ton beau capitaine*. Paris: Seuil, 1987.

Seacole, Mary, *The Wonderful Adventures of Mary Seacole in Many Lands*, London, 1857, Z. Alexander and A. Dewjee, (eds.), London: Falling Wall Press, 1984.

Senior, Olive, *Talking of Trees*, Kingston: Calabash Publshers, 1985.

_____ *Summer Lightning*, London: Longman, 1986.

_____ *Arrival of the Snake Woman*, London: Longman, 1989.

_____ Gardening in the Tropics, Toronto: McClelland and Stewart, 1994.

_____ Discerner of Hearts, Toronto: McClelland and Stewart, 1995.

Shepherd, V., Brereton, B. and Bailey, B. (eds.), Engendering History: Caribbean Women in Historical Perspective, London: James Currey, 1995.

Showalter, E., A Literature of their Own: British Women Novelists from Bronte to Lessing, London: Virago, 1978.

Smith, L. and Padula, A., Sex and Revolution: Women in Socialist Cuba, Oxford: Oxford University Press, 1996.

Sidney, P.,The Defence of Poesie, in Feuillerat, A. (ed.), Works, Volume Three, Cambridge: Cambridge UP, 1965.

Smith, P.C., Anancy Stories, London: Robert Howard Russell, 1899.

Smith, S., 'The Other Woman and the Racial Politics of Gender: Isak Dinesen and Beryl Markham in Kenya', in Smith, S. and Watson, J. (eds.), De/Colonizing the Subject: The Politics of Gender in Women's Autobiography, Minneapolis: University of Minnesota Press, 1992.

Smith, V., 'Masks and Voices of the Female Hero: Tania la guerrillera as testimonio', Paper presented to the seventeenth annual conference of the British Society for Caribbean Studies, St. Stephens House, Oxford, July, 1993.

_____ 'What are Little Girls Made of Under Socialism? Cuba's Mujeres and Muchachas in the period 1980-1991', Studies in Latin American Popular Culture, 14, 1995, 1-15.

Spelman, E., Inessential Woman: Problems of Exclusion in Feminist Thought, London: Women's Press, 1988.

Stephenson, C., Undine: An Experience, New York: Broadway Publishing, 1911.

Stubbs, J., 'In Search of an Unchaperoned Discourse on Mariana Grajales Coello: Social and Political Motherhood of Cuba', in Shepherd, V. and Brereton, B. (eds.) Engendering History: Caribbean Women in Historical Perspective, London: James Currey, 1995.

Swift, C.R., 'Feminine Identity in Lady Mary Wroth's Romance Urania', in English Literary Renaissance, 14, 1984.

Tate, C., Domestic Allegories of Political Desire: The Black Heroine's Text at the Turn of the Century, Oxford University Press, 1993.

Thieme, John, 'Mixed Worlds: Olive Senior's *Summer Lightning*', *Kunapipi*, xvi(2), 1994, 90-95.

Torrents, Nissa, 'Women Characters and Male Writers: A Cuban Approach' in Condé, L.P. and Hart, S.M. (eds.), *Feminist Readings in Spanish and Latin American Literature*, New York: Edwin Mellen Press, 1991.

Travitsky, B., 'The Lady Doth Protest: Protest in the Popular Writings of Renaissance Englishwomen', *English Literary Renaissance*, 14, 1984.

_____ 'Placing Women in the English Renaissance', in *The Renaissance Englishwoman in Print: Counterbalancing the Canon*, Amherst: University of Massachusetts Press, 1990.

Walcott, Derek, *Remembrance and Pantomime*, New York: Farrar, Straus and Giroux, 1980.

_____ 'Mass Man', in *Derek Walcott: Collected Poems 1948-1984*, Toronto: Harper & Collins, 1986.

_____ *The Antilles, Fragments of Epic Memory*, New York: Farrar, Straus & Giroux, 1992.

Waller, G.F. (ed.), Lady Mary Wroth, *Pamphilia to Amphilantus*, Salzburg: University of Salzburg, 1977.

Warhol, robyn and diane price herndl (eds.), *Feminisms*, Hampshire: Macmillan, 1997.

Warner-Vieyra, Myriam, *Juletane*, London: Heinemann, 1987.

Willis, S., 'I Shop Therefore I Am: Is There a Place for Afro-American Culture in Commodity Culture', in Wall, C.A. (ed.), *Changing Our Own Words — Essays on Criticism, Theory, and Writing by Black Women*, London: Routledge, 1990.

Witten-Hannah, M.A., 'Sleeping with Monsters: Lady Mary Wroth's Complete Urania, The Book and Manuscript Continuation', in *Aulla XX: Proceedings and Papers of the Twentieth Congress of Australasian Universities Language and Literature Association*, 1980.

Wroth, Lady M., *The Countesse of Montgomery Urania*, London, 1621.

Young, L., *Fear of the Dark — 'Race', Gender and Sexuality in the Cinema*, London and New York: Routledge, 1996.

Notes on Contributors

ALBA AMBERT was born in Puerto Rico. An award-winning novelist, an essayist, short story writer and poet, she is currently Writer in Residence at Richmond, The American International University in London. Her most recent collection of poetry is *Alphabet of Seeds* (Mango Publishing). Her most recent novel is *The Passion of María Magdalena Stein* (Mango Publishing).

JOAN ANIM-ADDO is Head of the Caribbean Centre at Goldsmiths College, University of London. She is founder editor of *Mango Season* the journal of Caribbean women's writing. Her publications include *Haunted by History* and *Imoinda*. She is editor of *Framing the Word: Gender and Genre in Caribbean Women's Writing*.

AIDA BAHR graduated in Cuban Literature at the University of Oriente in 1981. She is a member of UNEAC (Cuban Writers and Artists National Union). Her books include *Hay un gato en la ventana*, *Ellas de noche*, *De los cuentistas de ayer* and *Rafael soler una mirada al hombre*. She is the director of Editorial Oriente, an independent Press in Santiago de Cuba.

PAULETTE BROWN-HINDS is an Associate professor of English and African-American Studies at the University of Cincinnati (USA) where she teaches courses on African-Caribbean literature, Caribbean literature and literature of the African diaspora. Her book, *Long Memoried Woman: Memory and Migration in 20th Century Black Women's Narrative* is forthcoming.

MARY CONDÉ is a Lecturer in English at Queen Mary and Westfield College, University of London. She is co-editor of *Caribbean Women Writers: Fiction in English*.

GIOVANNA COVI is a Professor at the University of Trento, Italy. She is co-editor of *Feminist Europa*. She has published extensively on Jamaica Kincaid. Covi's book, *Jamaica Kincaid's Prismatic Subjects* is forthcoming (Mango Publishing).

ALISON DONNELL lectures in post-colonial literatures at Nottingham Trent University. Her doctoral thesis examined Jamaican women's poetry 1900-1945. She is co-editor of *The Routledge Reader in the Caribbean Literature* aimed at bringing the region's early writings to critical attention.

DENISE DECAIRES NARAIN is a lecturer in the School of African and Asian Studies at the University of Sussex. She has taught at the University of the West Indies (Cave Hill) and the Open University. She is author of *Contemporary Caribbean Women's Writing: Making Style.*

MARIA CRISTINA FUMAGALLI is the author of *The Flight of the Vernacular: Seamus Heaney, Derek Walcott and the Impress of Dante.* She has also written on Erna Brodber, M. Nourbese Philip, Jean Rhys and Maryse Condé. She lectures in Postcolonial Studies in the Department of Literature at the University of Essex.

BERYL GILROY (1926-2001) was born in Berbice, Guyana (then British Guiana) and came to London in the 1950s. Her publications include the award-winning *Frangipani House*, the first of several novels, and the essay collection, *Leaves in the Wind* (Mango Publishing).

SAM HAIGH lectures in the department of French Studies at the University of Warwick where she teaches courses on Francophone Caribbean literature, culture and society. Her primary area of interest lies in Guadeloupean women's writing. She edited the collection *Caribbean Francophone Writing: An Introduction.*

CONRAD JAMES was born in Jamaica. He teaches Latin American literature in the Department of Spanish at the University of Birmingham.

PAULA E. MORGAN is Trinidadian and lectures in the Department of English at the University of the West Indies, St Augustine.

ROSHI NAIDOO currently lectures at Middlesex University. Her doctoral thesis focused on the works of Joan Riley.

BEVERLEY ORMEROD, who was born in Jamaica, introduced French Caribbean literature courses to the University of the West Indies, Mona. She is now Associate Professor of French at the University of Western Australia. She is author of *An Introduction to the French Caribbean Novel.* She is co-author, with J.M. Volet, of *Romancières africaines d'expression française.*

EVELYN O'CALLAGHAN is Head of the Department of Literatures in English at the University of The West Indies, Cave Hill Campus. She is the author of *Woman Version: Theoretical Approaches to West Indian Fiction by Women* and *The Earliest Patriots.*

M. NOURBESE PHILIP was born in Tobago and lives in Toronto. Her books of poetry include, *Thorns, Looking for Livingston: An Odyssey of Silence* and *She Tries Her Tongue; Her Silence Softly Breaks* (awarded the 1988 Casa de las Americas prize). She is author of *Harriet's Daughter, Frontiers: Essays and Writings in Racism and Culture,* and *A Genealogy of Silence.*

VELMA POLLARD is a linguist now retired from the University of the West Indies. Born in Jamaica, her works include *Considering Woman, Shame Trees Don't Grow Here, Homestretch* and *Karl* which won the Casa de las Americas prize in 1992. Her most recent poetry collection is *The Best Philosophers I Know Can't Read and Write* (Mango Publishing).

SHEILA RAMPERSAD was born in Trinidad and completed a doctoral thesis on Caribbean literature at Nottingham Trent University. Her research addresses questions of dougla identity in the Caribbean. She is an active member of Women Working for Social Progress and currently works with the Caribbean Association for Feminist Research and Action (CAFRA).

SARAH LAWSON WELSH lectures in English and Post-Colonial Literatures at University College, Northampton. She has published on Caribbean and Black British Literature and is co-editor of *The Routledge Reader in the Caribbean Literature.*

Index